SPIRITUAL AGGRESSIVENESS

Spiritual Leadership in The Pattern of Joshua

LEADING GOD'S PEOPLE
BOOK 2

ZACHARIAS TANEE FOMUM

First Regional Leadership Training Course.
1996 West Africa Regional Convention
Sea School, Faith Island, Apapa,
Lagos, Nigeria.
Wednesday, 14th — Sunday, 18th August, 1996.

Published by

A division of the Book Ministry of Christian Missionary Fellowship International

info@books4revival.com

CONTENTS

FOREWORD

Burdened with the need for competent and aggressive workers in the field for a growing work, Professor Zacharias Tanee Fomum gave these talks on *SPIRITUAL AGGRES-SIVENESS* to about 250 leaders from eight nations, during a leadership training course.

This course, which was on **"*Spiritual Leadership in the Pattern of Joshua*"**, took place in Lagos, Nigeria, during a period of five days from Wednesday 14th to Sunday 18th August 1996.

In this book, Professor Fomum cover topics like:

1. Greatness through might in character and might in deeds
2. Breaking new barriers with total violence
3. Marriage to hard work
4. Team work
5. Radical holiness for spiritual service
6. Aggressive servanthood
7. Bleeding pursuit of God

8. and many others.

The messages are written just as they were spoken, having been compiled from notes taken during the course, with very limited editing by the author. They have maintained their freshness and sharpness.

Contributions from various workers from the field make this book a very practical book on missions.

Read it. You will be blessed.

You will be challenged to become the type of leader that is needed for the Lord's flock on the eve of His imminent return

DAY ONE

OPENING REMARKS

Beloved Brothers and Sisters in Christ,

Grace and peace to you from God our Father and the Lord Jesus Christ. Amen.

I thank Christ Jesus our Lord, who has given me strength, that He considered me faithful, appointing me to His service.

It is my greatest pleasure, privilege, special joy and honour to welcome all of you to this first ever Regional Leadership Training Convention of the Christian Missionary Fellowship International taking place here in the Sea School, Faith Island, Lagos. Permit me, brethren, to welcome you delegation by delegation.

- If you're from Angola, please stand up, let us see you: 1
- Do we have a Gabonese here?: No
- Congo: 1
- Chad: 3
- Ghana: 6

- Togo: 3
- Ivory Coast: 27
- Republic of Benin: 40
- France: 2
- Cameroon: 28

I will now call Nigeria by their localities. Our brethren from

- Kaduna: 4
- Jos: 2
- Abeokuta: 5
- Ibadan: 9
- Is there anybody from Owerri?: No
- Lagos: Many

We are one

Welcome, our Brethren, Welcome

We are grateful unto God for this Coming Together

When the idea of a regional convention was first mooted, it was going to be low-keyed in scope, covering one or two countries only. It was conceived mainly to relieve our Brother, Professor Zach Fomum, of having to teach in Nigeria, then in Benin, and perhaps afterwards also in Togo. Why not let us have a combined teaching meeting with participants drawn from these three nations? And so the planning commenced on this premise.

However, soon enough, the geographical coverage was to expand. Other countries in West Africa were to join in the meeting, namely: Ghana, Ivory Coast and, if we had missionaries there, also Liberia. Later on the list of countries from which delegates were to be drawn further expanded to include Chad, Cameroon, Gabon and Angola. At this stage there was mild excitement, especially with the prospect of brethren coming from Cameroon. The brethren in Lagos had heard about people like Dr. Joe Mbafor, Papa Atogho, Brother Emmanuel Bayiha, etc. And now they could expect to meet with these same people face to face. It was a very exciting prospect. But still our plans centred around a convention of about 150 brethren, all told. We had been informed to expect 20 brethren from Cameroon. We imposed the same number on the Church in Benin. As far as we were concerned, Togo and Ivory Coast were to send about 4 to 5 brethren each. As for Gabon, if two brethren came from there, it was perfectly alright. But then, the Lord went ahead of us. Having initially expanded the geographical spread, He began also to expand the number of delegates. The first inkling was when we received a fax from Brother Calvin announcing that 12 brethren were on their delegation. We were happy. Then another fax message came from Pastor Boniface Menye announcing that he was coming with a delegation of 29 brethren from Ivory Coast, and that they were arriving on Tuesday at No. 1 VIP Quarters, Surulere.

On Sunday afternoon, we learnt that the Cameroonian delegation would consist of 35 brethren, although now reduced to 28. At this point, we knew that the Lord had indeed taken over from us in the matter of the number of participants. When, therefore, on Sunday evening Pastor Bossoun called from Cotonou and excitedly announced that he would be arriving this morning with a delegation of 40 brethren, we were in no doubt as to who was now in charge! Praise the Lord!

The Lord God: He doeth all things well and He doeth what seemeth right to Him. Hallelujah!

Our convening this meeting on this island, for a number of us in the Lagos Assembly, has a nostalgic value. It was here on this island that early in February 1994, a few of us gathered for a weekend retreat with Brother Zach. On that occasion, Brother patiently shared with us his vision of presenting to the Lord by the year 2045 one billion people who will render total obedience to Him. The vision was explained and clarified.

Before then, even though most, if not all, of us prided ourselves as 'followers' of Brother Zach, we neither shared in this vision nor were committed to him beyond having the satisfaction of, once in a while, receiving him as a man of God in our midst and intently listening to his messages. This done, we would wave him goodbye and wait for another opportunity to once again welcome him in our midst sometime in the future.

So during that retreat, we brought our minds to bear on issues such as consecration, commitment and life goals so that the heart may find its place and take on its true colouration. There was a great deal of mind-searching, and exposure of hidden doubts. Tears flowed from many eyes, and in one particular case, uncontrollably throughout the night. At the end of the retreat, relationships were re-defined, commitments were made and the Church in Lagos was born.

It is not surprising, therefore, that during the planning stages of this leadership course, the Lord steered us to return to Faith Island as the Convention site. Praise be to His name for always showing us the best way.

The preparation for the Convention has tasked and challenged our capabilities and resources. But the Lord is forever faithful. He stirred us through it all.

If the physical preparation was tasking, the spiritual preparation was even more so. Apart from the fasts and prayers, the toll on the health of the brethren was very devastating. But we waded through. Lastly, the Lord Himself led us into some deep spiritual preparation in the area of hospitality. As we confronted the Bible doctrine on hospitality, many previously-held tenets were shattered, unthought-of benefits were discovered and the power of hospitality was revealed. Some of these truths were initially unpalatable and indeed devastating, but as we confronted more and more the doctrinal issues, the light of God was shed into many hearts.

Brethren, we may not be able to offer you samples of Abrahamic hospitality during this convention, but this one thing I know: Lives have been deeply touched and hospitality is a settled issue in the lives of the Lagos brethren.

I am grateful to God who has helped us to make some modest spiritual progress within just over two years of our existence as an Assembly. At the beginning of this year, after five brethren decided to go on a 40-day fast, the Assembly seemed to have been caught in a fasting fever. Practically everybody, from the highest down to the least person, fasted, as much as they could, in support of the brethren. Soon afterwards, many of the brethren successfully undertook a 40-day prayer crusade. Although the Assembly goals for this year now appear unattainable, we nevertheless feel that these costly spiritual investments have laid a foundation for future growth.

I thank the Lord our God who is our wonderful help through these years. I thank Brother Zach Fomum for his special love and care for us. He has encouraged us tremendously in this Assembly. The words the Lord spoke to us in February through him, during the inauguration of our public worship place, ring current in our ears.

To the Church in Yaounde, we pay special tribute for sending us missionaries and for being an inspiration to us. I also thank CPH, Yaounde for the great support they have been to our own CPH here in Lagos. We acknowledge the missionary couples sent to us. Truly, they have provided for us models of practical Christianity. Praise the Lord!

As touching to the vision given to our Brother, the Lagos Assembly has primarily pitched on two fronts. The first is the penetration of Brother's message in the nation through the saturation distribution of ZTF books in Nigeria. To this end, we established a branch of the Christian Publishing House here in Lagos. The Lagos CPH has now published four ZTF books, including the latest, "The Practice of Intercession," which will be dedicated during this convention. The goal of CPH, Lagos is to distribute 250 million books in the next 40 years, if the Lord tarries. That should make it one of the largest publishing houses in Africa. Permit me to once again acknowledge the immense help CPH, Yaounde has been to us in this our effort. No opportunity for sending books to us is ever lost by them. This is wonderful. Please accept our loving thanks for your love.

The second area is our resolve to see Asia, and in particular India, conquered for Christ so as to contribute their quota to the 1 billion souls who render complete obedience to the Lord Jesus Christ. In this regard, 60 percent of all our income is dedicated to that cause, and any assembly established anywhere in Nigeria will be encouraged to follow that example.

As time goes on, I believe that the Lord will lead us into other areas where we shall be equally or even more useful to

Him. This is why I consider this leadership course to be of utmost importance. It is in this sort of gathering that God will speak to His people as individuals, as assemblies and as a Church. It is my prayer that as He speaks during this course we shall all be open and sensitive to the Spirit of God to know His mind for us. Indeed, it is my expectation that I will be a different person at the end of the course from what I am today. He has done it once before for me at this same venue and my expectation is, therefore, no less this time. I am convinced that this is the expectation of everyone present here today.

In addition, I expect new relationships to be forged, new bonds of friendships established and old ones renewed and strengthened. I expect that we will go away with a sharpened vision of the task ahead. I expect that out of this, better defined individual and corporate goals will be fashioned. I expect new commitments to be made. I expect that each delegate will return to his post and bear fruit for the increase of God's Kingdom. I expect that a sense of unity of purpose and urgency will bind us all together with a chord that cannot be broken, a chord of love, and in this strength go out, with the help of God, to conquer the world for Christ in holiness and fear of God. I expect mighty things to happen to us at this convention.

I love you all. We love you. The Lagos Assembly says WELCOME!

God bless you.

INTRODUCTION

As you are making resolutions, be separating the resolutions from the rest of your notes. SEPARATE WHAT YOU MUST DO FROM THE REST OF THE NOTES. In fact, your meditations these days ought to be on what you must do, with a strategy to execute what must be done.

- Only acts bring change.
- No message is understood until it is acted upon.
- Clearly made plans are an indication that one intends to act; but until there are acts, it could be dreams. This particularly applies to the things that you can start acting upon here.
- When action is delayed, it may never occur at all.

The Enemy will snatch the word that is not acted upon immediately. People who want help should write out what they must act upon and give a trusted friend; so that he will ensure that they obey. If not, there may be many resolutions that end only in resolutions. There is the thief who steals what is not acted upon.

Somebody ought to go away with a compilation of the things that he must act upon; so that if he fails, he at least knows. In Hudson city, Florida, in the United States of America, I took time to examine the last 5 years. I wrote out 209 things for action or for reaffirmation or to continue, and I carry them and look at them everyday. Until it is acted upon, a resolution doesn't mean anything.

The Lord Jesus Christ loves a lost world. Let us say: "The Lord Jesus Christ loves a lost world. And we too love a lost world. God the Father loves a lost world and He gave His only begotten Son for a lost world. I too love a lost world. I will give my best for the salvation of that world. God loves a lost world and God held nothing back from that lost world. I place my all at the disposal of the Father to be used for the conquest of the world for His beloved Son. I am important in my Father's hands for His global purposes. I am very important. My Father is counting on me. My Father is counting on me."

> *1. God said, "You stand up, Paul, and dry up your tears,*
> *You must preach My Gospel for many long years;*
> *Go to Damascus, the Way that is Straight,*
> *You'll meet Ananias, and there you must wait.*

> **<u>Chorus</u>: I counted on Adam, I counted on Cain;**
> **I counted on Jonah, but he was the same;**
> **I counted on Judas, but he proved untrue;**
> **Go tell this world, Paul, now I'm counting on**
> **you."**

> *2. "Three days have gone by, Lord, and yet I don't see,*
> *But here stands my brother, He's talking to me.*
> *He says, 'Brother Paul, the Lord in the skies,*

Has sent me to heal you and open your eyes.'"

3. "I'll send you to the Gentiles, I'll send you to Rome;
But, Paul, you must suffer until I call you home;
You'll sleep in the desert, you'll be shipwrecked at sea,
But keep right on preaching this Gospel for Me."

*Go tell this world, **Bossoun**, I'm counting on you.*
*Go tell this world, **Agbor**, I'm counting on you.*
*Go tell this world, **Seraphim**, I'm counting on you.*
*Go tell this world, **Obiaga**, I'm counting on you.*

Put your hand on your neighbour and say:

Go tell this world..., I'm counting on you.

Place your hands on yourself and say:

"My God is counting on me!
I will not be like Adam!
I will not be like Cain!
I will not be like Jonah!
I will not be like Judas!
I will be like Paul!
I will be like Anna!
I will be like Timothy!
I will be like Moses!
And I will be like Joshua!"

"I counted on Adam, I counted on Cain;
I counted on Jonah, but he was the same;
I counted on Judas, but he proved untrue;
*Go tell this world, **Theodore,** I'm counting on you."*

God is counting on you!

I just want to tell those people who are involved in church planting that growth from the beginning is very slow. After that, it becomes explosive. So don't measure growth by the first two years. You have been building a foundation and foundations take time. Only a fool hurries over the foundation. The building will never be able to stand on a foundation that was rushed through.

There are no closed doors with God!

Even when doors seem like closed,

God is just preparing to open a wider door.

Every door with God is an open door.

It is only a matter of time.

So whatever looks like a closed door in your life,

it is so that a wider door might be opened.

Hannah's womb was closed so that it might open to give the nation of Israel a prophet - Samuel. What if it had been opened to produce people of no consequence? God said, "Wait, I will close it first, so that when it is opened, a prophet might emerge for the nation."

I want us to pray that the Churches that have already been started and those Churches yet to be started should know a massive visitation of God for growth in depth and growth in numbers.

I want each one of us to pray, saying,

> **"God, grant me growth in depth of loving You. Grant me depth in knowing You. Grant me breadth in**

serving You.

Lord, grant me new heights in knowing You and serving You. O God, grant me to hunger for depth, breadth, height in knowing and serving You."

The growth is dependent, first of all, on the growth of the leaders

1. in their knowledge of the Lord,
2. in their love of the Lord,
3. in their service of the Lord.

What happens to the leader will happen to the people.

Every leader at whatever level should pray, saying,

**"What happens to me will happen to the people.
I will not limit God and I will not limit the
    people of God.
I will let God have all of His way in all of my life,
so that He will have His way, so that He will
    have all of
His way in all of His people."**

And God must have all of His way in all of His people. It is not God having all of His way in some of His people. It is God having all of His way in all of His people. The apostle in Colossians 1 from verse 28 says:

"We proclaim Him, admonishing and teaching everyone with all wisdom, so that we may present everyone perfect in Christ."

Everyone with all wisdom; so as to present everyone perfect in Christ! Everyone perfect in Christ:

- The leader perfect in Christ.
- The flock perfect in Christ.
- The strong sheep perfect in Christ.
- The weak sheep perfect in Christ.
- The weak flock perfect in Christ.
- Everyone perfect in Christ. Hallelujah!
- The goal of God is to have everyone perfect in Christ.
- The purpose of God is to have everyone perfect in Christ.

Could I illustrate this with one of the Yaounde leaders who ought to have been here but who is not here. Our problem was how he would get into the canoe and come out of the canoe. Brother is handicapped in his feet, but his hands are very firm and strong. Yet there is a limitation.

It is not enough that the leader is perfect.

It is not enough that the leaders are perfect.

It is not enough that part of the flock is perfect.

The purpose of God is that the whole Body might be presented to the Lord perfect in Christ.

Every pastor is charged with the responsibility to present the whole flock perfect to the Lord Jesus Christ without exception. If my legs have been cut, even if I have my very strong hands, I am handicapped! God's answer to a Church that is not handicapped is that the shepherds will labour to present everyone perfect in Christ. So they are to:

- teach everyone,
- encourage everyone,
- rebuke everyone,

- stir everyone,

in order to present everyone perfect in Christ.

Therefore, the shepherd dare not give up anyone. The person who gives up people is not a shepherd. The shepherd's heart grows to include all the flock: the weak, the broken, the troublesome, all, and to present them perfect in Christ.

What a task! Who is equal to such a task? We are not able. However, we must do it. Therefore, knowing that we have no sufficiency of our own,

We must have sufficiency that is from above.

Yes, we must have sufficiency that is from above.

We must have the power from above operating.

We must have the supernatural power of God operating in full measure.

Then we shall be able to present the whole flock to the Lord in splendour, without spot, without wrinkle and without blemish. We shall be able. Oh, if you are a shepherd, lift up your hand and say:

"I shall present the whole flock to the Lord in splendour, without spot, without wrinkle and without blemish, because the supernatural power of God will move mightily through me."

In fact, the supernatural power of God must flow through me because, either the supernatural power of God flows through me or I have failed hopelessly. I will not give up one sheep. You have all been invited to this convention because we expect that you will all become shepherds. You may shepherd one or two or three or four or five people. You are a shepherd.

Lift up your hand and say, "God, I will not give up one sheep. The weakest sheep shall be the object of special attention."

I want us to pray that for all the shepherds, the weakest sheep will be the object of special attention; so that the weakest sheep also might be presented to the Lord perfect in Christ.

What are we trying to communicate? We are trying to communicate the fact that the Work by human power will fail hopelessly. Yet it must be done. Therefore there is absolute necessity for us to turn totally to the Lord, receive His power, and operate in that power; that we turn to God completely; that we turn away totally from ourselves, because in our own strength our failure is guaranteed. But in Him and with Him we are more than conquerors through Him who loved us.

I am not able but He is my ability.

Every human being is an exclusivist - he throws out some people. Some people just look at some and say, "No, you are excluded." Others say, "Your nose is not the type of nose that I want." Others say, "You chew your food... so you are excluded". The others say, "You pray too loudly." Others say, "You pray too slowly. I don't want to pray with you again." In Adam we are always excluding others. If you know yourself well, you will agree that you are always excluding others.

There were three people who came together saying they wanted to form the perfect Church. When one person was away, the other two of them said, "No, we are not even very sure of that person." Then the one brother said to the other, "And I have my doubts about you." So he stood there alone, the perfect Church.

Can you imagine, if Zach Fomum had come here and was just a head, a head bouncing here and there — what would you have done? Some would have broken the window and some would have drowned in the sea, trying to run away. Or if you meet somebody and he is just one eye, a very fat and very big and very accurate eye, and another person is just one mouth, all of the person has been reduced to one big mouth. If you just meet a mouth, will you say, "This is the most wonderful mouth that I have ever met"? What if you just see a hand floating in the air, and it is coming towards you to greet you? That is what individualism is. That is what the person who is the 'alpha' and the 'omega' is. If he is the eye, he may be an excellent massive eye, but without the other parts, it is a frightful thing. May God help us to see that!

My beauty lies in my being part of the whole. And my usefulness lies in the fact that I am a part of the whole. Look, Brethren, pride eats very deep into us. We think we can do it all alone.

Some years ago, I got to the U.S. and somebody gave a book to me about a famous Nigerian. At the lower part of the cover was written: "The Man who Single-handedly Brought all Nigeria to God." Single-handedly! So I began to imagine this eye that was also the nose, that was also the mouth, that was also the feet, and the toes and the nails, ...

In the next message, we shall see the need to be a servant as the way to spiritual aggressiveness. In 2 Corinthians 2:12-14 the apostle Paul writes: "Now when I went to Troas to preach the gospel of Christ and found that the Lord had opened a door for me, I still had no peace of mind, because I did not find my brother Titus there. So I said good-bye to them and went on to Macedonia. But thanks be to God, who always leads us in triumphal procession in Christ and through us spreads everywhere the fragrance of the knowledge of Him."

Paul, the great apostle, went to preach the gospel. He went to Troas and, by the grace of God, a big door was opened to him.

The great apostle was in a place where God had opened a great door. He could have said, "Now, God has opened this great door. I will do it."

A great apostle saw a great door opened by God, but he did not find his helper, Titus. He closed the whole matter and went away. He went away from the door that God had opened because a small Titus was not there. One would have said, "Ho! This is a terrible failure! An apostle who runs away from open doors because a person of no consequence called Titus is not there. Oh this man does not know how to lean on God. He is leaning on Titus and going away!" You would have said, "This is his last failure. He is finished!" But Paul says in verse 14: "But thanks be to God, who always leads us in triumphal procession in Christ and through us spreads everywhere the fragrance of the knowledge of Him." Thanks be to God, who always leads us in triumphal procession. The fact of leaving that open door because Titus was not there and going to look for him so that they might minister together, was the triumph of the gospel. And Paul says, "Glory be to God who always leads us in triumphal procession," the triumphal procession of looking for our brother, the triumphal procession of knowing that we are not the whole Body but we are just part of the Body, that without the other members of the Body, the victory cannot be won!

Paul is saying, the matter of leaving the open door and going to look for your junior co-worker — that is spiritual triumph. That is the triumph of the gospel! The triumph of the gospel is manifested in the great apostle leaving an open door, opened by the Lord, in order to go and look for his younger assistant; so that the stupendous glory of God might be manifest in the Body and not just in individuals; so that the stupendous glory of God may be seen in the Body.

Listen, if you are the hands and they say, "There are mighty fishes there," in stead of saying, "O.K., I'll first go and get eyes because I cannot see, before I come and do the fishing," will you be the fool who will go there blind and start to fish? The wise person will say, "O.K., thank God for the fishes, but let me go and get my eyes so that I can see." I may be the strong hands, I may be the very able one, but I must go and look for my brother who is the eyes, so that we might do great exploits, where there are many fishes provided by our God. Therefore waiting, going away for some time, becomes the only way to victory. Therefore, the going to search for the younger brother, the going to seek the small helper is victory, triumph, the only way to succeed. May God write on our hearts that we cannot do it alone. We must look for our Titus, and for our Timothy. We must look for the Body. God's great blessings have been given to the Body, and we are only individual members of it.

I cannot win without my brother. Say:

> **"I cannot win without my brother. I must seek my brother if I want to avoid failure."**

The one and only way to avoid failure is to become a helper. Then victory is inevitable.

I will be that helper and I will go and look for my helper.

Doors can wait, but the need for the helper cannot wait.

Opportunities can wait, but the need to function as a team cannot wait.

We shall stop there, and as we go on we shall see how this provides a foundation.

DAY TWO

A CORRECTIVE COMMENT

When you are translating somebody you put off your own personality and put on his own. When you see somebody talking with his whole body and you stand there with your old personality, you are misrepresenting him. You are to carry out the person's acts:

- If he jumps, you jump.
- If he is excited, you are excited.
- If he bounces, you bounce.

Unless you are ready to put off all of your personality, you do not qualify for the office of translator, because when the message comes out vigorously through one person and you are reducing its intensity in your self-love, you are a dangerous being.

If the man goes down, you go down.

If he dances, you dance.

If he is angry, you are angry.

If he is happy, you are happy.

Yes, that is the price that must be paid in accepting the office of translator. It is the putting aside of your personality. Because you can really do what the person is doing, you can become the person, if you will only die to yourself; and if you don't die to yourself you don't qualify to minister anything. We are putting an axe under the root of some people's self-love and their determination to be their own individuals. If you want to maintain that...what I will call your personal madness, then you cannot enter into the office of co-ministry.

The next thing we want to say is that: There are two ministers of critical importance - the one speaking and the one translating. Sometimes people stand up and pray for the speaker as if he were going to speak in one language, then immediately speak in the other language and then come back and speak in that other language. I had about the most confusing experience of my life when somebody tried to do that. It was in Hong Kong. The person would preach in English, then translate into Mandarin, and then go back to preach in English. Even you yourself will forget what you said. I asked, "What is wrong with this man?" They said that he is a man who does not know how to delegate. He does everything himself. So he is crushed by everything in the Ministry — he has to do everything, everything himself. He does not trust anybody. He does not believe anybody. He has put himself out of the Ministry because there will come a day when he may stand there and just collapse, and there will be nobody to pick him up.

There are two ministers of the New Covenant. When you pray, pray for both the minister and the translator because, unless each is an instrument of God, the meetings will not reach where God intended them to reach. I have heard God for this morning, but if my brother cannot be the channel through which what I have heard from God will pass, then God's purpose for the meeting will be blocked. He is just as important as myself for the success of this day.

And if you come to make announcements or to translate announcements, it is part of the Ministry of the Word. If you come to introduce, it is as important as the Ministry of the Word. So there is no time to be off-hand or off-guard. So each time you come here, you are coming as a competent minister of the New Covenant, because if what you are saying is not of Kingdom importance, it should not be said. And we want to say, throughout these days, we are on retreat. What is not of Kingdom importance should not be spoken. If eating food is not of Kingdom importance, it should not be eaten. But if eating food is a holy task and building a healthy body is a holy task, then eat food for the glory of God, drink for the glory of God and sleep for the glory of God. If giving somebody a hug is a holy duty, give it with all of your might. Whatever you do, do it for the glory of the Lord, and do it unto the Lord.

Lift up your hand and say: "I will do everything this day unto the Lord. I will treat my brother and sister as if the Lord were personally present, physically represented by them, and I was reaching out to Him through them. In Jesus' Name, Amen."

2

RECAPITULATION

BROTHER ZACH:

What did we learn in the last lesson? If you want to answer, you stand up and answer clearly.

BROTHER THEODORE:

I learnt for myself that the triumph of the gospel is when a senior worker can surrender opportunity in order to seek his junior co-worker. That is what I learnt for myself.

BROTHER ZACH:

In fact, the question is, "What did you learn?" Because there ought to be 250 messages for the 250 people, each person receiving a message that depends upon:

where he is in his walk with God,

where he is in his battles with God,

where he is in his service for God,

how much he has obeyed in the past,

how his heart is prepared at the moment to move ahead in the school of obedience.

So, it will be your own message, what you can receive, what relates personally to you. That is why Brother Theodore is talking about that which came to him as he is and where he is. What did you receive yesterday?

BROTHER BONIFACE MENYE:

I received yesterday that the blessings of God have been given for His entire Body. And that for me to inherit them, I need to always look for the Body, that I need to always look for my brethren, even the weakest.

A BROTHER:

What I learnt yesterday was that, it was said that even the weakest are to be the object of particular attention, i.e. whoever we are, whatever be our degree of faith, we should not neglect the weak.

BROTHER MARK AJAKPO:

For me, I learnt that the growth of those whom I lead, as a leader, depends on my own growth. And consequently, I can see that if I will not grow, I hinder God from having all of me and I hinder God from having all of those whom I lead, and as such, I hinder God's purpose. It is a challenge for me and I have really seen the critical need for me to grow and continue growing.

ANOTHER BROTHER:

Praise the Lord! Yesterday I learnt something precious. I saw that, as a spiritual leader in a locality, if I do not pay a higher price than the others, I am not qualified to be a real leader. Secondly, I also learnt that every leader must make a great effort, must pay a great price to present each sheep perfect to the Lord.

BROTHER ALBERT NJAMEN:

Yesterday, I understood that I need to seek to be a helper in the Body of Christ to someone; that someone needs me to accomplish what God has put in his heart. And the message of yesterday for me was that I have to be a helper in the Body of Christ.

You have to be a helper in the Body of Christ or "I have to be the helper of this person?" Because there are some people who can get drowned in the Body. He sees the Body, the Body, the Body without seeing anyone. You should reduce this great message to you as the helper of one person.

BROTHER BOSSOUN KOUMABÉ:

Yesterday I received that I should no longer exclude others and even the weakest sheep has to receive from me the most serious attention. And I will from today make the list of those sheep I have excluded and the weak sheep and begin to give them serious attention.

BROTHER FIRMINO:

Yesterday I learnt to be patient with those I lead, not to seek a Church of perfect people, but to help the others and bring them to the level I can. And I have a responsibility because what I am is what they can be, those whom I lead, to move ahead.

BROTHER ZACH:

Did you say you do not need to seek a Church of perfect people? That is dangerous because the apostle Paul says that he has to present everyone perfect in Christ and you are saying you are not going to seek a Church of perfect people! All our confessions were that we have to present the whole flock perfect in Christ. But you are concluding that you will not seek a perfect Church. Whether you want to seek it or not, God demands it of you. I think what you wanted to say was that you will not leave some behind. That is important, but it does not mean lowering the standards in order to take everybody. Taking everybody along does not mean lowering the standards so that everybody will go along. The standards must remain God's standards, but the leader must bring everyone to God's standards. And there is no room there for patience. The theme of this Convention is SPIRITUAL AGGRESSIVENESS.

This is not a Convention for people to be patient! We have not come here to teach people how to be patient! We have come here to teach people how to be aggressive! You will have to aggressively carry the weak sheep to the perfection of God!

SISTER SUSAN:

I learnt for myself yesterday that I will not be a wicked sheep. I will follow and render total obedience so that my leader will not spend all his time giving me special attention; so that the Church will move on.

BROTHER ZACH:

Praise God! And you are already speaking as someone who already knows something about leadership. God bless you!

BROTHER MOÏSE FIOGBE:

From what the Lord told me yesterday, I understood that the growth of the Church, the people I lead, depends on my growth and that all that happens to me will certainly happen to the flock.

And that I have to do all to pay the price and grow in love, in the knowledge of the Lord, in order to be able to lead the people in that same direction.

BROTHER ZACH:

What Brother Fiogbe is saying is that the Church's growth is directly proportional to the leader's growth.

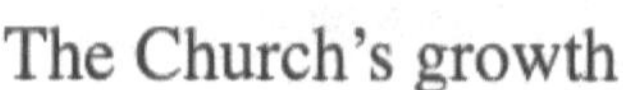

The Church's growth

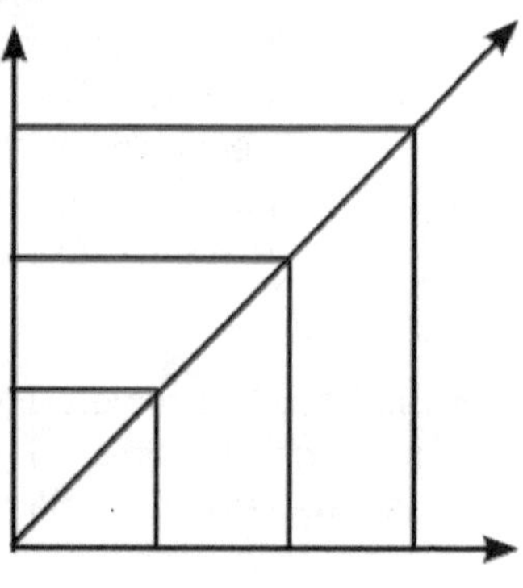

The Leader's growth

If the leader does not grow, the Church is stagnant.

If he grows a little, then the Church grows a little.

If he grows averagely, the Church grows averagely.

If the leader grows to the extreme or to the maximum, the Church's growth will be at the maximum.

- The Church's growth is directly proportional to the leader's growth.
- The Church's growth in depth is directly proportional to the leader's growth in depth.
- The Church's growth in numbers is directly proportional to the leader's growth in that dimension.
- The Church's love for the Lord depends upon the leader's love for the Lord; it is directly proportional to the leader's love for the Lord.
- The Church's seeking of God is directly proportional to the leader's seeking of God.

- The Church's hatred of sin is directly proportional to the leader's hatred of sin!!
- If the Church loves the world, it is because the leader loves the world.
- The Church's growth in sanctification is directly proportional to the leader's growth in sanctification.
- The Church's growth in perfection is directly proportional to the leader's growth in perfection.
- The stability of the Church is directly proportional to the leader's stability in the Lord.
- The Church's vision is directly proportional to the leader's vision.
- The Church's sacrifice is directly proportional to the leader's sacrifice.

Listen!

- The easiest way to bury a National Work is for the leader to be indulgent.
- When the leader loves the world he has buried his Work!
- When the marks of sacrifice are lacking in the leader's life, they will be lacking in the Church.

There are missionaries here. When a missionary makes himself comfortable, he has buried the Work! He will produce a comfort-loving Work, and that is no Church. We say it again:

When a leader loves comfort and is indulgent in comfort, he will produce a comfort - loving Work, and that is not a Work of the Cross.

If the leader offers to live on a hundred thousand whereas he could sacrificially live on seventy, he has destroyed his Work!

We say that again: If a leader can sacrificially live on 70,000, but he could also with more comfort live on 100,000, and he chooses to live on the 100,000, his Work will perish eventually. If it doesn't perish in numbers, it will perish in quality. If a leader wants to buy a shirt, he must first ask: "How will this shirt affect the Work?" Whatever the leader offers himself, he must think about how it will affect the Work.

Work that is not rooted in the Cross will lack depth.

I just came back from preaching the Word in the United States. The Church in America is generally very sick. In one place where I was preaching, I told them we have a prayer room for America. The pastor said, "I beg, when you go, pray that this Church will be delivered from the American spirit." It is the spirit of comfort, of ease and of indulgence. It is the spirit of the Church that wants to be entertained. The sermons must entertain, the programme must entertain. The marks of the Cross have been removed. No all-night prayer meetings exist.

There is a Church there which is about fifteen years old. They have had one all-night prayer meeting. That was the one I led two years ago. The pastor told me, "That meeting changed all of our Church and changed all of our lives." But they have not had another one. They don't want the transformation to continue. And because they do not want the transformation to continue, when I lived with one of the Elders, I was told that recently, they were marrying a woman who was getting married for the third time. Her first marriage was to a believer. It ended. Then she married another believer, and the marriage ended. And then they were blessing her with her third man - in the Name of Jesus. That is what prayerlessness produces. In the same Church of five hundred believers, I was told that last year there were eight divorces; that means sixteen out of five hundred really because two people are involved each time. And three of the people who were divorced married other people in the same Church. What is that? That is what prayerlessness produces. That is what low consecration produces. You can start by amassing clothes, chairs and the rest. You will go on to accumulate women one after another — progressive monogamy!

Unless there is harsh personal discipline applied by the leadership, the Work has been surrendered.

Unless the leader lives on the minimum in order to give away the maximum, he has abandoned the Narrow Way.

Unless the leader personally decides to live on the minimum in order to give away the maximum, he has turned away from the Narrow Way.

They said that in America the pastors are millionaires; that the easiest way to grow rich is to become a pastor. Many pastors have pleasure boats at sea. A brother who is a pastor came and picked me from Florida to take me to Georgia. He suggested that he could come with me to Africa and that he was leaving the brother with whom they were working. I said, "Why?" He said that they gave this man tons of things to bring to Nigeria for the Churches. One of the top companies in America gave tons of brand new men's underwear. Yes, and they were brought in by ships. An agent was appointed to do the selling. This brother said, "Zero franc entered the Work." Then there was a quarrel between the missionary and the Nigerian leaders because they say that the missionary banked it in his Swiss account. And the Nigerian leaders were rebelling, not because the money did not go to the Church, but because he did not give their share, because he ate it alone.

And then they say that there are Ministry leaders in the U.S. with Swiss bank accounts. A lot of it must be exaggerated, but I also read on paper the confession of a leading minister who had two pleasure boats and enormous property—in the name of the Crucified.

When you start to increase your material gains, you are diminishing the impact of your Ministry. We shall look at that later on, but what we are saying is this: Everything in your life:

- where you live,
- how you live,
- what you wear,
- all that you have,

will have an impact on your Ministry.

Which one of you has heard about Mother Theresa? I passed near her home in Calcutta. They wanted me to go and see it, but I didn't have time. After praying about it, next month when I shall be in Calcutta, I shall go and see it in order that I may say what I saw. This woman had a Nobel Peace Prize, but all the money, all the profits were invested in leprosariums. Someone gave her a brand new Cadillac, with leather seats. She auctioned it and put the money into building leprosy settlements. I read that she always travels in third class carriages on the trains in India and that she has just two dresses. And this is a woman who meets Presidents. A few years ago, she was at the Presidential Breakfast in the U.S. Immediately she stood up, she said,

"Woe unto those who commit abortion! And woe unto those who help others to commit abortion! And woe unto the nation where abortions prevail!" And that is America.

She could not be bought. What could you buy her with? What can you give her to keep her quiet? And the President was sitting there and he is one of those who are pro-abortion. If she came there hoping that they might give her some money, she would be afraid to offend the President because it might influence the packet negatively. She sleeps on a mat. The journalist who was interviewing her asked, "Is that life not too severe?" She said, "That is between God and me." That is between God and me.

Without ruthless sacrifice, without radical sacrifice, there will not be great Christian careers.

For our missionaries, I know that 25 years from today, their Work will manifest very much whether they have lived in a spirit of sacrifice or a spirit of worldly indulgence. I thank God for what happens at the beginning but I am looking at the long race because that is what is determinant. Those who live on the barest minimum will, 25 years from today, have massive Works rooted on the Cross. The example is the Lord Jesus Christ.

I was told of an American preacher who said that Jesus lived in extreme luxury, and that when Jesus said, "The Son of Man has no place to lay His head," it was because there was no Holiday Inn in that village. Holiday Inn is one of the top hotel chains. I just said, "This Bible is given for the rise and the fall of many." That preacher said every poor preacher should repent because he is not living like Jesus or like the apostles. He said that they brought all the money and put it at the apostles' feet. They sold everything and put it at the apostles' feet. But he refused to see the fact that after they laid it all at the apostles' feet, Peter and John said, "Silver and gold, have I none."

I went to see Sister Polly. She is a sister I have known for some years. She is now bedridden at 75. While I was there, Benny Hinn, who had come to this country, was on TV. He said he asked people to study the problems raised in the letters that were coming to his Ministry, and classify them into: Number One, Number Two, Number Three,... He said when they brought the results he was so shocked that he said, "No, go and do the research again. You have just got it wrong." But they came back with the same results. The first need raised by American believers for prayer is money and how to get out of debts. That is the thing that most believers are raising as prayer topic: "O God, give us money. Help us to get out of debts." I said to myself that this America dream is a lie. It has failed. In the richest nation in the world, those who are said to be citizens of heaven, who are supposed to lay no treasures for themselves on earth, their number one problem is money and how to get out of debts! Even in the primitive African village, that is not their problem. So if the richest nation has money as its number one problem, then the love of money is really the root of all evil.

My host told me that America is the most indebted nation in the world. They owe fourteen trillion dollars! Fourteen and twelve zeros - that is the American debt. And he said that four trillion dollars were owed in credit cards. He said, "You have your Visa-card and all those cards, it is your debts that you are carrying."

They also said something that was interesting: that the Saudi Arabians, the Kuwait people and the Japanese came and bought a lot of things in America. Now they are very sorry because when you possess property in a debtor nation, you are a loser.

Just to give you a glimpse of it, about twelve years ago, I started an account in the U.S. They were giving 6% interest for any amount in it, but you could write four cheques a week. That same account now gives you 1% interest. So those Arabs and Japanese who put their money there have had it.

The love of the world is personal ruin.

The love of the things of the world is personal ruin.

The wealth of a person is determined, not by what he has kept back, but by what he has given away.

It is how much a man has given away especially for the cause of the gospel that establishes his wealth.

I met a brother who was 38 then. I was told that his wealth was $50 million. Someone sat him down and taught him on tithing and sat him down and talked to him again about tithing. But he would not tithe. Then, you know, two years ago, there was a small crack on Wall Street. It was very short and brief. He spent the whole day phoning New York just so as to know where he was. In the evening he got the results. He had lost only $5 million in that split brief crack in Wall Street. When one brother heard about it, he told him, "That sounds like a tithe." It is only that that tithe has not gone to serve the Kingdom of God. It has been burnt by the Enemy. He still would not tithe. He got engaged at 38. The girl asked for a car that would suit the wealth of a man like him. She asked for a car of $24,000,00. Then she asked for a change of dress. After those two requests the man cancelled the engagement saying that that girl would be too expensive. He is still single today. He cannot even get married because of his money.

Everyone involved in leadership must ask:

What is the impact of my lifestyle on the work?

What is the impact of my life on Church growth in numbers?

How much have I stored away in the treasures of heaven?

It will tell the story; not now, but in 25 years.

George Muller who was living in extreme poverty, gave $180,000,00 into God's cause - that was the money that had been given for his own personal needs in the course of his long spiritual ministry. He could have kept this and been enormously rich, but he gave and gave and gave and lived on the barest minimum. I read it. He wrote the whole story of his giving in his autobiography and said, "Someone may ask, 'Why am I exposing this?' It is because I want the lovers of the Lord to follow my example. They need to know about it in order to follow it."

Models must be known.

And Muller has been influencing believers till this generation. And he will continue to leave an impact on believers till the Lamb comes.

I think about C.T. Studd, the world cricketer, who turned away not only a cricket career, but also turned his back to his massive wealth, actively giving it to the gospel, such that at his wedding he had only $5.00 because he had signed massive sums to the gospel. We read about him today. And the World Evangelisation Crusade that he started is in at least 80 countries today. **He, though dead, speaketh.**

Had he kept the money, nobody would hear about him today. And the World Evangelisation Crusade would never have been born. And when he came to the Belgian Congo, what is now the Democratic Republic of Congo (former Zaïre), he built a one-room hut in which he lived. His writing table was on one side... Even the missionaries wanted to rebel because, as they said, he was making conditions too hard. Oh! But C.T. Studd had caught the vision of what missionary life means. It is that

If a man goes to a place and lives above the level at which the people are living, he has betrayed the Ministry and built a grave for himself, and will be of no consequence.

When a missionary lives the lifestyle that the others are not living he has buried his Ministry. In fact, he has buried everything. Whatever he calls his work has failed because people may begin to covet his house, or his car, or his furniture, or his kitchen instead of coveting his God.

If a missionary ever causes someone to wish he were a missionary because of his condition of living, he has done the uttermost harm to the gospel!

Brother Peter Schneider, a brother whom you know, is a German missionary in Cameroon. His wife got an inheritance, and when he was working he saved some money. He added this inheritance of his wife's to the money he had saved and bought a small house in Ulm. And because he is an architect, he gave it touches that made it look really nice. Then in the Churches associated with his mission some began to say, "Ah! It is wonderful to become a missionary. In a few years you have a house, when people have been working for twenty years and don't have any." And the thing was spreading and blocking people to his message because when he came they said, "Yeah, the rich fellow. Yeah! The missionary field has made him rich." When people are saying such things they won't listen to what you're saying, whatever you're saying.

Brother Peter told me he had to call the mission leaders and expose to them his finances to the last franc. That is the crucible into which the Work is born and then it grows.

There is a tendency in the world to say, "Just make it more comfortable! God is not against ease! Just make it more comfortable!" Brethren, that spirit is not from heaven and it is not the voice of the Lamb. "Just add another shirt. Just add another pair of trousers. Just add another piece of meat. Just add another this! Then another hour of sleep. Just add another hour of sleep. Another hour of relaxation."

And the best are transformed into mediocres!

And a work of finest quality is reduced to a work of no consequence!

What have you done with the sharp edges that you had at the highest level of your consecration to God?

What have you done to the sharp edges that you had?

- the sharp edges of unusual simplicity;
- the sharp edges of unusual sacrifice;
- the sharp edges of unusual refusal to compromise.

What have you done to those sharp edges?

A brother said in Yaounde, "When I just believed, I thought that every believer who took a debt was going to hell because the Bible says: 'Owe no one anything except love.' But now I find myself in debt. Then I ask myself, 'What has happened?'"

What has happened to the high standards that you had about the call of God? What has happened to that rugged commitment to the simple life because of the perishing souls of men?

You used to say, "Vanity of vanities!" Now it is no longer vanity. It is God's blessings. You have now coined a way of clothing your love of the world by saying it is God's blessings. Are you seduced? The sharp edges have gone. Unbelievers can now listen to your message and remain comfortable. Unbelievers can now come to your home and not be disturbed. You have renewed some of the friendships that were broken. You have said the Narrow Way must be broadened. You have backslidden.

When a backslider goes to the mission field he goes to be a curse to the people of that nation.

When a backslider - a man who has lost the sharp edges that he had, a man who has lost the radical consecration that he once had - when he goes to the mission field, he goes there to advance the cause of the Devil and to block the purposes of God, and to ensure that that nation will never be where God meant it to be. He goes there to ensure that the right person will never be sent there.

Where are the sharp edges? Where are your sharp edges?

Listen, Brethren, when Gideon was going to battle for God, when he was going to battle against the enemies of Israel (and the enemies of Israel were idolaters) Gideon had to confront the fact that in his father's house there was an idol. And he had to destroy that idol before he could destroy the idols in the land of the enemies of Israel!

Have you destroyed the idols in your own heart?

Have you destroyed the idols in your family?

Ho! It was a terrible day because there was an idol in Israel, and yet the Israelites wanted to go and destroy idols in the lands of the others! So it was important for Gideon to first demolish the idols in his father's house.

What of the idol in your heart?

What of the idols in your heart?

The love of ease is a terrible idol!

The love of the things of the world is a horrible idol!

The desire to be seen is a horrible idol! So is the desire for clothes and the love of the many things that will soon pass away!

Gideon had to pull down the idol that was in his father's house, to destroy it and bring it to nought, before he could go and deal with the Midianites.

How can we possess the land, and possess the people of the land before we have possessed our hearts completely for the Lord?

Oh Brethren, the idol in Israel had to be destroyed first! Gideon had to first bring that idol down before he could go into God's battles. He had to destroy that idol before he could go into God's battle. If he had gone without destroying the idol, he and the enemy would have been one. They would have been both idolaters. And which idolater should destroy the other? Oh, the idol had to be destroyed!!

To those of you who have served the Lord for some time now and who at the beginning of your walk with God smashed the idols and brought them to nought, I want to give you a warning today:

At the end of Gideon's life he gave the Israelites another idol.

He asked them to bring their earrings and the rest and he built an idol. From the beginning he destroyed the idols.

There were radical sacrifices, radical separations and total investment for the Lord Jesus Christ. You followed Him along the pathway of radical separation and painful sacrifice. It cost you almost everything and almost your whole life. You risked everything on the altar for Him. Then you began to know God's victories. And then you built an idol. You went back to your vomit and called it God's blessing. You abandoned the way of sacrifice. You wanted to be like the others. Are you then surprised why the work is stagnant? After the initial growth, nothing more seems to be happening. The conversions are less radical and the marks of the Cross more difficult to see. The joy of the Christian way is no longer found among the believers. There is murmuring, gossiping and all the rest. Dissatisfaction is the order of the day. If you are honest, ask yourself, "How is this different from the religious systems that are around?" You have backslidden! You are a wicked backslider - maintaining a physical position before men, but with the position in God's heart lost. You blame the nation where you have been sent. You blame the people, whereas the problem is you. You are no longer where you started. Then the things of the world did not make sense to you. Now you are possessed by your appearance and by what you must buy. You are possessed by your house - how it must be furnished. You say, "I must make the leader's place dignified," but not dignified with the Cross. The Cross is no longer dignity. Yet it was meant by God to be the highest dignity.

The believer's highest dignity was to be found in the Cross.

The greatest joy of the believer was to be the Cross. The one music that thrilled the believer was to be the music of the Cross. And the Cross calls for a sacrifice, to a life of self-denial that knows no limits.

You are no longer where you ought to be or you have never been there. From the very start, you compromised. From the very start, you faced the Cross, the Narrow Way, and you compromised. From the very beginning, you negotiated the demands of the Narrow Way. You would not go the whole way. From the beginning, your wicked heart told you that you could love the world and love the Lord Jesus Christ. Look, from the beginning, your wicked heart told you you could gain the world and gain the Kingdom. From the beginning, you looked at the supposed ministers of the Gospel instead of looking at the Minister of the Gospel — the Lord Jesus Christ. From the beginning, you acquired what the Lord never acquired. You made the things that were not the joy of the Lord become your joy. You listened to whispers from the land of the Enemy. The devil said, "Love the world. It is God's blessing. It is prosperity." And it is as if God told you, "I did not prosper My Son, I did not prosper Jesus, so I did not give him good things, but I will prosper you, I will give you what I did not give Jesus!" And when people begin to ask God to give them what God did not give to the Lord Jesus Christ, they become wicked enemies of the Cross. We say it again:

And when people begin to buy what Jesus would not have bought;

And when people begin to seek what Jesus would not have sought;

And when people begin to desire what Jesus would not have desired;

And when people begin to want to possess what Jesus would not have wanted to possess, they have turned to become God's fiercest enemies.

Yet in their deceit, they want to build a work approved of God. What seduction!

Do you enjoy the music of the Cross, the music of a very simple life, the music of self-denial because of the Gospel?

Do you enjoy the music of self-imposed poverty because what could have been kept has been invested in the Gospel?

Paul loved the music of the Cross.

Song :

> *Forbid it, Lord, that I should boast,*
> *Save in the Cross of Christ my Lord:*
> *All the vain things that charm me most,*
> *I sacrifice them to His blood.*
>
> *Were the whole realm of nature mine,*
> *That were an offering far too small:*
> *Love so amazing, so divine,*
> *Demands my soul, my life, my all.*
>
> *See! from His head, His hands, His feet,*
> *Sorrow and love flow mingled down!*
> *Did e'er such love and sorrow meet,*
> *Or thorns compose so rich a crown?*

Thorns composing so rich a crown!

The music of the Cross is that music that is found in thorns -

- thorns borne because of the Cross,

- thorns borne because of sacrifice for the Gospel,
- thorns borne because of that which is given away because of the Gospel,
- thorns borne because of that which is invested into others because of the Gospel,
- the bleeding of the heart because of that which has been given away in order that the Gospel may get to others,
- thorns composing a rich crown,
- thorns composing so rich a crown,
- thorns, a crown of thorns!

Ease! Indulgence! Is that the idol you have now built? When the Lord first called you, you did not have the wealth of the world and the Enemy has seduced your heart to think it is in the Lord that you should acquire that which must soon pass away. You have made the Gospel and the Ministry of the Gospel a way to gain that which you did not have when you first met the Crucified One. Do you not see that that is your own destruction? Listen, Brethren:

What did you possess when you met the Lamb?

Has your encounter with Him stripped you of what you possessed?

Or is life in the Lamb the life to gain, gather, amass that which you did not have in the world?

No wonder, the intimacy with God is gone. No wonder, the people you lead to the Lord are more and more worldly and more and more dissatisfied. They are compromising everything. They look at your life and they do not see the marks of the Cross. They only see marks that say, "This man is using God to gain the world. In the world, he could have nothing.

Now, in God, the world has filled his house and filled his heart."

With regards to worldly goods, where were you when you met the King of the Cross?

Did Jesus come down from heaven to give you the things of the world? Is that what Jesus came to do? Did He come down from heaven to ruin you with the things of the world?

In the Lord, you now covet things that you did not even desire in the world. You have made it the place of covetousness. You now desire things that you did not even desire before in the world. And you want a Church in splendour, without spot, wrinkle or blemish. Yet you would not let the Church arise. Your leg is tied to the world. And, seeing the progress or the greatness of others, you are not disturbed by a holy restlessness that says, "No, I will not die a mediocre." Your leg is tied to the love of the world. Your hand is tied. Even when you preach the Gospel, your mouth is tied. There are some things about which you preached in the past that you can no longer preach about now. Your conscience can no longer allow you to preach them because your life opposes that message that you yourself first preached. You have silenced your mouth. Could anything worse happen to a man?

Could anything worse happen to a man that with increasing years his message is becoming smaller and smaller because his life is shutting his mouth more and more? If it is not a manifest style, it is a desired style. He desires the world. He desires the things of the world. He is not content with himself because of his many desires after the things that must soon pass away.

Gideon destroyed the first idol and he left the second idol for the people. The legacy that Gideon left to the nation was an idol. In the final analysis, it would have been better for them to have remained subjected to the Midianites than to know a temporary freedom that led to more permanent bondage.

The music of the Cross. Oh! The Narrow Way that was chosen and the Narrow Way that is now abandoned. Worldly things now cause you endless worries, whereas before you used to say, "The people of the world are mad!" Now, who is mad? The world is even covetous of your possessions. The world now covets what you have. The world now says that you are more worldly than they are.

You went to a nation to block God because if you had not gone, eventually a consecrated man would have gone. But because you went, that person will never go and God's purposes in that nation will be ruined. You forgot the place from which God picked you, and you have become a personal wreck.

Some people should pray. But if God is not speaking to your heart, if there is no real evidence that God is speaking to you, if God is not causing you deep worry of heart, if there is no sense of saying, "Woe to me, I have backslidden!" or "I have never known the Way of the Cross. I have never known the music of the Cross. I have made the Christian life a life of debauchery to acquire that which the Crucified One would never have acquired. I am richer now in the things of the world than before I knew Jesus, but I am so poor in God. My knowledge of God is shockingly small," to destroy the initial idol, and the idol that you later on built, then you had better keep quiet.

I want us to look at New Testament leadership. I want the missionaries to look at it first. Then I want national leaders to look at it. And I want leaders of Churches to look at it. I also want all who aspire to leadership in the Kingdom of God to look at it.

<u>1 Corinthians 4: 8-13</u>: "Already you have all you want! Already you have become rich! You have become kings - and that without us! How I wish that you really had become kings so that we might be kings with you! For it seems to me that God has put us apostles on display at the end of the procession, like men condemned to die in the arena. We have been made a spectacle to the whole universe, to angels as well as to men. We are fools for Christ, but you are so wise in Christ! We are weak, but you are strong! You are honoured, we are dishonoured! To this very hour we go hungry and thirsty, we are in rags, we are brutally treated, we are homeless. We work hard with our own hands, when we are cursed, we bless; when we are persecuted, we endure it; when we are slandered, we answer kindly. Up to this moment we have become the scum of the earth, the refuse of the world."

Is this the Gospel we are supposed to represent, being top ranking people? The apostles were poorly dressed compared to the world. But satanists in the name of God have said spiritual leaders are people to tell their message by their clothes, to get all of the world, to be seen by their dressing. That is the devil's message! The apostles were poorly dressed - in some versions it is said, "They go naked," but it is just that they were poorly dressed. They were either homeless or living in tents. They were living at the simplest level possible. They were not the honoured of the world. They were the scum of the earth, the refuse of the world. There was nothing in them that the world should desire them. No one could have wished to change positions with them. But the Enemy has seduced many who call themselves after Him, and Pentecostalism is the most seduced philosophy of our generation. They are lovers of money, lovers of the world, and lovers after the world in the name of prosperity. God did not prosper Jesus.

God did not prosper the Paul who wrote that. God did not prosper the early apostles who said, "Silver and gold, I have none." God did not prosper them. Yet the Gospel is on their foundation. Look at your heart that desires more and more, and has acquired more and more. And you want to fill the city and the nation with your kind.

Where has a sword gone through your heart so that the thoughts of many might be exposed?

In the world you didn't have much. You started the Christian life hardly having anything. Now demons have seduced you to say, "Gather the world and possess the world in the Lord Jesus." Is that what you came to Jesus for? We want to ask you:

What did you come to Jesus for?

You came to prepare for heaven; now you are seduced to prepare for the world.

You came to prepare for heaven; now your worry is the world, how to have more and more of it.

Where were you when you first started?

What did you have?

It is now gain! When you were a simple believer, you had limited things. Now you have been seduced into thinking that now as the leader you should have more. And you deceive yourself that it is so as to serve God. And God is weighing your wicked heart. The Gospel has become an instrument of covetousness. There is no peace in your heart! There is no rest! No wonder, the fruit of your ministry lacks depth. You lead people to Christ and you are the one to tell them that they are Christians because there is no evident change. They see no change but you use Bible verses to deceive them that they have become believers. What will be required at the gate of heaven will not be a Bible verse. Where are the marks of the Crucified One in you or in them? It is this whole matter of reproducing your kind!

Have you been a blessing to God?

Your kind that is being reproduced, is it a blessing to God?

Mr. Missionary, with a world-laden heart, what are you doing to that nation?

In Burkina Faso, they say it is a land of people of integrity. As we were looking for a missionary to go to Burkina Faso, we said the person must, first of all, be deeply rooted in integrity. If he is a person for whom 2 + 2 can be 4.1, even the unbelievers in Burkina Faso will pick him out for a crook. I am told, a Cameroonian went there and, thinking that there weren't enough seats on the plane, he decided to do it the Cameroonian way. He passed a thousand francs note under the table. The man took it and gave him back publicly and told him, "We don't do this here." These are the standards of the world. Are they your standards? Maybe the world should preach a message to you that you have exaggerated the whole matter of loving the world.

Some years ago, I went to Douala with a brother who works in Christian Publishing House, Yaounde. The police stopped us to check whether we had paid the tax. And this brother had not paid taxes for about two years or so. He had specialised in cheating the government, stealing from the Cameroonian government. Then a pastor in the city went to plead for him because the police said they would take him and go and lock him up until he paid his tax. The policeman said, "Ah! Mr. Pastor, you are the one who ought to have been saying that this man should pay his tax. You are now saying that I should let him go free!"

When the world begins to preach to believers,...

A sister bought a Mercedes Benz car in our Chemistry Department. The striking thing is this: The Head of Department decided to have a personal interview with her to ask her how she got money for a Mercedes Benz car with all the salary reductions.

Now when the world is worried about our possessions, is it because we have followed God better than the apostles? If the world begins to be worried about our possessions, is it because we have followed God more than the apostles? It is because we have kept what the apostles would have given away for the sake of the Gospel. I have to confront the fact that:

Regardless of what I give, if there is any keeping of what the apostles would have given away, I have disqualified myself. I am demoted. I have demoted myself because God is not just looking at what I have given; He is looking at what is left.

He is weighing my lifestyle.

He weighs what I eat.

He weighs what I wear.

He weighs my expenditures.

and the information that comes out determines the extent to which I could be promoted spiritually in the future.

Is that why you have been demoted? You were a leader of 1000, now you are a leader of 100. Or you were a leader of 500 and now you are a leader of 200. Or you were a leader of

100 and now you are a leader of 5. God has demoted you! God has demoted you by cutting down the impact of your leadership, and cutting down the people you should be leading. Is that why there is no increase in your numbers?

God cannot increase the leadership of a worldly man.

Whatever his growth in number is, it will soon stop.

By the grace of God, the brethren are still in the Assembly, but they have turned to another leader. God is bringing you to your size, according to the things you love. People who came after you are now the people who control the others. You turned away from the Narrow Way and the Lord has turned away from you. It is as if very soon you will be led by the people you led to the Lord. Among the men and women of the glory are people who believed many years after you. And if your name were to be mentioned among them, they would know that it is a lie. You lack splendour because little by little, a step at a time, you are now looking exactly in the opposite direction.

Among the people of the glory are people who believed many years after you.

- among the men of fasting,
- among the women of fasting,
- among the men of prayer,
- among the women of prayer,
- among the people of sacrificial giving,
- among the soul-winners,
- among the restorers of backsliders,

in truth, you are not one of them. You are just the conductor in the front. You are like a monkey who entertains. You are like *Jacob*, the monkey in the Zoo in Victoria.

You buried all on the altar of self-indulgence and the love of the world, and the love of the things of the world. You have been going round in circles for many years.

In Yaounde we place the Elders according to when they became Elders. But listen, there is another list according to :

- their spiritual weight,
- their standing before God,
- the marks of the Cross written in their lives,
- what they have sacrificed for Jesus,
- what they have denied themselves of because of the Lord Jesus Christ.

And everyone knows that that list is different from this one. And it is that list that matters.

Have you ever asked yourself, "Where am I?"

Have you ever asked somebody to tell you where you are? Have you ever asked somebody who cannot be bribed, to tell you where you are on the real list? Your work may be progressing, but have you confronted where it would have been had you been total in your consecration? Maybe you are rejoicing because of twenty people whereas were you to be more consecrated, there would be two thousand. You have taken twenty for two thousand.

You know King Solomon made all those gold shields, which were held when he was going into the temple. They were stolen and Rehoboam made other ones of bronze. When he too was going into the temple, they also held them. This fool could not distinguish between gold and bronze. He thought that they were the same thing, provided somebody held them. Each time I get to these Bible verses, I am totally overwhelmed by how a man can be so deceived. They take gold away and you replace it with bronze. Then you take steps as if...Brethren, do you see the extent to which a man can be deceived? If this man had been honest, he would not have made those things. He would have just walked simply into the temple. But he did not want to face the facts.

1. You have something like the prayer life to substitute for real praying.
2. You have bronze praying in place of gold praying.
3. Your spiritual father had gold praying; you have bronze praying.
4. Your wife has gold praying; you have bronze praying.
5. Your disciple-maker has gold giving; you have bronze giving.
6. You have bronze consecration in place of gold consecration.

Are you an Elder of bronze amidst the Elders of gold? And you say, "We are all Elders ." When they say, "The Elders are meeting," you also go. They are Elders of gold; you are an Elder of bronze.

You are an Elder's wife or a missionary wife of bronze.

Your husband, a man of gold; you, a woman of bronze. When they say Elders' wives are meeting, a few women of gold gather. You also appear and say, "My husband is Number One, Number Two, give me the big seat. I will be the President of the association," - of women who don't know what they are looking for or of an association of dishonest women, because if they were honest they would say, "Leave the chairman's seat. You are bronze."

Let us pray that everyone here who has replaced gold with bronze and is content with it in whatever area of his life, should be convicted.

The reference to the shields of gold we are talking about, in Solomon's case, is (2 Chronicles 9:15-16). The Bible says, "King Solomon made two hundred large shields of hammered gold; six hundred bekas of hammered gold went into each shield. He also made three hundred small shields of hammered gold, with three hundred bekas of gold in each shield. The king put them in the Palace of the Forest of Lebanon.

2 Chronicles 12 verse 2: "Because they had been unfaithful to the Lord, Shishak King of Egypt attacked Jerusalem in the fifth year of King Rehoboam."Verse 9, "When Shishak King of Egypt attacked Jerusalem, he carried off the treasures of the temple of the Lord and the treasures of the royal palace. He took everything, including the gold shields that Solomon had made. So King Rehoboam made bronze shields to replace them and assigned these to the commanders of the guard on duty at the entrance to the royal palace. Whenever the king went to the Lord's temple, the guards went with him, bearing the shields, and afterwards they returned them to the guardroom."

He was guarding them. To him bronze was treasure. And bronze is of lower quality than silver. In King Solomon's day we are told that silver was cheap. Even that which was cheap was not even available in Rehoboam's day. And it was just one generation after.

Have you backslidden in your own lifetime, just in one generation, just in one lifespan, from gold to bronze, from single-hearted commitment, to somebody fat with the love of the world? Do you not see from where

you have fallen? Do you not see that in your life you now permit things that ten years ago you would have considered that any person who did such things would find heaven difficult to attain?

Now your wife does the things you thought girls who did such things should not be married at all. She dresses in the way that if you had seen a girl dressed like that, you would have jumped through the window, but now that kind of dressing is not only found in your heart but is found in your bed, and the courage to say, "In the Name of Jesus Christ, I stop this thing," is not there. And your children are also like that. It is total disorder. And the children say, "Papa don weak" = ("Papa has become weak").

You now allow your husband to do things of which you said, "A man who does such things cannot be my husband." The type of men of whom you said, "A man like this will offend everything of God in me," is the one you now call: "Darling." Everything is totally confused.

I read a commentary about the Church on Random Road, in China, in Watchman Nee's days. It was their main Church in Shanghai. From the beginning there were the rigours of Watchman Nee. The author says that when the Church was now 4000 members, miniskirted girls began to be there. Girls who in the past would have been considered fit only for a brothel were now coming to sit under Watchman Nee's teaching of the Gospel.

Even if naked women came to an evangelistic meeting, we would allow them, but when you soak semi-naked women in water and call them believers, and sit such to teach them, it is because you have lost God. When the things that infuriated you in the past are now accommodated, it is not because you have matured. It is because you have backslidden.

Where is the rigour of the days when you first found the Lord?

I think of a sister. Some years ago, she was going to pray with Sister Emily. They said they were going to pray for four hours. She asked, "Is it four hours of real praying or just four hours in the place of prayer?" That was about ten years ago. The other day I saw her fat with pregnancy, but also fat with backsliding. I don't know when I last saw her in the place of prayer. In her own lifetime, she has become a backslider, meanwhile she is reproducing, reproducing backsliders. Her children will be born again backslidden.

Have you backslidden in your own lifetime?

Before, you could take a thirty-day partial fast. Now, one-day partial fast is like a cross. You are invaded by hunger as if by armed robbers. Hunger to you is like armed robbers.

You used to spend nights in prayer alone. Oh! but you are now a man, and a personal all-night prayer is no longer in your programme. It was the thing that was there week by week, but now after one or two hours of praying alone, you are yawning. You cut the personal all-night prayer from ten hours to eight hours, then to seven hours, then to five hours, and now it is no longer there. The personal all-night prayer has disappeared. Now you say Jesus fasted for all of us, and Jesus is on the throne praying for all of us.

Have you backslidden in your own generation?

Before, when money entered your hands you thought about the souls of men. Your dream was how to give more and more. Now your dream is how to buy more and more things. It has been clearly shown that in most Ministries, as the facilities have increased, as the rooms have increased, the Holy Spirit has disappeared.

Brother Peter Schneider showed me two buildings in Germany - the old building and the new one. The old building was at the beginning of the Work, where people prayed and prayed and prayed. And the new building was put afterwards when the Fire had gone out, because when the Fire is out, people are concerned or preoccupied with buildings. They plan more and more buildings. They plan more and more structures, more and more computers, more and more tape-recorders, etc. thinking that these can substitute for the absence of God, or that these things can bring God back. They cannot.

Do you know any marriage that has become more intimate as goods have increased? I am yet to find one.

Have you backslidden in your own lifetime? Your meditation book is now full of new positions because you have abandoned the original position and found new positions to allow you to continue away from the Cross. Your life is no longer a model. You don't disturb anybody any more. You are no longer insulted. You are even respected. Your family is now totally at peace with you because the sharp edges of the Cross have been abandoned. The family meetings to which nobody dared to invite you in the past because your presence made them so uncomfortable, you now attend and have the president's chair. Your sisters and brothers, who dreaded you, find your companionship fun. They want you. Have you backslidden in your own lifetime?

In order not to deceive ourselves, write in your book:

Areas in which I have replaced gold with bronze:

1. ....

2. ....

3. ....

4. ....
5. ....
6. ....

so that when you come to look at your notes you will see them in a conspicuous way. When you do it, allow some space to add what the Holy Spirit will show you later on.

There might have been golden commitments to someone. Now there is none or there is very little. There might have been golden service, golden gifts to God and to man. And now you have become Mr. Stingy. You have got a degree from Stingy University. Maybe you were always there on time for the prayer meeting; now you come late and go away early; and sometimes you are not even there. Before, you were the one who prayed on almost every topic; now, for you to stand up and pray, it needs a horse to lift your buttocks. Before, you had the gift of tongues and you exercised it; now, the gift is dormant. Before, you exercised your body; now, you are just clumsy from no exercise. Before, you were slim and nice; now, you are like someone prepared for the Agric Show. Before, your things were orderly; now, everything is scattered. Before, when there was dirt on the collar of a shirt , you didn't wear it; now, you wear the same shirt over and over so that they see that you have become Christian dirt.

In America where things are very cheap - with two dollars you can buy six socks - one Reverend Brother there removed his shoes and his socks were laughing with holes. It is not poverty. Of course, the man knows nothing about sacrifice for God; so it is not because he gave. It is just the lack of the power to take care of himself.

Before, you bathed everyday; now they need to catch you to bathe you.

Your beard has become disorderly. Everything has crumbled. You have no more standards in anything.

As one sister has said, she starts following the husband from the door to pick up his socks. She picks up this one and then the other; for he starts throwing them from the door. Then he removes his pants and throws them anywhere in the room.

These are not errors. There is a problem inside.

The more a man loses God, the more disorderly he becomes, because God is a God of order.

Before, you loved those who love the Lord; now, their presence offends you. And you have never had a team. People come and go away because you lack what it takes to keep people around you. It takes God to keep people around you. The aroma of Christ has disappeared, so there is nothing to keep people there. You are a gossip centre, so when they have gossiped and gossiped with you they go away because they now want the company of a spiritual man in order to grow. Even the one who loved you most is no longer interested in you because you are like Ichabod. The glory has departed. That thing of Jesus which used to make you sweet and attractive, which made that person linger around you, is no longer there. It is just the world now; so that when he sees you he is immediately offended. After hearing two or three sentences from you, he must go away because what you offer is offensive.

When you were consecrated you and your wife knew no disagreements on money, but now as you have reduced your giving to God, you quarrel more and more. It is just the reality.

People have less and less quarrels as they give more and more to God. But as they keep more and more for

themselves, they have an increasing range of disagreements.

One wants the deep freezer, the other one wants the refrigerator. One wants a bed, the other one wants a cupboard. One wants a car, the other one wants a boat.

The more people have, the more they disagree.

The next list is the things that you have never put on. Write down:

I have never purchased the gold of:

1. **Long fasts:** You have deceived yourself that God made you for short fasts and that you would die if you did a long fast. And you make as if burial grounds were all full.

2. **Long prayer seasons:** You have never taken yourself to pray every night for ten days, every night for twenty-one days, every night for thirty days or every night for forty days. You have just said, "No, these are for the specialists. They are not for me. I am a simple believer." It is wickedness for a person to say, "I am a simple believer!" Who is not a simple believer? Who is a complicated believer?

The tragic lack of spiritual ambition!

The tragic lack of a desire to do great things for God!

The tragic lack of striving after God's best!

The tragic lack of monuments!

You are just there, good-for-nothing, yet endowed with enormous capacities. When they talk about forty-day fasts, it is as if you will do your own in heaven. When they talk of twenty-eight-day fasts, you will do your own the month before Jesus comes. When they talk about twenty-one-day fasts, you will do your own when the Church has been handed back to the Saviour. When you hear that some people pray for forty days, you say, "Well, we have different gifts." Now, which is your own gift?

I am amazed by the ease with which believers shake away challenges! You hear that somebody is giving 50% to God; you are content with your 11% and say, "After all, all people are not to do the same thing." Now what are you great in? You have refused the challenges that God brings along in your life. You ease yourself and say, "Ah! They are boasting. God will not record it for them." But what then is there to be recorded for you?

You hear that some Assembly is growing very rapidly. Instead of going to ask, "Brother, what is the secret?" You say, "Ah! they are half-converts." You seem to think that real converts should be very few, and that they are those who are found with you. You don't want to confront your barrenness. You say, "When the numbers are big, they are carnal. We are the deep ones." Deep in barrenness!

One sister drove over a very long distance to come and listen to me speaking. She said, "In the last four to five years no one person has been added to our Church, but our pastor looks very devoted." I said, "He is devoted in what? In ensuring that nobody comes to the Church? He is devoted in closing the door to potential converts. No fruit, cut it down!"

Refusing to be challenged, you speak evil of those who are distinguished or you say, "Well, my own gift is elsewhere." Where is it? Name it. People who don't want to name things are people who have constructed their own dishonesty system. Paul said, "Are they apostles? I am more." Now, take a bit of folly for once and write and boast. Some people's head is always there because they have nothing to boast about. If Paul had had nothing to boast about, he would not have lost his head. Can you lose your head? When you lose it, what will you talk about? You lack the power to see great things as possible. You lack the power to attempt great things for God. You have no massive projects in view. You have no projects such that unless God intervenes, failure is guaranteed. You are striving after nothing.

My wife tells me that when they were in the secondary school they used to have some exercise: "A hop and a lift, a hop and a lift." Running away from vigorous exercise. You have never been angry in prayer. There has never been the desire to pull down the heavens, to tear down the barrier and get God down quickly. You have never prayed and got near fainting.

Brethren, I have had that experience only once or twice. One of them was just twenty minutes of prayer. After that, I was more tired than I have ever been in any prayer. A brother in France said the doctors had examined their baby in the womb and said the baby would be handicapped. So they had been advised to commit an abortion. He said, "I have said, 'No' to that advice. If that baby will only be able to say, 'Jesus Christ is my Saviour,' that is enough." When I read the letter, I was aflame, I was angry. In twenty minutes, I had exhausted all my energies to the finish. The child is perfectly normal and is seven years old now.

No anger in prayer, "Our Father,... Who art in heaven..." When a man of prayer is praying with you, he has to cry out to God for patience. When he hits, hits, hits, you take your hand like... (You know, when they are trying to repeat the scoring, a goal that was scored PANG! They now get the man to play very slowly and the ball is going at the most reduced pace.) You are like that. You are playing with somebody who smashes but your own praying is like that after - slow motion. By the time that you have prayed your one sentence the other person is dying. He needs somebody with whom when he smashes, the person will smash, smash, smash and smash! If when the man gives two blows, your hand is still going out to look for the first blow, before he prays with you next time, he will pray alone first to ask God for grace to bear you: "My...my God,...I wor...ship You. A...men." The sharp edges are not there. The aggressiveness is not there. The anger is not there, so that your praying is sending people to sleep. It is the music of sleep. And you have been doing that for years, yet you have been in the company of aggressive men and women of prayer. And your wicked heart tells you that you shall not make any change because it is your habit, it is your character. Go to Cotonou and there you will see how people are praying like fire. You do not put your all into your praying. You do not pray with all your spirit, soul and body. You make as if your mouth were full of butter: "Bah, bah, bah, bah." No fire. And your whole life has been without fire. Your burdens are there today; tomorrow they have evaporated. You have never known sustained burden. You have a new burden everyday because the old one has gone. Like a baby, you are easily distracted. Like a baby, you lack the power to keep at one burden, to keep smashing and smashing and smashing until the walls collapse. Being so easily distracted, you have never put on what you ought to have put on, and yet you are happy. Some say, "If I can only make it to heaven."

They lack holy aggressiveness.

They lack holy ambition.

They are disturbed by nothing except food and clothes.

They have never put on aggressiveness.

They have never put on fierceness.

No one fears you except because of your self-love; when someone steps on your toe, then you rise like a serpent. But nothing about things going wrong in the Kingdom of God disturbs you.

Say, "I have never put on the following:" (Make the list.)

1. ---------------
2. ---------------
3. ---------------
4. ---------------

You have had an unusual capacity to insulate yourself from being disturbed by the people God has brought your way to provoke you.

God brings men in your life who ought to disturb you and set you right.

But you are insulated and therefore remain untouched. You build all the reasons to ensure that you are not provoked. The books you choose to read are only books of encouragement. You like testimonies, but you don't imitate the people whose testimonies you read.

Are you disturbed by the progress of others?

Do you feel a holy disturbance that says, "I will not die a mediocre! If this man could do this, I will rise and do something about it"?

Can you be disturbed?

Can you be provoked?

Who has provoked you?

Where are the marks of it?

Contentment with mediocrity soon turns to jealousy.

Once I was in Ibadan. There is a man there, opposed to the baptism in the Holy Spirit, but the wife got baptized in the Holy Spirit. After she got baptized, she began to lead very many people to the Lord, and she had such an intense burden to pray. She would pray, pray and pray. Both of them were believers, yet one day when she was praying, he went there and said, "Ah! You are not different from any other person!" The man ought to be provoked by a woman who was always praying and he was not praying, but instead when she made a slight error, he would rejoice saying, "You are not different from all of us." That was how to harden his position against the baptism into the Holy Spirit. Who was supposed to be different - the wife or the man?

If your wife is like you, you have already failed - because you should be a gap ahead.

Any man who is not a shoulder higher than his wife has failed. If you are not a shoulder higher than your wife

- in your consecration,
- in your service,
- in the intensity of your devotion,
- in the intensity of seeking God,
- in the intensity of finding God,
- in the intensity of knowing God,
- in the intensity of loving God,
- in the intensity of making God your total satisfaction,

you are a mediocre. Where will you stand to speak to her?

So this man was saying, "My wife, you are not better than me," out of jealousy, but he was at least admitting that the wife was at his level, that he had lost leadership. But he had not only lost leadership; the woman was very far ahead. If a man is content to be at the same level with his wife, where is the leadership? Manhood is not trousers or ties. You know there are women who wear trousers and ties and coats. If it were the clothing that made manhood, we could by one announcement change things.

Manhood is the power to be ahead in everything that pertains to God.

God places people in our lives to push us to great heights. And the unholy contentment is the undoing of many.

God brings people into our lives so that we imitate them and therefore rise to heights.

You know an area in which a person is distinguished, and instead of going to ask him, "Brother, how have you done it?" the corruption of your heart does not allow you to ask him. Somebody sleeps little; you sleep the whole day and the whole night and even when you are not sleeping, you are half asleep; and you will not ask him, "What is the secret?" You don't want to know lest you have to change. You have decided to settle for mediocrity. I joyfully reread a Bible verse and found that it said that the baptism of the Holy Spirit means that rivers of living water should flow forth; NOT a river. Before the baptism, the Holy Spirit is like a spring welling up to eternal life.

John 4:14 "But whoever drinks the water I give him will never thirst. Indeed, the water I give him will become in him a spring of water welling up to eternal life."

About the baptism in the Holy Spirit, John 7:37-39, says "rivers": "On the last and greatest day of the Feast, Jesus stood and said in a loud voice, 'If anyone is thirsty, let him come to me and drink. Whoever believes in me, as the Scripture has said, streams of living water will flow from within him.' By this He meant the Spirit, whom those who believed in Him were later to receive. Up to that time the Spirit had not been given, since Jesus had not yet been glorified."

It is as if I had never discovered the "s" in "rivers." I discovered it in the U.S. and I danced and danced although I was in an upstair house. "Rivers! rivers!" I said, "Ah!"

- rivers of the pastoral ministry,
- rivers of the evangelistic ministry,
- rivers of the teaching ministry,
- if need be, the rivers of an apostolic ministry,
- if need be, the rivers of a prophetic ministry,
- rivers of giving to God,
- rivers of fasting,
- rivers of prayer,
- rivers of restoring backsliders,
- rivers of academic excellence,
- rivers of professional excellence.

Rivers! Not just one. Rivers!

So I sat down and I decided on the many areas in which the rivers shall flow. And some that were becoming small, I decided to dig out the obstructing things and deepen them and widen them. Rivers! A very mighty river on this side and another mighty river on that side! Rivers! Hallelujah! It is in the purpose of God because it is the supernatural work of God. God has ordained that we move into the supernatural, and that there be many rivers flowing out of us. Rivers! Hallelujah!

Our labour is to present to the Lord Jesus Christ people who obey Him in everything.

So if you want an easy-going place, this is the wrong one. And there is no day that you will stop wrestling because the more progress you make, the more progress you have to make. To make as if one has got to the end of the battle is to miss it completely. Some of you are shocked if a senior leader confesses his sin. That confession is just telling you that he is going higher and higher because the nearer you are to Jesus, the more you see how sinful you are. The farther away you are from Jesus, the more you say all is well even when nothing is well.

AGGRESSIVE SERVANTHOOD

Joshua!

We are going to have seven books on leadership.

1. This one will be called : Spiritual Leadership in The Pattern of Joshua

2. There is: Spiritual Leadership According To Moses.

3. *"Vision, Burden, Action"* is: Spiritual Leadership According to Nehemiah.

4. There will be: Spiritual Leadership According to The Pattern of David.

5. There will be: Spiritual Leadership According to The Pattern of The Apostle Paul, which will be what we shall have in the World Convention next year.

6. And the last book on the series will be: Spiritual Leadership According to The Pattern of The Lamb, Jesus Christ, because when you get there, you can go no further.

After that, we shall look at: <u>The Character of The Spiritual Leader</u>—not his ministry but his character—because there are more failures in character than there are in ministry. A crook can do great things once or twice, but it requires distilled character to live day by day according to the Cross.

The first thing we want to look at is: Aggressive Servanthood

---

As we go on, you will find out how best to put it. In the background, you see Moses as the servant of Jethro for forty years. When you meet a man, ask:

- What is in his background?
- At whose feet did he sit?
- With whom did he rub shoulders?

For Joshua's spiritual heritage, you have Moses. Moses was a servant for forty years. He was Jethro's servant. Moses was like a Doctor from the University of Egypt, but in Jethro's house he became a shepherd. Jethro didn't say, "Dr. Moses is going to shepherd the flock." He didn't say to the sheep, "Your shepherd has a doctorate's degree. Clap for him." Nor did Moses say, "Sheep, when I was in the University of Egypt, I got very high marks. See, I did great things in Egypt, I was mighty in my deeds and mighty in my words. Sheep, your shepherd almost became the next Pharaoh. Sheep, just with my empty hands, I killed an Egyptian and buried him in the sand because he was against my people. Sheep, I am very handsome. Your shepherd is very hand-some. Look at my face, my looks." Whatever Moses could have said that looked like a wonder in the world could have got only one answer from the sheep: "Meeee! Meeee!!

Meeee!!!" because that is all that there is in worldly things — "Meeee!!!!"

If Brother Jacques, the publisher, goes and tells his books or the machines, "Your Director was Director General of Forest Regeneration in the country. Clap! You are honoured. You are privileged." If the books could speak, they would say, "Meeee!!!!"

"Books, your publisher studied in Canada." "Meeee!!!!"

"Books, your publisher has a very good car." "Meeee!!!!"

"Books, your publisher has four children." "Meeee!!"

"Books, your publisher has the power to command people and to lead them." "Meeee!!!!!!!!!!!!"

As you increase the list of your accomplishments, the sheep are getting more and more hungry; so that if it were possible, the sheep would ask for more food: there would be more "Meeees!"

Listen, Brethren, it looks like a joke, but in eternity, all the glories of the world will make just the sense that saying that you were a doctor makes to sheep. May God imprint that on your heart!

Song:

> *Forbid it, Lord, that I should boast,*
> *Save in the Cross of Christ my Lord;*
> *All the vain things that charm me most,*
> *I sacrifice them to His blood.*
>
> *See, from His head, His hands, His feet,*
> *Sorrow and love flow mingled down*
> *Did e'er such love and sorrow meet*

Or thorns compose so rich a crown?

Were the whole realm of nature mine
That were an offering far too small
Love so amazing, so divine,
Demands my soul, my life, my all.

I would like us to pray that that "Demands my soul, my life, my all" should not be words only, but that it should be true that if the whole realm of nature were ours, that would be an offering far too small; for love so amazing, so divine, demands all that I possess: my soul, my life, my all.

What does "demands my soul, my life, my all" mean? Now write out what it means.

It demands your husband: you leave him to God, and never complain.

It demands your wife: you leave her to God, and never complain.

It demands your children: to give them to God and never force your wicked plans on them, wanting them to gain the world that you failed to gain, even though you wanted it so badly.

"Oh! I want my child to be first in the class, first in the class!" And I am not against children being first. But what will that "first" lead to? Will it lead to the Cross or away from the Cross?

Rather, your prayer should be: "Lord, I take off my hands from this child. I abolish my plans. God, if this child will glorify You by failing in school, God, may she succeed in failing."

Are you sincere that your child should be married to the Cross or have you worldly desires to see the child succeed before the world?

In your educating of the child, is it glory, heaven, the knowledge of the Lord, the service of the Lord, or is it a mixture: "Child, have the world, but have Jesus also. Have the world, but don't abandon Jesus. Let Jesus help you to win the world"?

A colleague once told me in Makerere that someone prayed in London, saying, "God, You are good; Satan, you are not bad either."

"My child, love the Lord, but make sure you succeed in the world." Finally, parents can be the most wicked people that ever existed in a child's life. Their divided hearts cause them to have plans for a brilliant sin-stained future for their children.

My wife and I had a TESSA account in Britain, an account that has existed since 1969 when I graduated from the university, because I used the money of the prize I got at graduation to start that savings account which I later on converted into the TESSA. Later on I said, "In order to be a responsible father, this one will be for the education of the children." The account matured last month. It is an account that matures after five years. And I said, "Well, Stephen is at the university. Elizabeth will be going to the Medical School," and I had a war. In fact, there is £11,200,00 in the account, the fruit of 26 years of savings. Then I said, "My father saved nothing for my education, and this year I am in Who Is Who In The World for my chemical contribution." My wife and I decided to turn the money over to the Missionary Fund. If the children cannot be more educated, 'A' level certificates at the General Certificate of Education Examination are very good education already. So that nobody may go to hell while I am planning the education of our children.

The words in the Bible are not beautiful language. They are rooted in practical Christianity. They are demands on a life. If you are reading the Bible honestly, it will be putting a question mark on your life! That is why to really read the Bible, only Spirit-filled men can cope. The others have hardened their hearts so much that they can read so many chapters and they are not touched.

Before I went to the university, I had some time with the father I loved so much. He told me, "I leave you in the hands of Jesus. I give you Jesus. I have nothing in the world to give you, but I give you Jesus." And I have lacked nothing. I have lacked nothing, and I have acquired all in the world that it was sane to acquire.

Be very careful about your ambitions for your children.

They might represent the height of the corruption of heart.

They might represent utter wickedness.

They might represent utter divorce from the life you seem to say you believe and separation from the One you say you believe.

My first daughter, Ruth, and the husband, Philip, will leave this month for Great Britain as missionaries. Their going represents the greatest price I could ever pay and I have had to pay so far in following the Lamb, because of my special relationship with Ruth. And they will go away with no knowledge as to when we may ever see ourselves again except on that Great Day when there will be no more parting.

> "Were the whole realm of nature mine,
> That were an offering far too small."

The realm of children.

The realm of possessions.

The realm of positions.

The realm of family ties!

> "Love so amazing, so divine,
> Demands my soul, my life, my all."

Have you secret plans for your children's success in a cursed world: a success that is not the overflow of the Cross?

Then of all people you deserve to be pitied.

Have you worries about your children's worldly future without greater and exceedingly great worries about their spiritual future? Have demons caused you to pay a greater price for your children's academic performance than for their spiritual progress and development?

The covetousness that is hidden in a man's heart often comes out in the children. You give them the world, but you have not given them Jesus. You are the worst thing that ever happened to your children!

And I have seen parents cause shipwreck of their children by making choices for their children that will guarantee a place in the world, and risk everything spiritually. The first question is not, "What will happen to her soul?" Or "What will happen with her spiritual development?" But "What diploma will she have?" If rats ate my many certificates now, I would lose nothing. Is that not amazing? If rats ate all of them, I would miss nothing. But to have sacrificed God to get them, would represent folly in the extreme.

What are you worried about as far as your children are concerned — the marks of the Cross in their lives or the diplomas of the world? Where are your plans for them? What is your vision for them?

When Sister Elizabeth from Ibadan told me she dedicated her sons to the Lord and to the cause of God in the mission field, I said those children could not be more blessed to have such a mother.

> *"Were the whole realm of nature mine,*
> *That were an offering far too small;*
> *Love so amazing, so divine,*
> *Demands my soul, my life, my all."*

What is your response to those demands?

The question is:

What risk have you taken for the Gospel?

What have you jeopardised by your investment into the Gospel?

What is there that was guaranteed but can no longer be guaranteed because of your investment in the Gospel?

What have you shattered by your commitment to the Gospel that will remain wrecked for ever, unless there is a miracle?

The Lord is touching hearts and making them tender. It is also the moment for decisions, to make them and announce them so that you don't go back.

<u>Song</u>:

> *Saviour, while my heart is tender,*
> *I will yield that heart to Thee,*
> *Suffer me to leave Thee never;*
> *Seal Thine image on my heart.*

Seal Thine image on my heart!! so that I might see everything through the eyes of the Lamb, so that I may see everything with the values of the Lamb.

What did you do with your children while their hearts were still tender? Did you fill them with the world or did you fill them with brilliant hopes of lives wasted for the Gospel?

Because China is a massive mission field, we encourage our children to go there. So we put up a map of China about seven, eight years ago in the house. And some of them chose Chinese towns to which they shall go.

Are you preparing your children for a brilliant sin-stained future or for a brilliant future in the service of the Lord?

What is your life prophesying to the children?

As one brother prayed, the idols on his heart or the idols on the heart of the parents soon get installed in the hearts of the children. Look at the idolatry of your heart. Then your child has all those idols and more, plus her own!

Idols not overthrown in the lives of the parents soon become idols on the hearts of the children.

That is why: A worldly wife or a worldly husband is the worst tragedy that can happen to a person.

Do you look at your partner and weep because of the partner's infatuation with the world and the fact that your children will be that twisted?

The idols on the father's heart and those on the mother's heart will soon be the idols on the child's heart. An unconsecrated partner is the worst thing that can ever happen to a person. It is the ruin of the progeny.

When I was in America, everyday I had a lot of time to pray. Sometimes I prayed for 11 hours, some days for 10 hours, some for 9 hours. My new cry to God is,

> *"God, let all my children go to foreign mission fields.*
> *Let them go where the Lamb has not been named.*
> *It will be the best way of investing their lives.*
> *Take them away from all ease, Lord.*
> *Take them away from all comfort.*
> *Take them away from worldly comfort.*
> *Take them away from the comfort of the world.*
> *Take them to the rough lands.*
> *Send them where they will sleep on mats."*

And, Brethren, when I was 11, my father told me, "For the whole of this month, you will sleep on the mat because someday you might need it." So for that month I slept on a mat. It was training with the vision of a seer.

What are you schooling your children in? Will your children be happy to hear that you have kept money for them or to hear that you have invested in the Gospel, and that you have given them Jesus as their Inheritance?

When I knew that John was backsliding because his zeal for Shanghai was almost no longer existent, I began to pray for him everyday. I begin to see sparks of the renewal of his love for the Lord.

When Elizabeth was 8 years old, she received a call to become a missionary doctor. She has just done the General Certificate of Education Examination at the Advanced Level. And recently, when we were talking together, I asked her whether if she didn't go to the Medical School in Yaounde she would study something else in Cameroon. She said, "No, I must go to the Medical School, whatever country I must go to in order to become a medical doctor, because God told me to become a missionary doctor." I was touched by her tenacity. She is 17 this year. But it was at the age of 8 when during a family retreat she went with the others to seek the purpose of God for her life. And when I met her, she told me God had called her to be a missionary doctor.

Seeing the call of God.

Prepared to be that at any cost!

What are you schooling the children in?

What do they hear, what flows unconsciously into their ears?

Before I went to the United States, I told her, "Look, there is immorality in your heart. You have too many clothes! Too many clothes!" Clothes speak of immorality: "See me!!!!" Clothes were meant to cover our nakedness. When they have another purpose, it is immorality: "See me!!!" She emptied half of her wardrobe as a treatment of the disease I was pointing to and did a 21-day complete fast, asking God to separate her from the love of the world and the love of the things of the world permanently.

There must be violent pulling down of idols. There must be aggressiveness in the pulling down of the things that tempt the heart!!

When you have put in a 21-day complete fast, drinking water only, to overthrow the stronghold of the love of the world in your heart, or to overthrow the stronghold of the love of the things of the world in your heart, it will begin to betray spiritual seriousness. Until then, it is beautiful jokes, even if they are long prayers.

What are you schooling the children in?

When they look at your possessions, what comes into their hearts - glory, the world to come, or this one that has been judged?

Now, considering the schools to which you send your children and the extra monies you pay,

What have you done to send them to advanced spiritual schools? What have you done to ensure that your children cultivate determinant relationships?

Some of our children were very close to Theodore. It was very good for them.

What do you inspire in people?

Who are the heroes of your children?

Who are their role models?

Whom are you actively helping them to be close to?

Any idols left in our hearts will be planted in the hearts of the children.

Song:

Saviour, while my heart is tender,
I will yield that heart to Thee,
Suffer me to leave Thee never;
Seal Thine image on my heart.

Saviour, while my heart is tender,
I yield that heart to Thee;
Don't allow me to ever leave You,
Seal Thine image on my heart.

Saviour, while my children's hearts are tender,
Cause them to yield those hearts to Thee,
Suffer them to leave Thee never;
Seal Thine image on their hearts.

I want to ask you,

1. **Are you a worldly parent, causing the image that is being sealed on their hearts to be tarnished?**
2. **What type of parent are you?**
3. **Are there great renunciations in your life to cause the image of great renunciations to be sealed on their hearts?**

Anyone who thinks that what is transmitted to children is just genes is deceived. The caprices of parents are transmitted. Their tendencies towards the love of God are transmitted. A divided heart is transmitted! The rich ruler's type of heart is transmitted. The Pauline heart is transmitted.

What have you transmitted?

Can you say, "My consecration has made what I transmitted a great blessing to my children"? A parent who is a perpetual baby blocks the children from rising to great heights. It would have been good if some parents never reproduced, because of the corruption of their hearts. The irony is that such people go and overpopulate the earth, producing their kind.

Do you feel like going near the sea there and weeping for your husband?

Have you wept very often for your wife when you have seen her infatuation with the world and you know that your children will be like that?

There is something in genetics, both natural and spiritual: If a hardworking woman marries a lazy man, the children will tend to take the laziness of the man and leave the woman's hard work. As someone put it: **Nature sides with hidden flaws.**

So, if you say, "I am strong here, let me marry a woman who is weak there," the children will pick the weakness.

The story is told that Socrates was very ugly but also very intelligent, and that there was a woman who was all beauty, but the cerebral hemisphere was very smooth. She was not intelligent. She was very foolish. One day, she came and told him, "Let's get married, so that the children will inherit your wisdom, your intelligence and my beauty, my good looks." He said, "Your speech just betrays you. What if they inherit my ugliness and your foolishness?" She was not wise enough to see that possibility.

Do you see then the need for radical renunciations?

Do you now see the curse of having played with the call of God to radical consecration for so long that it is totally engraved in the children?

You thought you were very smart, you were cheating God. God cannot be cheated. Man can only deceive himself and his progeny.

Do you now see the need for the whole matter of marriage to be taken more seriously in the Assemblies because of what may be inherited? Are you to be feared when it comes to considering your children as possible partners?

DEDICATION OF THE BOOK: THE PRACTICE OF INTERCESSION

Could we commit this book - "The Practice of Intercession" to the Lord and to the cause of the Gospel? It is the most practical of the books to teach you how to pray. I was just looking at prayer Bulletin Number Nine on Fasting Intercession for Cameroon. Request Number 8 says: "Lord, there are multitudes in our nation who have heard Your Gospel but take it lightly. Lord, pour Your Holy Spirit on all such so that they will be quickened to turn from sin and self to the Lord." Is that not a need in this nation, and a need in many nations? Very many have heard the Gospel and they take it lightly. There is need for the second touch of God to lead to conversion.

When I was in Pensacola, the owner of a radio station, Brother Steven Williams, said that he was just going to read this book on the radio to the people, chapter by chapter, page by page, paragraph by paragraph, prayer topic by prayer topic, if the Americans would learn to pray. He told me my books are the most difficult books he has ever read in his life, because they search your stomach, search your heart, search your head. But he said they are the most blessed to read also. He was reading this book for the third time, and he said he had read all the others on prayer at least three times. He had an operation recently and he said for all the time in the hospital, he was reading this book. And he said, "This is what America needs in order to avoid the judgment of God."

"The Practice of Intercession." We thank God that it has been produced in Nigeria. I just thought about the fast we took some time in the past, "With the love of Jesus Christ to the Moslems." We thank God that Christian Publishing House, Lagos has got the book out with something of the modern approach to covers, and even the production inside - inking and the like.

We want to commit it to the Lord, pleading that the praying Lord on the throne might use this book to produce people like Him to wrestle in the nations. In it there are topics like:

- Intercession for an individual,
- Intercession for individuals,
- Intercession for a family,
- Intercession for an Assembly or Church,
- Intercession for a city,
- Intercession for a nation,
- Intercession for a continent,
- Intercession for Planet Earth.

A full-time ministry of intercession; which may be what God is calling you into; which is what Henriette Mbarga has been in for nearly 8 years now is a full-time ministry of moving God to move someone, and the like. Yes, it is a full-time ministry of intercession. There are many full-time prophets and many full-time apostles, including some who have only led two people to Jesus, but they have become apostles.

In Limbe, we met a Cameroonian who had loitered in Nigeria for a few years. When I met him I said, "Brother, who are you?" He told me, "I am Apostle Somebody." I said to myself, "Wow! One of those rare occasions one has in life to meet an apostle!" I said, "Brother, how many churches have you planted?" He said, "None as yet." I began to think that we were in danger. I said, "How many people have you led to the Lord?" He said, "Two," and he was an apostle! I was just stupefied by the courage. The Devil must be working for a man who has led two people to the Lord to call himself an apostle.

I am seeking some full-time ministers of intercession. In fact, I desperately need two people as full-time intercessors for the continent of Africa. We shall give them the chain where they are to shed their tears for the continent of Africa, day by day.

It is as if we had enough full-time pastors, although we don't have enough. It is as if we had enough full-time evangelists, even though we don't have enough. But where are the full-time ministers of intercession? Comparatively, it is as if there were too many pastors. For every full-time pastor, we need a full-time intercessor.

Let us intercede that God should use the book to set the Church aflame to pray, to inflame the leaders to pray to alter

- the history of individuals,
- the history of families,
- the history of quarters,
- the history of cities,
- the history of churches,
- the history of nations,
- the history of continents,

through the vigorous instrument of holy intercession.

Let us pray that the book should fall where it must fall and that the seed should germinate to produce a praying people.

Praise the Lord! The book costs N 450.00 = 3,000 CFA francs. The American hardcover is 9,000 francs. So this is sold at one-third of the price and, as you know, in the U.S. now paperback costs 50% of the hardcover. They normally cost around 60% of the hardcover. So this is an extremely good price. When you buy it, protect the back and you can use it for the next ten years.

A Nigerian in Great Britain wrote to me. She wanted this book to be sent to her at her expense. She said that the one she had has been used and used until the cover and the pages are worn out from much use. We thank God for such users. It means that the Lord gave the Word, and they are chewing it. That is what we need today. The problem is that we don't have eaters of books.

Watchman Nee's book, "What Shall This Man Do?" that got into my hands just when I was laying hold on the Ministry - I read it during four months. In the first reading, which I did on my knees, I could read only a page or half a page at a time. The book was concentrated stuff. But I have read it eight times through now.

Deep books are not for superficial people. Superficial people will not get much out of it. If you buy this book, take it on a weekend for your first reading. Afterwards, begin to read a page at a time so that it might stir your spirit to go and pray. Whether we win in the future or not will depend upon how much we pray. Ask God to make you a lover of the books on prayer. It is absolutely important, and we have many of them. Very soon we shall have "Moving God Through Prayer." We are waiting for it to come from France. We are waiting for "Practical Spiritual Warfare Through Prayer." The Lagos Publishing House in Nigeria intends to produce "Practical Spiritual Warfare Through Prayer." And in the U.S. when they heard that we had written "Waiting on God in Prayer" many people wanted to read it because such titles are not found in current literature, and many people don't know what it is about. By God's mercy we have been allowed to know something of what we write about from experience. You cannot read the books on prayer and remain the same. I was reading what Oswald Chambers wrote. He said:

Prayer is the greater works.

The Lord said, "Greater works than these shall you do because I go to the Father." He said many believers think that they will pray so that the greater works happen. He said prayer is the greater works.

The day before yesterday, I began a new series of teaching in Yaounde, teaching the leaders on the theme: What Prayer Does To The Praying Person. It will come out as a book because many people do not know what prayer does in the praying person. Next Tuesday, we shall have the second message.

The person who does not pray is a caricature. He cannot know God. His character is out of symmetry with God.

Why? Because Prayer is the place of change.

One man enters into a prayer closet, another man comes out of it.

The most dramatic changes take place in the prayer closet.

Pray that men and women should love prayer literature.

Brethren, let me tell you what happened. This year, I read 24 books on prayer from Spurgeon to Moody to Watchman Nee, all this year. Oh! and Spurgeon wrote. You can't write deeply on prayer if you are not a man of prayer. A man who writes on prayer without deep experiences in the School of Prayer is a dangerous crook.

One man gave me two books. I decided not to take them because the man has nothing in his life that reflects a bit of what the topic is about. He wrote Volume One and Volume Two. But the two books could have been squeezed into thirty pages. And he was selling each for $5.00. His co-worker said, "We wrote it because we want to make money." The book was on angels. He deserved to be beaten by angels.

If you have not made history in prayer, where else will you make history? Prayer is the greater works. Pray with clear goals for answers, using the dimension of praying with the spirit.

I said to myself, "Before this year is out, I must pray six hours at a stretch in tongues," that is, I start praying in tongues and I do not stop until I have prayed for six hours. I have been developing little by little, from 15 minutes to 20 minutes to 30 minutes,... When I left for the United States, I was at 1 hour 15 minutes. I came back at 2 hours of praying with tongues non-stop. I will not leave for India unless I am at 3 hours non-stop. I will keep training. By the end of the year, I must be able to pray at a stretch in tongues for 6 hours.

You remember when we were in Cotonou the other year, God was talking to us about intensity in prayer. Now, He is talking to me about intensity with duration - sustained intensity. Because to blow "Bang" is great. But to make "Bang!!!" for a short time and to give "Bang!!!!!" for 1 hour, "Bang!!!!" for 2 hours, and then "Bang!!!!!!!" for 6 hours...!!!!! Listen, Brethren,

Prayer is like physical exercise; you train the body for it.

I got a magazine in Delta Airlines. They give it free. They were interviewing people who were going for the Olympics. The person with the minimum record said he was putting in 8 hours of training a day. Eight hours a day and into training his body in order to win a perishable medal! But we are training for the imperishable reward of God.

Sustained intensity cannot come any other way than by practice. There is no other way to sustained intensity, or to fierce fighting for long periods except by goals set and goals pursued and goals accomplished.

Sustained Aggressiveness! Sustained Intensity!

- It is one thing to stand up and give 50% to God.
- It is another thing to have years of giving 50% to God.
- It is one thing to pray for a season.
- It is another thing to have a life of sustained seasons of prayer.
- It is one thing to carry out a long fast.
- It is another thing to have a life plastered with long fasts,
- a life plastered with prayer crusades,
- a life plastered with heavy gifts to God,
- a life plastered with sustained evangelism.

If we had written only one book, it would have made no impact. For those of you who pray, last week in Yaounde we dedicated the 74th book entitled; "How To Lead A House Church." Next week, we will dedicate the 75th book entitled:

"A Missionary Heart And A Mission Life." Both of them are thick books.

Sustained intensity in prayer and fasting is part of spiritual aggressiveness. A long fast every year is sustained, then you decide to have two long fasts a year, then you work at three long fasts a year. Whether the Enemy likes it or not, he will collapse. Before, it was heavy blowing once a year. Now it is twice a year; then when you get to three times a year, his reserves will be knocked out.

The Bible says in <u>Deuteronomy 1:6-7</u>

> *"The Lord God said to us at Horeb, 'You have stayed long enough at this mountain. Break camp and advance into the hill country of the Amorites; go to all the neighbouring peoples in the Arabah, in the mountains, in the western foothill, in the Negev and along the coast, to the land of the Canaanites and to Lebanon, as far as the great river, the Euphrates.'"*

You have stayed too long, you have stayed long enough at this mountain! You have stayed long enough at this mountain! You have remained at the same place for too long. It might have been a great place but you have stayed there for too long.

Ruth Ndasi has done a 40-day fast every year for many years. If she had continued like that, she would have stayed too long at that place. One long fast a year, one 40-day fast a year!! It would have been great, but it would have been staying too long at that place. So this year, before her marriage she did a 40-day fast to support our Ministry. Then she did a 40-day fast to support the husband's Ministry. And she plans to do a 40-day fast when they get to London. Already two 40-day fasts a year is intensified aggressiveness. It is changing the speed of knocking the Enemy. And something more glorious:

Last year when she fasted, her disciple fasted thirty days with her. This year when she did 40 days, her disciple, Somma, also did forty days. She and her disciple are on a 14-day fast now to pray that they will be in London this month. Brother Joe Mbafor began to ask, "How can we send this disciple to join them there so that there is a fasting team?" And they really need fasting teams because some of the people there fast between breakfast and lunch. Some of them eat breakfast and eat supper, and it is a fast.

You have stayed too long on that mountain! You have been going around that mountain for too long! I want to ask you:

- **Where does your strength lie?**
- **Where does your spiritual strength lie?**
- **Is it in prayer?**
- **Is it in fasting?**
- **Is it in giving?**
- **Have you just been maintaining a routine in that domain?**

At the beginning it was only one fast a year! One 40-day fast a year, one 28-day or one 21-day fast a year. And now there are two a year! Then from there, three a year!

You have stayed on this mountain long enough. Another version says, "You have been going around this mountain for too long." You have been going around your giving God 25% for too long. You have been going around your giving God 20% for too long. You have stayed around your 7-day prayer crusades for too long. You have stayed long enough around your 2 hours of prayer a day. You have stayed too long around that place. The Lord is saying to us, "You have stayed long enough, too long on this mountain! Break camp and advance!" That is aggressiveness! Break camp! Shatter, your constructions! Break camp and advance. There is need to break camp! Shatter the camp! That is aggressiveness! Advance towards the hill country! Hey, some people have never broken camp, they have never advanced! They have been going round, round and round the same place for too long. That small church of 50 or 60 or 100 people, they have been turning around that small Church for too long. Break camp and advance, and move to 100 people and to 200 people and to 300 people and to 400 people and to 500 people.

The Elders in Douala, we have heard that you have been around 1000 for too long! We command you in the name of the Lord Jesus Christ to break camp and advance into the 2000 area. And it is the Lord who calls us, who commands us to do it! Break camp and advance!

Sustained aggressiveness! Was it Sister B's voice I heard praying for a 21-day fast? Don't do it, my dear sister. Your fasting level is to go on till you collapse. Don't accept anything less than that. That is how to abandon the heights.

Many brethren do not know the theory of long fasts. They don't even know the theory of fasting. We are going to include it in the book entitled 'Practical Helps For Fasting Believers'. Actually, we are going to write seven books on fasting. I got this message from the Lord; it is not Zach Fomum's analysis. The Lord was teaching me that which I could read from no book. He said, "Partial Fasts is Hitting the Devil at this level."

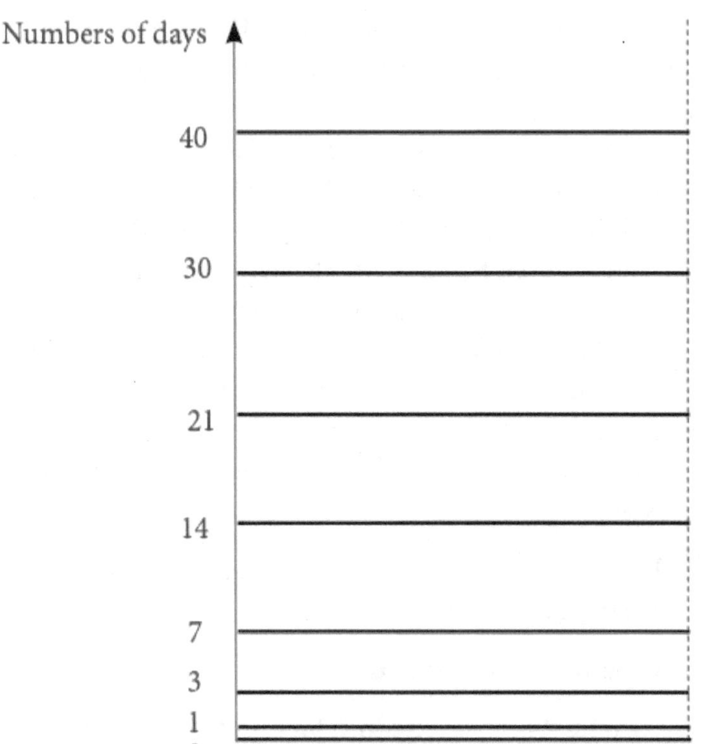

So you hit all the demons that can be hit at this level. Even if you do a million partial fasts, you will only be hitting the Enemy at that same level. In three-day fasts, you will strike all the demons from there down. In seven-day fasts, be they one, two or more of them, you will destroy increasing numbers, but of the same kind, and then right down. So the man who does a 7-day fast has done all the destruction that the person who can do 3-day fasts does. The same goes for fourteen-day fasts, 21-day fasts, 28-day fasts, 35-day fasts or 40-day fasts. And He said, "In the 40-day fast the Enemy is taken in the full range; all the power of hell is confronted. So if you are just thinking about quantitative warfare, you take these small demons and destroy all of them." But He said, "If you get to 40 days, you have attacked the host of hell in its total range." He told me, "That is why My Son went for one 40-day fast while He was in your world. And He took the Enemy full scale." But He said, "Remember that He is fasting since He left your world." In the book we have talked about the longest fast in history. This year is 2000 years since the Lord was born, and He lived for 34 years. He started His ministry at 30 years of age. So the Lord has been fasting unceasingly for 970 years. And He said to me, "If fasting were optional, the Lamb would not be fasting from the throne. If prayer were optional, the Lord would not be praying from the throne; because the Lord does not do anything except that which is absolutely necessary."

The Lord only does that which He must! Anything that can be left, He leaves it.

Fasting and prayer are musts.

That is why from the throne the Lamb fasts and prays.

I want to say, looking at Scriptures, that the five most potent weapons against the Enemy (I am not putting them in order) are:

- Fasting,
- Prayer,
- Giving to God,
- Death to Self, and
- The Will of God.

Listen, anyone who goes into sustained fasting, is a man or woman of power.

These people who do long fasts, because they take the Devil full scale, they may have many weaknesses in their lives, but when you meet them you just know that "they surpass you." There is something released in fasting that just puts you ahead of the others. They may talk about your weaknesses, but you are just ahead of them. Why? You are taking the Devil full range.

When you have been to the top of Mount Everest and you get to the top of Mount Cameroon, or even to the top of Mount Kilimanjaro, at the end of it you will be unfulfilled because you have known better days. When people who have known heights come down to do things below where they once walked, they are not fulfilled. They multiply all such stuff; they multiply their one-day, two-day, three-day fasts, but remain unfulfilled.

I saw a man in Yaounde carrying six giant rats on a stick and he was moving with confidence as if he had done something great. I thought he should leave the road and be walking in the bush. When you kill six giant rats, have you done anything special? And he dared to be proud, moving with confidence that comes from giant rats! When I saw him, I was angry. I was even more angry because he seemed to be moving like a man who had done something. He could have hidden those rats in a bag and not carried them like a man who was displaying a conquest. Had it been that the man was carrying a baby lion, I would have joined those who gathered around him to ask him, "How did you do it?" If you kill giant rats, hide them, for fear that it sticks on you that you are a giant-rat hunter, because that name "giant-rat hunter" can stick on you.

When I was 14, I asked one of my teachers, "What is the biggest degree one can get?" He told me it was the Ph.D. I said, "O.K., I shall get it." And he told me the number of years that it would take to get it. So I wrote my name and I put the year. I said, "In 1972, my name will change to Dr. Fomum." I missed it by six months. Listen, don't go for giant rats.

Sister B., you have been to the top of Mount Everest in fasting. If Mount Everest is a 40-day fast, and Mount Kilimanjaro is the 28-day fast, and Mount Cameroon is a 21-day fast, when you are on the top of Mount Cameroon, you will think about the top of Mount Everest and you will not be fulfilled, because

God has put something in us that longs for spiritual heights. And without spiritual heights, we are unfulfilled.

Listen, Brethren, you have to force it! Since 1976, every year, my wife and I have given God a bigger percentage and a larger sum, forcing it against the decreases in salary and devaluation, because

God has given us a will to will and the will must be used to will that which God wills and see God execute it.

So Sister, go on until you collapse; but this time you will not collapse.

There was a man whose wife gave birth to the first child and it was a boy. The second child was a boy, the third child a boy, the fourth child a boy and the fifth child a boy. He is a Cameroonian, and he comes from a tribe where a baby boy means that you have done it. The wife became pregnant again. When I met him, he told me his wife had given birth. I asked him, "What sex is it?" He told me, "What other sex can my wife give birth to?"

Be the person whom when you say you are on a fast, nobody will bother to ask: "How many days?" because: "Which other fast can you do?"

Part of spiritual aggressiveness is settling in your heart that you will not stop short of the winning point or the collapsing point. That is aggressiveness.

Sister I.G. is hypertensive and diabetic. But she did a 40-day fast, drinking only water. I am not telling you to go and imitate her if that is your condition. Get your healing from the Lamb. What I want to say is that in the laws of spiritual aggressiveness the consequences are ignored until the victory is accomplished. The laws of aggressiveness demand that the consequences be ignored until the victory is attained.

The laws of spiritual aggressiveness demand that the consequences be ignored until the victory is attained.

We are where we are in our giving to God just by stubbornness — a stubbornness to increase the percentage every year, and to increase the amount every year.

God has given us a will. We will it. We use it. Some people have hung their own will up and said God should will for them. God will not will for you; you must rise up and use your will.

Brother Joe Mbafor and I belong to the same research team. One of the reasons why I didn't come on Tuesday was that I had to write a letter to accompany our most recent publication. He knows that we have stayed where we are just by stubbornness, using our money to buy chemicals, where others have allowed things to collapse while they waited for money to come from other sources. We need a drum of ethyl acetate and a drum of ethanol. We are going to pay for it from our pockets because we will not allow the research group to collapse because fools are misusing the research monies. Listen,

The world belongs to the stubborn.

Those who say it must happen, will see it happen.

We are trusting God that He will give us some compounds to sell that will make us recover our money and make a profit. But we have to sacrifice first. Some people want the blessings to come before the sacrifice.

Victory is won by forcing things!

Some people had too easy a childhood. I remember when we were children, we used to play a game that consisted in knocking each other with the shoulder. One day, we knocked till 2.00 a.m. to get the champion. Some people were from college, the other ones were from the primary school. The primary school people said, "We will bring this your college thing to nothing." We had to knock to defend the matter of being in secondary school. By 1.30 we were still wrestling for the crown. During break, those of us from secondary school went and discussed afresh. We said if we allowed ourselves to be beaten, we would never open our mouths again in that quarter. When it was 2.00 o'clock our flag was flying high when we were going away - by sheer determination, by a stubborn refusal to accept a "No!"

By a stubborn refusal to accept a "No", mighty battles are won.

The world belongs to the stubbornly determined!

Matthew 11:12: From the days of John the Baptist until now, the kingdom of heaven has been forcefully advancing, and forceful men lay hold of it.

The Kingdom of heaven has been forcefully advancing — forcing all obstacles! From the days of John the Baptist, the Kingdom of God has been forcefully advancing! Is it advancing in your heart?

- **in fasting,**
- **in long fasts,**
- **in long prayer crusades,**
- **in bleeding giving,**
- **in bleeding dying to self,**
- **in bleeding adoption of the will of God,**
- **in bleeding fasting,**
- **in bleeding praying,**
- **in bleeding sacrifice,**
- **in bleeding dying to self,**
- **in bleeding redemption of time, redeeming time in order to invest it into the cause of the Gospel.**

Song:

When I see the Blood,
When I see the Blood,
When I see the Blood,
I will pass over you.

There is the trail of Blood marked by :

- sacrificial praying,
- bleeding praying,
- bleeding fasting,
- bleeding giving to the Lord,
- bleeding dying to self,
- bleeding putting on of the will of God,

that brings the powers of hell to nothing.

The trail of Blood — Where is it in your life? Where is the bleeding? Is it in fasting?

Sister B. collapsed, was it on the 36th day? And she stood up and finished the fast. A small woman. "Small no be sick." And men cannot fast. They look so big, they have such big muscles but they love food. We the men, shall go away from this island, covenanting to separate ourselves from food. When they did the fast here, three men and two women completed the 40-day fast. When they did it in Douala, it was Brother A. alone who saved the men from a total scandal. He is the only man who crawled through. He even told me that he crawled through because his wife refused to agree with him that he should stop it. That refusal was historic because at the end of the fast it would have just been women.

There is an evil going on! The men are gradually handing over the leadership to the women in fasting, in prayer, even in giving. In Yaounde, Sister E.K., Sister E. N., Sister H.M., Sister C.B., are the names that are frequent in the prayer circles. And you could continue with others - Sister I.G., Sister H.K., and you could continue. But listen, I am not going to surrender the leadership to women. In India, I will finish my third 40-day prayer crusade for the year. The first one of 42 days we did it together. The next one of 44 days I did it alone. And the third one of 400 hours I will do it alone. I cut ten days off to put them in when I shall be in India. But it will be 400 hours of prayer and there will be one more at the end of the year that will end up with 10 days of locking myself up with God alone. I am not going to surrender the leadership to women.

Have you surrendered the leadership to women?

At any cost I will do a long fast before the year ends. And during the ten days of locking myself up alone with God, I will be fasting. Next year will be aggressive returning to many long fasts and many long prayer crusades. Brothers, who has bewitched you to hand the leadership to the women? Leadership in fasting! Leadership in prayer! Who has bewitched you to give up prayer and fasting to become a sneaky diplomat that speaks words: "C'est moi qui ai le commandement" = "I am the one in command"?

Men command by fasting. They command by prayer. From the time of John the Baptist until now, the Kingdom of heaven has been FORCEFULLY ADVANCING…!

May God write it on your heart. May He stamp it on your heart that the Kingdom of God advances forcefully, that the power of the Enemy is so present that only force will crush it and create room for the victories of our God.

4

FORCEFULLY ADVANCING!

Overthrowing every obstacle! That is how it has been advancing. And if it is not forcefully advancing, it doesn't advance at all. It is forcefully advancing, and forceful men lay hold on it. Forceful men and forceful women take it. The others have no part in it. The Kingdom of God has been forcefully advancing! And forceful men lay hold on it. The others are disqualified. Stubborn forceful men and forceful women, who will not give up until the Enemy has collapsed, take the Kingdom. If the door will not open when it is shaken, they will smash it with their feet and they will transform all of their being into a stone and smash it until the door opens. The Kingdom of God has been advancing forcefully and forceful men take hold of it. There are quarters in Lagos that will yield when forceful men lay hold on it. The expansion of the Church in Lagos and the expansion of all the Churches is waiting for violent men to enter into the arena.

Jean-François, one of the evangelists we have, went on a 40-day evangelism crusade, led 37 people to the Lord and many of them joined the Church. That is aggressiveness. This whole matter of saying, "I will go out for one hour a week," is a wicked joke.

From the days of John the Baptist, the Kingdom of God has been advancing forcefully, and forceful men take it. Why have you allowed the Enemy to take the marks, to chip away the sharp edges from your life?

- The sharp edges of fasting,
- the sharp edges of praying, sustained praying, long praying, aggressive praying,
- the sharp edges of bleeding giving,
- the sharp edges of bleeding holiness.

The Kingdom of God has been, we can say, aggressively advancing.

Only those who attack the Enemy will possess what he has kept.

What sharp edges have you added to yourself since you went to the mission field, or has the Enemy removed the ones that you took along?

You hit the Enemy and he removed those sharp edges. Now you are like a lion that has lost its claws. You will start eating human beings and goats.

We went to Queen Elizabeth's National Park in Uganda. The day we arrived there, a lion ate an old man. The lion was too old to run after swift animals and the man was too old to run away from the lion.

You have retired from spiritual aggressiveness.

We live in a generation that knows nothing about price.

My father had one brown tooth. I asked, "Papa, what happened to your tooth?" He said, "When we were children, the mark of handsomeness and beauty was to have a gap in your upper front teeth. If you had it, you had made it. If you didn't have it, you did all to introduce it." So they developed a technique of heating an iron tool and chipping off the teeth. He had the gap but one tooth was a bit brown. I told him, "Papa, you are very handsome even without that." He said, "No, beauty is what people say, not what people think." Don't you see it in the world of dressing? Something is very clumsy but they say, "This is the fashion of the moment," and everybody is in for it. He bore in his body the determination to get the beauty marks. But what of the beauty marks of Jesus? Where has your life been chipped? Chipping is like cutting a piece off a stone. Just like you chip off stones in order to give them shape.

Where has your life been chipped in order to pass the beauty test of God?

People will go to extreme measures to bear beauty marks of the world.

Where are the marks of heavenly beauty in you?

There is a sense in which the Devil fears Sister B. He says, "This one, I knocked her to finish her but she stood up and finished the fast." It is good that the husband finished the fast because he might have needed stilts to climb on in order to talk to her. If he had stopped that fast at 28 days and she fainted on the 36th day and then stood up and finished it, then he would have borrowed stilts. There are many men who now need to borrow stilts to talk to their wives, whereas the man should just be a shoulder high so that the woman needs stilts, if she must have some, to talk to him. I know of that fast that the Church in Lagos took, where so many people fasted that big records looked like small things. Twenty-one-day fasts are hardly spoken of. Yet those people put aside 63 meals. The thing is that when you are a leopard in a country of lions, they don't know about you. But get to some other country, the people will be falling at your feet. Once I did a 28-day fast and went to America. When I shared this, somebody came and was touching my flesh, saying, "This flesh, 28 days without food." Americans are very expressive people.

The sharp edges are put in by harsh determination.

Brother J.G. collapsed at the end of a 28-day fast. Brother E.B. has collapsed twice during fasts. Forceful men lay hold of it! They didn't just say, "Men", but "Forceful Men."

Where are the marks of a forceful man in your life?

What are you forceful in?

Now write it down: I am forceful in this.

I am forceful in this.

I am forceful in this.

Now, some people know the gentle, meek and mild Jesus. Oh! But they don't know the Lion of Judah. They don't know the One who is qualified to take the scroll and break the seals!

Where do you have fellowship with Jesus the Lion?

In what department of your life do you know fellowship with Jesus, the Lion of Judah? Or is the Lamb all you know?

So according to you, the seals must not be opened because you do not know the Lion of Judah. You know only the Lamb of God that taketh away the sins of the world.

In the U.S., for the first time I understood my own story because, in a sense, it was confusing. At the age of 10, on reading the tract: "Someone Died For You", which my father gave to me, I invited Jesus to come into my life. And I was filled with heavenly joy. I ran over to the next quarter to tell my friend, Reuben, that Jesus died for him. And I knew a hunger for the Word. I used to read the Bible right into the middle of the night, 1.00 a.m., 2 a.m. I took an old Bible of my father's. Whatever my father underlined in his I also underlined in mine. I didn't know why he underlined it but I said, "If he underlined it, then there was a reason, so I will copy him." By the time I left the primary school I had read through the Bible twice.

And in Secondary School we went out for evangelism. I didn't understand the Gospel, but we went telling the people about God. It is one thing to receive the Lord Jesus Christ; it is another thing to understand the plan of salvation. I didn't understand the plan of salvation, but my sins were washed away. And we loved to pray. On Sunday, there was Christian Fellowship - singing of songs, Bible quizzes and the rest. And when everybody went away, there was a small group, about seven of us, who considered ourselves as the ones carrying the school spiritually. We would stay and pray until we fell asleep; and we did pray. We prayed for the teachers, and for the students, that they would become like Christ.

In High school, I was distracted with the need for Africa to be liberated from colonialism and imperialism, and God became secondary. We still went to the public morning prayers at 5.30 a.m. I still preached fiery messages. When students knew that I was to preach, many of them didn't come to Church. There was a book in the library entitled, "The Monk Who Shook The World." They would borrow it and come and put it on my bed. I would throw it away. They would go and borrow it again and put it on my bed. "The Monk Who Shook The World." I didn't want to be considered a monk. Some people used to call me "Monk Fomum", yet my heart went after the world. That is why on 1st October 1966, the Lord showed me the corruption of my heart. As I look back I notice that. He didn't show me the Cross. He showed me the corruption of my heart because I was His child who had allowed the heart to corrupt. I now understand it like this:

In 1955, I came to Jesus as my Saviour.

In 1966, I came to Jesus as my Lord because it was then that I gave Him the master-key of my life and told Him that I would follow Him at any cost. Oh! But I was cheated. I ought to have come to Jesus as my Lord and Saviour in one go. I would have saved 11 years and particularly those 2 years in High school.

Where are the bleeding marks in your life?

Have you given up that which is easy to give up?

Where are the crippling marks?

Has your giving put permanent crippling marks on your economy so that there is no way you will ever be rich again on earth?

What about your prayer life, your fasting life or your reading of the Word of God?

The Kingdom of God has been advancing forcefully. The thing is that of the brethren I know, many of them are backsliders. They once knew heights in specific areas of their lives, but they backslid from there. They once knew heights of harsh abandonment. They were distorted in the direction of total consecration. They could not walk straight but by slowly compromising, they now walk like everybody else. They are no longer different. The price they paid in the past is forsaken. Everything great is now only history. Great sacrifices are only in the past. Great acts of bravery are only in he past. Unusual sacrificial gifts are only in the past. Personal nights of prayer alone are only in the past. For whole nights of prayer, even in group prayer crusades, they are not there every night. Personal prayer crusades of 21 days, 28 days, 35 days, 40 days are not there. They now know 3, 5, 6, 10 days of praying. They have just backslidden. There is no area in which a steady gap is being created year by year. They have been going around that mountain for too long. They have become old without fighting God's battles. The Kingdom of God has been advancing forcefully and forceful men lay hold on it. There is something you could not say because it was too dirty or too worldly, but now you say it. There was some make-up, some way of dressing, some way of making your hair that you could not stand. There were some clothes that you could not buy because they were too expensive, but the corruption of your heart now says all prices have gone up. You have backslidden.

In what are you a forceful woman?

Write down: I AM TAKING THE KINGDOM OF GOD FORCEFULLY BY:

1. -------------------
2. -------------------
3. -------------------
4. -------------------

5. ————————————

I KNOW BLEEDING IN THE FOLLOWING AREAS:

1. ————————————
2. ————————————
3. ————————————
4. ————————————

The worst thing that can happen to a leader is that he himself is not a man of violent praying, but he gathers women of violent praying to pray for him. Such a man has committed spiritual suicide. He is now walking on stilts.

The worst thing that can happen to a man is that he is a leader who does not fast, and he gathers fasting women around him who fast for him. Fool! What will you lead the women with? When the woman says, "Aie! Aie!" on the 30th day because she does not know whether to stop or continue, the fool goes there and says, "Continue." Do you know what is happening? If she dies the next moment, what was your recommendation based on? How can you recommend people to move across barriers that you know nothing about? You know nothing about this. How do you know whether it is indulgence or it is the person coming to his own limits? How do you know whether the person should be encouraged to continue or the person should be encouraged to stop? When people around you are doing things that you do not know and you don't know that you have abandoned leadership, and that God is looking for the next leader...

The leader must make some history in fasting.

He must have some history in prayer, some history in giving that commends him as a consultant in those realms.

You can say, "Jesus, You who did the 40-day fast, help me in this difficult stage," but you leave the Lord aside. If the leader doesn't know what the 40 day fast is about, how will he know what you are going through? Someone's leadership may not allow him to be a man of constant 40-day fasts because of many other things, but he must have been through it at least once in order to be able to lead those who will do it very many times. If he has never confronted the Devil at full range praying 8 to 10 hours a night alone, for 40 nights, how can he inspire people to do 40-day prayer crusades? How can you stand with them when the battle is fiercest, when you know nothing about what they are going through? If a man has given to God until his heart is breaking and he turns to you for counsel, and all you will use is your head because you have no experience, you will be a false guide because you have never known what it means to stand in peril because of sacrifice for the Lamb.

Listen, when you have a new revelation: "Reduce your days of fasting, reduce your giving to God, reduce your level of praying," you know where it is from - from Satan or from the flesh. When the revelation is: "The times are hard now, give God a bit less," it is the radio announcement that precedes your demotion. When you hear, "Oh! Don't bother about 40-day prayer crusades; now do many 3-day, many 10-day and many 15-day prayer crusades," it is saying, "Don't worry about lions, just get many giant-rats, very many of them, have a house full of them."

I did a 44-day prayer crusade waiting on God. That was the second one after the one we did together. By the 10th of

September, I shall have finished another one of 400 hours, and there will be one more. Brethren, is there any reason why I should do four 40-day prayer crusades this year and you don't do one? Are you busier than me? I am jumping from one nation to another in conditions that make prayer crusades near impossible.

One reason why I strive to give ever-increasingly to the Lord is because of my leadership. I cannot give the same percentage this year as last year because I will be prophesying a stagnation in the gifts that are coming to the Ministry that God has given us. Because my gifts are prophetic, at any cost, there must be a higher percentage and a greater amount every succeeding year. If you do not know,

Leadership is fundamentally prophetic.

A leader is a prophet.

By his deeds he tells his people what must happen.

The leader's giving must be prophetic of what must happen to the people he leads.

The praying must be prophetic.

The fasting must be prophetic.

His labours must be prophetic.

His marriage to hard work must be prophetic.

Everything must be prophetic!!

When I receive some of the reports from the mission field, I ask myself, "Who bewitched us to send these people to the mission field?" Because there are no prophetic fasts and there is no prophetic praying. If a missionary's life is not a 40-day prayer crusade followed by another 40-day prayer crusade, a long fast followed by another long fast, the man is a wicked man, because the **taking of a nation is by violent mighty deeds.**

When a lion gets into a place and begins to roar, all the other animals escape. But I don't even hear of a missionary going on a 40-day prayer crusade. I rarely hear of them taking long fasts. Who has bewitched you? Who seduced you to think that you could take nations otherwise?

I am amazed that you Douala Elders have not gathered to weep because you have been in this realm of around 1000, 1100, 1200, 1300 for many years. You have not gathered to weep and you will not pay the price that takes the Church to the 2000 bracket, and pay the price that takes the Church to the 3000 bracket, and so forth. Because there are barriers, there is something that keeps the Church turning around the 1000. And a Church can keep turning around the 5000 or 6000 until there are violent actions that compel the Enemy to cede and new brackets are entered into. The same thing could happen to a Church that is 10 or 20 or 30 or 40 people. When the Elders do not have a session to meet and weep, saying, "We have been going around this mountain for too long..."

Breaking new barriers is total violence.

Brother W., the fact that you people did not have a weeping session to weep because no Elder was among those who did the 40-day fast means that somehow some screw has got out of position. You instead met to celebrate. Is it these women who are to lead the Church? You met to celebrate. There was no Elder among those who did the 40-day fast. You met to celebrate the handing over of the Church to women, some of them very young women in the Lord. And you had a thanks-giving session! It should have been weeping day because the

Elders were put out of office. If each Elder had had a 40-day prayer crusade, we might have said, "Well, O.K., maybe it compensated." Who has bewitched you people? It is as if the qualification to become an Elder were exemption from long fasts, or exemption from 40-day prayer crusades.

There are a number of Elders waiting to be ordained the coming Sunday in Yaounde. I ask myself,

Who are the men of fasting there?

Who are the men of long prayer crusades?

Who are the men of bleeding gifts?

What will they add to the Eldership beyond mediocrity?

When a man goes to the mission field and he has never had a 40-day prayer crusade, he has never had a 40-day fast, or a 28-day fast, or a 21-day fast, or a 14-day fast, will the gates of hell quiver? When a giant-rat person who has systematically avoided obtaining sharp edges through painful paying of the price is sent to a nation to go and fight with lions, I want to tell you,

Faithfulness is good but faithfulness alone doesn't take nations.

Faithfulness may keep what has been taken.

But it is wild aggressive combatting that breaks new grounds and establishes the Kingdom of God.

So if your spiritual diet is a maintenance diet, you will maintain that which you have not got; you will maintain the nation as not belonging to you. In football you score before you start to defend and play for time. Have the demons in that country had to have a meeting to find out: "This man who has come is hitting us too hard, and his weapons are deadly. What shall we do?" Don't be deceived. People say they have their ministry, "This ministry!" I say, "Is it anchored in 40-day fasts and 40-day prayer crusades?"

Mrs Fomum, I am waiting for your 40-day fast for the children of Yaounde. I am waiting for another 40-day fast for the children of the nation, and so forth. I am waiting for a 40-day prayer crusade of 400 hours; because somebody told me that he had a 40-day prayer crusade of praying one hour per day. I said, "What deceit!" - A 40-day prayer crusade of praying 3 hours a day! This person has not even given God 15% of his time, because if he gave God 15% of his time for prayer, it would be 3.6 hours a day. That would just be giving a tithe and an offering. For somebody of corrupt heart, that is a crusade! So his normal life, he calls it a crusade. May the wickedness of your heart be exposed! Brethren, I want to say that I spend a lot of my time thinking about these things, meditating upon them, questioning, searching my heart and asking God questions.

A 40-day prayer crusade should have 400 hours of prayer to warrant the word "crusade", because a crusade is a sustained intensive war. It is intensive and sustained, so that everything else is suspended or almost suspended.

You come out of such a prayer crusade like a man who comes out of a fast, with the aroma of God. But when you have 40 days during which you pray 5 hours a day you have just done normal praying.

It is this battling to put in the maximum number of hours in the minimum time. It is the battle to accomplish the maximum number of hours in the minimum time, the battling to put in the maximum number of praying hours in the minimum time, that causes some-

thing which the Devil cannot handle, to come out. It causes something to flow that the Devil cannot contain.

If you can have 400 hours in 20 days, which means 20 hours of praying per day, it will be bleeding praying at the extreme. Hell will not know how to handle it.

It is the maximum number of blows in the shortest possible time.

May God write this on your heart. And, Brethren, you will read these things in no book, but they have been distilled from the laboratory of spiritual experience and the revelation of God.

If a student takes 16 years to do an 8-year course, do you call that a crusade? Yes, it is a crusade - in wasting time. He is a crusader - fighting for the waste of time. But if studies that should take 8 years are finished in 4 years, brilliance and greatness are offered to the world. Some people seem to have been born to be wicked, such that they always take the smallest number of hours that will make them most comfortable. This day we denounce that wickedness in the name of the Lion of Judah! If that is your heart, know that you have a wicked heart, a heart that disqualifies you from God's battles!

Because I gave an assignment of long prayer hours to someone close to me, the person complained and kept away and lost 10 years. And he won't say, "Woe unto me for the 10 years lost! I will triple everything and cry out to God to restore to me the lost years." A hop and a lift! One brother asked me, "This tithe that they give to God, is it before taxation or after taxation?" He was afraid lest God should cheat. He wanted the minimum. Can you understand it? I don't, I can't.

Crusades are the maximum numbers of hours accomplished in the shortest possible time.

And they can be done. When a man says, "I am not able," Hallelujah! He has arrived because Jesus can do it through him. But when he says, "I am able," and he will not turn to Jesus to do it through him, that is where there is a problem.

Cities are taken by violence.

Some of you know what it took to overthrow the Prince of Yaounde. Some of you know that in 1984 we prayed for three months; first of all, 6 weeks praying every night, then 5 nights a week; and you know about the 8-week battle. Then you want to go and take nations with "a hop and a lift". The Kingdom of God is advancing forcefully and men of violence lay hold on it.

There must be a mad determination in the direction of what God wants to do, defying physical barriers, defying social barriers, defying economic barriers.

In spite of mountains of opposition, the winner presses on to God's heights and comes back as God's winner.

Brethren, I wish there were an easy way out; then I would have given it to you. But the easy way would have been the way to easy country, to giant-rants.

The Cross, the place of death; the Cross, the place of sacrificing all, is the centre of the universe.

God cannot take you beyond where you have decided to reach by your will, because God has given sovereignty to the human will.

What you say you cannot do, God will say, "Amen". But it is not because you could not do it. It is because you would not do it.

And God will force nobody.

You are able!

When big men who have big armies to support them, settle for small things, seeing small girls, who believed long after them and have no supporting armies, do great things such as long fasts, long prayer crusades, they must repent. And may that repentance come soon!

I don't know if you are like me. I do everything to win. When I play table tennis I play to win. When I play scrabble I play to win. I don't know how to play just for the sake of it. It is the backstroke in tennis that confuses the opponent. That is the joy of tennis. It is not making cock-cock, cock-cock, cock-cock, cock-cock, cock-cock, cock-cock. Even a chimpanzee can do that. You are not a chimpanzee. You were born for backstrokes. Decide that you will strike and begin to learn to strike. Don't say, "I cannot strike." The man who strikes - did he fall from the moon? You do not want to pay the price. Yes, that is the problem. Some women just sit down and say, "Bring me this! Bring me that!" When a child is in that house, that child is in for trouble. She may be as thin as thinness but her thinness makes her buttocks appear like ten tons. Some are just not willing to pay the price of standing up. When they wake up they want to lie down and pray. When they want to choose the days for the prayer crusade, they choose the days that will save them from the fierce battle where great things happen.

We know from hard-earned experience that from the 30th to the 35th day of the fast, when it is as if something were walking on your head, it is there that the Enemy is receiving the most fatal blows. But the Devil says, "I beg you, stop it before you get there." He cannot stand that. Some of you know what I am talking about. It is as if something were walking on your head. Now, it can happen even in 21 days. But it happens at critical points when so much is going on in the invisible. You don't know whether you want to defecate or urinate. You don't know whether you should be under a shower or.... It seems as if you need everything, but you don't know what you need. It is as if you were attacked from all the domains. It is because you are doing havoc in the unseen. That is why when you are ending the fast the Devil tells you, "Promise that you will not do it again." Sometimes it is as if everything were offensive. Everybody has a very strange stinking odour. Your capacities for smell have been so purified that you smell the slightest smell from a distance. The nights are long and wearisome. You literally almost want to cry, "May day come." And in the unseen, there is mourning in hell as if the firstborn son of Pharaoh were being slaughtered. That is the price.

In prayer, you get to the point where it is as if, if you opened your mouth again, you would die. Everything of your organism just says, "Keep quiet!" That is the time to really rise and pray, because you have entered into the area of total destruction and every prayer is smashing and bringing to nought the kingdom of darkness. But there are very few who know warfare at that level. They stop after 21 days of purification, the days when prayer is mainly noise, while God is preparing the heart to destroy the Enemy. In prayer, the first thing is that:

Prayer changes the man.

Then

Prayer smashes the Enemy.

Then

Prayer woos God.

So at the first level in praying, the praying man is conquered or changed. At the next level, the Devil is defeated. At the final level, God is wooed.

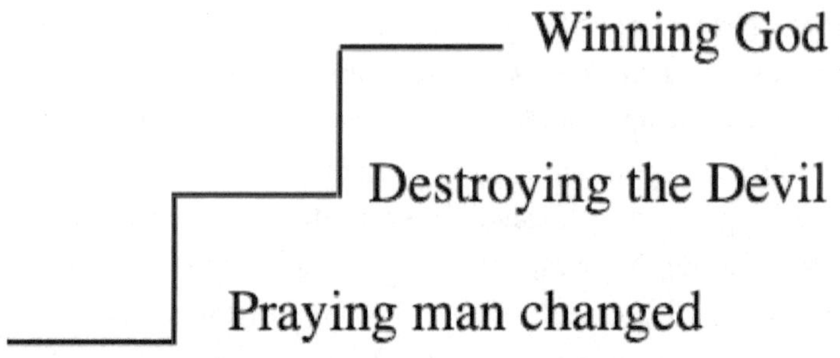

God is won in the last few days of a fierce conflict. So the person who keeps it to the comfortable zone, never enters into conflicts with the Devil. And he does not come out as a friend of God. He stopped too soon.

As I opened the Scriptures in the U.S., and exposed the fact that they were entitled to 120 years, because that is the age to which God reduced our lifespan, I saw people become young and boisterous. One brother had thought that since he was 67, he had only 3 years to go. When I told him this, he smiled and stood up strong. Among the unbelievers, they say, "Don't ask a woman's age." Believers live in the truth. They have nothing to hide. I know a girl who was 21 three years ago. She just clung to 21. She was afraid to become 22. Our sister U. is 47 and she looks like a 37-year old girl. That tells you that the 120 years are just round the corner... So how many more years? 73 years plus God's benefits. Jehoiada lived to be 130. And I want to tell you, it is yours to choose. David died at 70, in one of those his bad moments, <u>Psalm 90:3-10</u>:

"You turn men back to dust, saying, 'Return to dust, O sons of men,' For a thousand years in your sight are like a day that has just gone by, or like a watch in the night. You sweep men away in the sleep of death; they are like the new grass of the

morning - though in the morning it springs up new, by evening it is dry and withered. We are consumed by your anger and terrified by your indignation. You have set our iniquities before you, our secret sins in the light of your presence. All our days pass away under your wrath; we finish our years with a moan. The length of our days is seventy years - or eighty, if we have the strength; yet their span is but trouble and sorrow, for they quickly pass, and we fly away."

<u>Verse 8</u> "You have set our iniquities before you, our secret sins in the light of your presence." So David was saying all God does is put our sins before Him and look at them. And if God does that to anybody, there is no hope for him.

<u>Verse 9b</u> "We finish our years with a moan." No wonder the conclusion comes.

<u>Verse 10</u> "The length of our days is seventy years - or eighty, if we have the strength; yet their span is but trouble and sorrow, for they quickly pass, and we fly away."

Now, David was talking in his low moments, whatever the problem he had at that time... But God said that He gives us 120 years.

<u>Genesis 6:3</u> "Then the Lord said, 'My Spirit will not contend with man for ever, for he is mortal; his days will be a hundred and twenty years.' And God has not reduced them since then. When God has said a thing, don't go and listen to what man has said, to then go and put away what God has said and take what man has said. We accept what God has said, — the 120 years plus the bonus like Jehoiada. So we are going to ask 73 more years for our sister.

5

THE LIFE OF JOSHUA

J oshua became a servant of a man who was a servant. He became the servant of Moses and Moses had been the servant of Jethro for 40 years.

Whose servant are you? I want you to take a new page and write there:

I SERVE THIS PERSON. I AM THE SERVANT OF THIS PERSON.

Don't talk about serving God because when you can't serve man, you can't serve God. You may be serving yourself. Say:

I AM SERVING MYSELF BECAUSE I AM POSSESSED BY MYSELF.

And the Holy Spirit must agree with what you are writing. And if somebody who is not serving you says he is serving you and you agree when it is not true, you are a false witness.

Moses was the servant of his father-in-law for 40 years. That is why God gave him Joshua who served him for 40 years.

Wicked men who have never served anybody want to be served!

In heaven the highest rank is for the slave - the slave of all men. And the next rank is for the servant - the servant of all men.

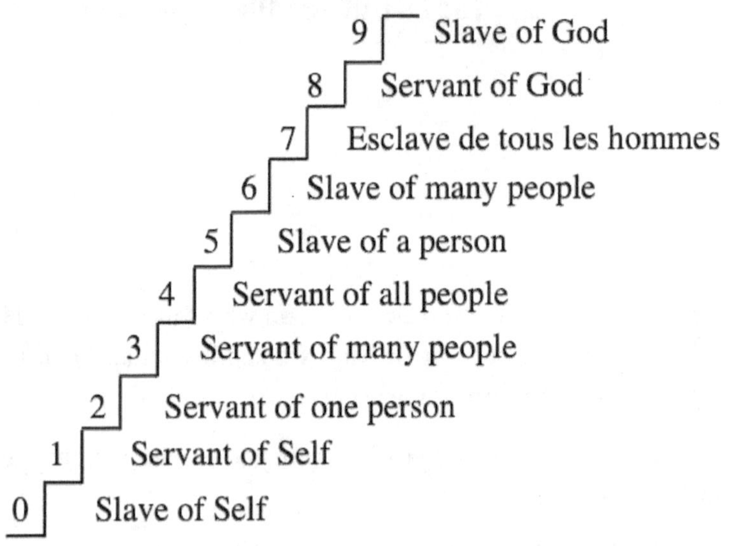

Different levels of serving

But let us show you the pathway there. You start as someone in Adam by being the servant of self: You serve yourself. You have no radical commitment to another! You can do things for others but when your self-love is touched, everything blows up. You can serve others, provided the serving of others is the serving of yourself. After that, at a higher level, you can be the servant of one person. With more progress, you can become the servant of many people. With progress, you are made a servant of all men, of all people. After that, you can be promoted and become the slave of one person. Then you can progress and become the slave of many people. And at the height of it, you become the slave of all men. Those are the seven steps.

A servant is there, looking for problems and solving them. He goes around looking for problems and solving them. The one who waits to be consulted is a good-hearted man. He is doing good to the household of God. Listen,

Servants are preoccupied with practical issues. They may go ahead and do other things, but no servant graduates from practical things.

Let me use the illustration of Brother Yonke so that some of you should learn because your deception is very high. Brother Yonke is very high up in the list of my servants, even though he is far away in the city of Douala. He is not at my disposal, but he investigates to find out if I have a problem. Let me even talk of what happened just recently. He decided to come to Paris when I was coming from the U.S. in case I had a problem there. And it was important that he came, because there was a problem with the confirmations of the flights which, as a man in the profession, he solved by being there. And immediately I saw him, I gave him my passport and gave him everything and I didn't bother about them any more. He found out where we were to sit in the plane. He found out what I wanted to eat and what I wanted to drink. In order to ensure that I don't rumple my coat, he has bought three pullovers for me. Each time I enter the plane, he takes the coat and hangs it somewhere and gives me a pullover to wear. I had thought I would be fasting in the United States, but I found that I could not fast and carry out the prayer crusade at the same time. But when I was entering the plane he put two jogging slips in my luggage. When I wasn't fasting, I needed to jog in the United States. He had provided for this. My special travelling bag was provided by him so that I can get everything into one case.

Since we got here, he comes to carry my books to and from the meeting place. He ensures that my shoes and my clothes are in order. He comes early in the morning to see if I am awake. He comes late at night to see if everything is in order. Theodore would be doing the same thing if he were not carrying the burden of the Convention. Even with that burden, he has been coming and doing various things. Brethren, that is service. And you see, **there is always room for a servant and always something for a servant to do.**

Brother Yonke calls me almost everyday to find out what is happening. Consequently, he is the most informed person in Douala about what is happening to me. And when we travel, he sits by me with his note-book to note down the things that he must do.

A servant is preoccupied with the interest of the one he is serving.

When I was going to the United States, I had a free ticket from Yaounde to Paris and back. He went and negotiated it with his boss. For this trip, I had a free ticket too.

Burdened to serve, he labours to know what button there is to be pressed. This is a servant.

When we could not catch the plane in Congo, for him the worst thing had happened on Planet Earth. Before I came back, he had written out what must happen, and did it in three copies: one which he sent to Sister Esther for prayer, one to my secretary, and one to me about the details that must go to ensure that it never happens again. And Brother Theodore does the same things.

It is preoccupation with a person in his entirety.

When we leave here on Monday, I will be carrying the roots and the bark of an Erythrina species that we have not yet worked on. Theodore has become a botanist in order to help me in my career.

So when you just cheaply call people servants when they don't deserve it, you deceive them; and the person will never become a servant, because he is deceived. And because of the critical importance, the Bible says the servant shall be great in heaven.

Mark 9:35. "Sitting down, Jesus called the twelve and said, 'If anyone wants to be first, he must be the very last, and the servant of all.'" Then in Mark 10:43-44 "(Not so with you. Instead), whoever wants to become great among you must be your servant, and whoever wants to be first must be slave of all." Servants will be great in heaven and the slaves of all shall be first. Because the matter is of such critical importance, to deceive a person is to help him to acquire low marks there.

It is a total commitment to put oneself apart.

These two men I'm talking about are very important men. They could be preoccupied with their importance.

It is a total putting away of self in order that someone else may have the place.

It is the total putting away of oneself so that another might have the benefit in a sustained way — day in and day out, week by week, year by year — without frowning, without anger, but rather with an inward joy.

It is not an occasional thing. It is a total affair.

It is a commitment to ensure that someone else becomes the best that he could ever be.

It is leaving no stone unturned which when turned would be to the benefit of that person.

It is an act of the will.

It is a commitment of the disposition of your heart.

It is a massive price paid.

It is not something that is enhanced or limited by geographical distance.

Even if the servant were on the moon, he would still serve from there. We have even written a book entitled: "The Overcomer As A Servant Of Man." It is yet to be published. As someone has said,

It is exaggerated concentration on one person.

It is a holy restlessness about the welfare of another.

Because this affects all men and affects all the Work in all of the cities and in all of the nations, because it has eternal impact, may people be honest about their own hearts, and let God be true and every man a liar.

The last thing is that none of these people will fight me, they will not resist me, they will not attack me with their thoughts or overthrow me with their ideas. If a suggestion is not accepted, there will be no war. But some bosses pose as servants. If they make a suggestion and you reject it, there is war or there are moods.

Somebody who gets moody about his service is not a servant.

And you see, Brother Constant has been carrying the books, and the other things,... When Brother Theodore steps in to do something, there is no fighting or pushing away between them. There are some people who come there and say, "May no one else come here." They instead want to pocket you, possess you, crush you and own you. They are not interested in you. They are using you.

The servant joyfully leaves space for another servant, glad that another person is bringing in what he has not brought in or helping him to bring in what he may not be able to bring in, or just that another servant should have the space to serve.

Because of the eternal consequences, because this is the way to great heights, we repeat : Moses was a servant of Jethro for 40 years and God appointed him the leader of His people. Joshua was a servant of Moses for 40 years and God appointed him. When a boss is appointed, it is temporary, until a servant arises.

Because it is the way to appointments of consequence, because God the Father Himself is a Servant, because God the Son is a Servant, because God the Holy Spirit is a Servant, not being a servant is rebellion. It is the loss of the best.

6

THE PROFILE OF JOSHUA

Servant of Moses

There are many things in the life of Joshua that betray the fact that he was a servant. And, I don't know one woman who is the servant of her husband.

Oh! that I would know. It seems as if the whole matter of being a boss, finally comes to its fullest expression in womanhood. I know a few brothers who are servants. I don't know any sister. I am not saying sisters don't do things. There are many sisters who do things and even sacrificially, but let another sister want to serve, they will knock her away such that she could go and drop in the Atlantic. That is the proof that they are not serving you, they are using you.

A servant is glad to see another servant.

It is not often that I am told off. But the people who have had enough courage to tell me off have all been women. The fear of God and the fear of man is absent! I want to ask you sisters: What did you marry these men for? To rule over them? To force your ideas into them? If your ideas are not taken, there is war. It could be violent speaking out or violent withdrawal.

I also want to say to these missionaries who have served nobody and who now want to be served, may the corruption of your heart trip you! How will you handle a servant when you have never served? How can you handle servants when you have never begged to serve, and begged and begged and begged until you were given the opportunity to serve?

Whose interests are you totally engrossed in that you expect others to be engrossed in your own interests?

Whose Ministry are you totally burdened about so that others will be burdened about your own Ministry?

In whom have you invested money, time and all else so that another person should invest money, time and all else into you?

You want to be the starting point, the first original. It is destructive pride, and it will hinder the Work, because **a Work without servants is like an engine without oil.**

Back to Joshua:

Even his name "Joshua" was given by Moses. Whatever name his father had given him disappeared.

<u>Numbers 13:16</u> "These are the names of the men Moses sent to explore the land, (Moses gave Hoshea son of Nun the name Joshua)." He was so dependent upon him that even his name was the one that Moses gave. He had his original name "Hoshea"; Moses gave him the name "Joshua". Moses changed his name. His commitment to Moses was such that he embraced the name that Moses gave him. And God back it by calling him by that name.

<u>Numbers 14:30</u> "Not one of you will enter the land I swore with uplifted hand to make your home, except Caleb son of Jephunneh and Joshua son of Nun." That is God speaking. It is God confirming this name. When a man is already a leader in his tribe and then you change his name...

Even though it looks like an act of folly, **Joshua was jealous for Moses' glory.**

<u>Numbers 11:24-30</u> "So Moses went out and told the people what the Lord had said. He brought together seventy of their elders and made them stand round the Tent. Then the Lord came down in the cloud and spoke with him, and he took of the Spirit that was on him and put the Spirit on the seventy elders. When the Spirit rested on them, they prophesied, but they did not do so again. However, two men, whose names were Eldad and Medad, had remained in the camp. They were listed among the elders, but did not go out to the Tent. Yet the Spirit also rested on them, and they prophesied in the camp. A young man ran and told Moses, 'Eldad and Medad are prophesying in the camp.' Joshua son of Nun, who had been Moses' assistant since youth, spoke up and said, 'Moses, my lord,

stop them!' But Moses responded, 'Are you jealous for my sake? I wish that all the Lord's people were prophets and that the Lord would put his Spirit on them!' Then Moses and the elders of Israel returned to the camp."

To Joshua, there was to be only one prophet. Somebody else would have said, "Aha, thank God there are others to prophesy so that this man's authority will come down." But Joshua's loyalty, his commitment, was that there be only one prophet — Moses. He had nothing to gain, but just wanted that there should be order, that the voice of God should only come through the one he was serving. It is not that he was anxious to prophesy. He had no secret desire to be the prophet but just wanted that God's voice should come through Moses. And they said he was Moses' servant since from youth. From his youth he was a servant. All his life he was a servant.

How many years have you wasted and never learnt to serve?

You could have been a servant since you believed, but until this day, you are still a dangerous boss. How you have wasted your own time! How your wicked heart has betrayed you! And do you see? You can hardly find someone to really serve you.

You know what Joshua said? "My lord, Moses, my lord. Moses, my lord." Do you see the exalted way in which he held Moses? "Moses, my lord." He didn't say, "Ah, they may think that I do not know that there is God."

Pride is the worst thing that can possess a person.

The proud heart is the dwelling place of the devil because the devil is the father of pride and the controller of the proud of heart. And God hates the proud of heart and pulls them down.

"My lord, stop them." He was not presumptuous. He didn't go there and say, "Stop!" He knew he was a servant. "My lord, Moses, stop them." He was not trying to impose his own authority on the people and say, "Don't you know that I am Moses' servant? I command you to keep quiet!" He said, "My lord, Moses, stop them!"

Proud hearts are very afraid lest they over-give somebody honour. May God convict you of the corruption of your heart! And what are most of these people proud about? You look and say, "But what has this person to be proud about?" And I have found that : **Pride is inversely proportional to greatness.**

The more a person' greatness is zero, the prouder he is.

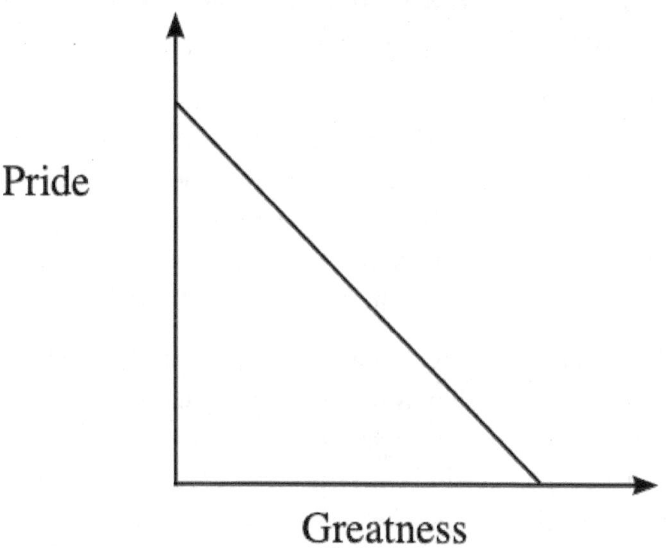

When the person is very proud, his greatness is zero. If his pride is very small, his greatness is very high. If his pride is very small, his greatness is the maximum. Think about your pride - it tells you something about your importance. I have found the emptiest people the proudest. The people who ought to run and hide are the most boastful. Joshua humbly said, "Moses, my lord, stop them." = **A holy jealousy for another's glory.**

What filters into my ears is that there is no doubt to the people who deal with Theodore that Theodore is under authority, that he is not an originator. It is quite interesting because he who was already an Elder in Yaounde is the one who has more to consult about, and those who hardly know are those who ask no questions. They feel they know everything.

The pride of a man's heart is his undoing.

The proud cannot ask even when they don't know until they have made a shipwreck of it all.

Joshua, in this utter submission to Moses, in this calling of Moses "lord" and serving him as a servant serves a lord, was not a man of no consequence. He was the Field Marshall of Israel. He was the Number One man in the army — the Commander-in-Chief of the Armed Forces. He commanded the Armed Forces when the Amalekites attacked.

Exodus 17:8-16 "The Amalekites came and attacked the Israelites at Rephidim. Moses said to Joshua, 'Choose some of our men and go out to fight the Amalekites. Tomorrow I will stand on top of the hill with the staff of God in my hands.' So Joshua fought the Amalekites as Moses had ordered, and Moses, Aaron and Hur went to the top of the hill. As long as Moses held up his hand, the Israelites were winning, but whenever he lowered his hands, the Amalekites were winning. When Moses' hands grew tired, they took a stone and put it under him and he sat on it. Aaron and Hur held his hands up - one on one side, one on the other - so that his hands remained steady till sunset. So Joshua overcame the Amalekite army with the sword. Then the Lord said to Moses, 'Write this on a scroll as something to be remembered and make sure that Joshua hears it, because I will completely blot out the memory of Amalek from under heaven.' Moses built an altar and called it The Lord is my Banner. He said, 'For hands were lifted up to the throne of the Lord. The Lord will be at war against the Amalekites from generation to generation.'"

<u>Verse 10</u> "So Joshua fought the Amalekites as Moses had ordered, and Moses, Aaron and Hur went to the top of the hill." As Moses had ordered! Amen! He did not fight the Amalekites according to his own ideas. He fought the Amalekites as Moses had ordered. He was under authority. Oh! but he was such a mighty general, the leader of the forces. The mower of the Amalekites, a servant!

May God convict you of your empty pride! You are not serving anyone, are you better than Joshua? Of which army are you the Field Marshall?

<u>Verse 13</u> "So Joshua overcame the Amalekite army with the sword." People think that a servant is a person who is not able.

There is no question, Brother W. is one of the ablest men I know. He could take a continent. His undoing is that he doesn't know how to be a servant. He has not learnt how to take his abilities and place them at Brother M's service, and be his servant. He has not learnt what this mighty general — Joshua — did. And we call you "general". I got it from your disciples and I agree with it. In my heart I know you are a general. Listen,

Submission, serving is not that which is to be carried out by people who are nothing.

That is also Brother N's problem. He is a very able man! But he is not JDD's servant, and therefore he can't get where he could have got.

A person who can give himself the woeful responsibility of finding faults in the person whom he should be serving is finished.

Joshua was not called to submit because Joshua could not lead on his own.

God has ordered that those who are great should establish their greatness by being servants.

God has established that those who are great and who will continue to be great should establish their greatness by being servants.

The one who would not be a servant has put a knife into his own greatness, and there are heights to which he will never attain.

God in His sovereignty chooses to make us submit to people whom perhaps we would not want to submit to.

And the choice of God is always perfect. He chooses and places people where the self-life will be most exposed.

Sometimes you may have to submit to somebody whom you think you are better than. Already, the fact that you think that you are better betrays you. It means that you don't know yourself. It means that perhaps you are looking at an aspect where you are strong and bending your back because of that, and not confronting the fact that the person is strong where you are utterly weak. But you will not see it, you cannot see it. Somebody may be strong in mighty deeds. Of necessity, God must get him to submit to somebody of mature character because

Character before God is of higher value than great deeds.

Often we measure people by great deeds. God measures them, first of all, by character.

It is in God's purpose that great deeds be embedded in mature character.

So if you think that you are so able that you can't serve, may God have mercy on you! If you don't see whom you should serve, it is because you see the idol self, and that is all you see.

Joshua was doing the practical issues. When Moses went to the mountain to pray, he went to do the practical matters.

A servant is involved in practical things, even though he will do other things.

He may be a master-planner, he may be a man of great vision, but a servant is the polisher of shoes, the washer of clothes, and a doer of other such practical things. He is the servant at table. And proud hearts know no such thing. They say, "Give us an office, we will control it and help you and be your servants." Or, "Make me the Number Two man, so that I prepare to take over from you." That is why when Jesus wanted to demonstrate it, He took a towel and washed the disciples' feet. He was not serving them by propounding great doctrines. He washed their feet and made breakfast for them. And when these things are absent in a man's life, his sickness is very serious because they are the spontaneous outflow of the life of God.

The real servant doesn't bother about position. What his rank is doesn't matter. He is just glad to be able to serve. It flows from the rivers that the Holy Spirit puts within a person.

I was glad in Newnan because there was an opportunity to wash plates, cups and spoons again, and I seized every oppor-tunity to do that. Those of you whose pride would not let you do practical things, of all men you deserve to be pitied!

Moses said to Joshua, "I will go and pray. I will go and be with God. Go and be with man." Joshua didn't say, "Hmmm, when it comes to the place of death, you send me and then you go to the mountain where no bullet will get to you." Do you know, Brethren? Joshua was not jealous about the fact that Aaron and Hur went to the mountain.

This is the destruction of the sisters around me - wanting to serve, provided they are the only person in the serving kingdom. Obviously, they want to serve themselves, then others interfere. Sister U, and all the other sisters, as the Ministry of your husband grows beyond what you can handle as a servant, will you let other servants come in? Or will you say, "Everybody who wants to serve should come and line up behind me. Then I shall say, 'You do this, you do that,' so that you are accountable to me"? Then they will not be his servants, they will be your servants.

(7)

PRACTICAL WORK FOR ANOTHER!

T.A. used to empty the dustbin behind our house. Since he left E has continued to empty it faithfully.

To train another servant so that when you are not there, the service can continue, is a mark of great maturity.

Some people ensure that when they are not there, there is nothing; so that it will be seen how important they were. But the real servant wants to ensure that there will be continued service when he is gone.

Joshua was carrying the burden of practical work just to ensure that Moses succeeded. This whole humility of going to the place of physical death and not being jealous that others were going to the mountain with Moses is an exhibition of the quality of Joshua's commitment:

"I am prepared to serve you at any cost to myself. I am not seeking position. I am seeking an opportunity to serve. I am glad that there are those to go with you to the mountain. I will take my place in the valley

according to your appointment." That is the message of Joshua.

Practical Work For Another: Then Preoccupation with the Spiritual Affairs of Another - The Permanent Intercessor.

Exodus 33:7-11 "Now Moses used to take a tent and pitch it outside the camp some distance away, calling it the "tent of meeting." Anyone inquiring of the Lord would go to the tent of meeting outside the camp. And whenever Moses went out to the tent, all the people rose and stood at the entrances to their tents, watching Moses until he entered the tent. As Moses went into the tent, the pillar of cloud would come down and stay at the entrance, while the Lord spoke with Moses. Whenever the people saw the pillar of cloud standing at the entrance to the tent, they all stood and worshipped, each at the entrance to his tent. The Lord would speak to Moses face to face, as a man speaks with his friend. Then Moses would return to the camp, but his young aide Joshua the son of Nun did not leave the tent."

Where was Joshua's place? Joshua was permanently in the place of intercession. He did not depart from the tent. He was the resident intercessor of Moses, as if to say, the permanent intercessor of Moses. Can you consider the discipline that it required not to go out of the tent? Some people's buttocks are always itching; they go in and out and in and out. Joshua was in the place of permanent intercession. I want to speculate that Moses would come there and they would pray together and then he would go away and Joshua would continue to pray. His assistant did not depart from the tent.

He was a servant in practical issues and a servant in spiritual issues.

There are some crooks who say, "Ah! we are just spiritual people. If you have some spiritual issue, give us to think about it. We are too big and too great to do practical things." Joshua was in the battles, mowing Amalek and in the tent, he was interceding. Therefore, his service covered the total range: physical and spiritual, material and spiritual, before God and before man. So Joshua was Moses' servant before God and Moses' servant before man. Joshua was Moses' servant with regards to physical conflict and in spiritual conflict.

Let us pray that God should change those proud hearts that have no orientation towards practical work. Their pride is their undoing.

QUESTIONS AND ANSWERS

Brother JDD W: Is there a difference between a servant and a helper?

Brother Zach: Is there a real situation like that?

Brother J.C.: Yes, Brother.

Brother Zach: Tell us.

Brother J.C.: It is a sister who has offered herself to serve me, but really I didn't want it.

Brother Zach: Well, then just leave her alone. If somebody is bringing fire, you can run away from the fire. Yes, you have a choice.

Brother A.N.: Is it possible to serve a person you are convinced doesn't love you?

Brother Zach: That he doesn't love you? Are you looking for love or are you looking for service? And to be very convinced that he doesn't love you means that your attitude towards him is wrong. You can't serve him.

Brother Joe Mbafor: Brother's question is a question many people normally bring to the Elders, "This brother doesn't love me, so I cannot..." I wonder if it is not a projection, saying that he doesn't love you whereas you don't love him and you have not examined your own heart. Because, truly, when someone really goes with the spirit of a servant, not just that, "I want to go and force something down his throat," but with the real spirit of the servant, it is difficult to be rejected. It is really difficult to be rejected, when there is the right spirit.

Brother Emmanuel Bayiha: I would also like to say that your desire is not to serve. It is, "I." You say, "He does not love 'me'," because the centre is you, it is not him. Because if the person is the centre, you will not be repulsed by the fact that he does not love you. You will be so preoccupied with serving him that you will not even seek to know whether he loves you or not. That will not be your first preoccupation. And if you really serve him, it is sure that he will love you.

Brother Zach: It is a boss who says, "They don't love me." That is the spirit of a boss. A boss puts you on the balance and says, "You, do you love me? Let me see the temperature. Let me see how much you weigh." It is a boss who goes weighing people, weighting their love.

Brother Theodore: I was just trying to say, David served Saul while being actively hated, while trying to dodge from the spear of Saul as Saul was trying to kill him.

Brother A.M.: My question is in two parts. How can one serve, in a place like Meri where I am the leader and all the others are my spiritual children? Second part: How will I be able to serve from a distance the person whom I usually serve when near him? Being in Meri, for example, and Brother T.E. is in Yaounde. How can I serve him in such circumstances?

Brother Zach: When I talked of how T.A. and Brother Yonke serve me here; are they in Yaounde? Brother T.A. is even in another country.

Brother A.M.: I began to be a servant.

Brother Zach: Where?

Brother A.M.: In Yaounde.

Brother Zach: And since you got to Meri?

Brother A.M.: When I get there I serve, I do practical things in the house.

Brother Zach: Now, what is your question?

Brother A.M.: My question is to know, I am far from Brother T.E. whom I want to serve.

Brother Zach: But I talked of Brother Y who is in Douala, and Brother T.A. who is in Nigeria. They serve me more than people who are around me.

A Sister: I would like to know if it is normal that many people should go to serve one person. Would it not in the future create problems, conflicts between those people?

Brother Zach: Answer her question, Emmanuel; I didn't hear it. Answer.

Brother Emmanuel: You didn't hear? It is good that you hear the question. She is asking, "Is it fair that very many people should crowd around only one person that all of them will serve him? Will that not create tensions and conflicts?"

Brother Zach: The person who is seeing conflicts and tensions hasn't the spirit of a servant. He is an escapist. He is looking for a reason to keep away. Even if there are 1000 servants, there is always room for another servant. Oh! But even one boss is too much.

Brother P.N.: Please, you talked about missionaries who are going to the mission field who have not known how to serve. Now, at the point where we are, for example, myself, how can such a situation be redeemed? How can one handle people who want to serve him, to serve someone who did not learn to serve in the mission field? How can such a situation be redeemed?

Brother Zach: By the grace of God, God redeems. If your heart is right, there is always room to start. There are abundant opportunities on the mission field to serve. Joe and I already got some money from a plant that Theodore collected; and we did not forget him. He is our botanical representative here, even though he didn't specialise in Botany. There is always room to serve. The T.O. home has become my second home in the world. And if we were in the house there, you would know in reality that it is home. I think the question is, "Do I want to serve?" When that question is answered, there is a lot of opportunity.

A Sister (from Benin): Without passing through the stage of a servant, can one not become a slave directly?

Brother Zach: We started with servant of self. That is one step too high. There is the other level which is the slave of self. Actually, this is the lowest step - slave of self. Servant of self means that you choose whether to serve self or not. The slave of self has no choice. He is just in the bondage of self. The slaves of self and the servants of self are not the same. In fact, there is a big gap between the two groups. A slave has no choice. A servant has a choice. My Sister, you are asking, "Do I need to go to the primary or secondary school? Can I not start my studies at the university?" Do you want to skip?

Sister: No, I don't want to skip.

Brother Zach: In what class are you?

Sister: Servant of self. But there are some who skip classes.

Brother Zach: One cannot skip here. If people were more honest, they would acknowledge that they are still slaves of self. When the self rises, they have no control over it.

Brother F.M.: He whom I serve may need me about three times a month. And it happens that the Administration I serve gives me only one permission per month. What can I do to meet his needs?

Brother Zach: You are bringing up theoretical things. That is not the spirit of a servant. If somebody looks for you three times per month, you are not a servant.

Brother F.M.: I am far from him. We are not in the same locality.

Brother Zach: Even if you are far away, you can serve every-day. The questions are running away from the central issue. The problem is not mental. It is the heart. All the women who don't serve their husbands, is it a matter of distance? Maybe some sisters should tell us why they don't serve their husbands. As a marriage counsellor, I would like to know. Who wants to tell us?

Sister E.O.: I think it is because of the familiarity between the two of them.

Brother Zach: The men who serve me are very familiar with me. We rub shoulders. How can you serve someone you don't even know? I want women to tell me why they do not serve their husbands.

A Sister: What does the servant do when he sees weaknesses in the life of his boss?

Brother Emmanuel: Why don't you serve your husband? That is what the women are being asked.

Sister: It is pride. It is my pride.

Brother Zach: How far will your pride dominate you? It means you are a slave to your pride; aren't you?

Sister: I commit myself to abandon it.

Brother Zach: Are you committing yourself to abandon your husband?

Sister: No. To abandon my pride.

Brother Zach: When are you going to abandon it?

Sister: Right now, immediately.

Brother Zach: Why do women not serve their husbands? Brother Joe, you people should not answer. They will say that you are not a woman. Sisters, why don't you serve your husbands? You can do things for your husband without serving him. You can wash your husband's clothes as a boss.

A Sister: Generally, the man does not see that he has been served many times and generally he doesn't say, "Thank you."

Brother Emmanuel: The thing is that they don't believe they are not serving.

Brother Zach: My sister, do you serve your husband?

Sister: Yes.

Brother Zach: You don't, because you say he doesn't see and doesn't thank you. You are there looking for thanks.

Sister: I have not understood. The two, service and thanks.

Brother Zach: What do you want?

Sister: I want to serve him and I want him to tell me, "Thank you."

Brother Zach: You have not yet begun. You do your things to seek for 'Thank you', and if it doesn't come, you get angry.

Sister: That's it.

Brother Zach: Therefore, you are seeking your glory, you do things for him so as to glorify yourself.

Brother Emmanuel is saying that sisters do not believe that they don't serve. That is the work of the Enemy. They cannot even see. Which woman here thinks that she serves her husband?

Sister Prisca: I thought until today.

Brother Zach: Each time I've told Sister Prisca that she was not serving, she defended it to the last ounce of her blood. Have you received a revelation today? Yet she does very many things for me, for her glory or in the way she wants. The greatest problem is that women are deceived that they serve their husbands. Even the men who don't serve me but with whom we have a good relationship, if I step on their toes, there will be no problem. Step on a woman's toes, and you have had it. The thing is that they have designed their own projects on how to please the man, their own ideas. Woe betide you if you don't accept that what they have designed pleases you! In the United States, one man said, "How can I tell my wife that all that she has done does not please me? I just have to keep quiet. I have even to pretend that it is wonderful since everybody says that it is fantastic."

Until someone forgets himself, he cannot become a servant.

Brother Zach: Which woman serves and creates room for others to serve?

Brother T.A.: My wife fights nobody.

Question: Your wife fights nobody. What of the heart? Sister A, when those who do some things better than you come around to serve your husband, how do you feel like inside?

Sister A: I accept them.

Brother Zach: You make room for them, but how do you feel inside?

Sister A: I feel nothing.

Brother Zach: Then there's a problem. If you feel nothing it means that you are dead.

Sister A: I don't know how to put it but I don't reject them.

Brother Emmanuel: When somebody comes like Brother Zach says, do you say, "Hallelujah, the person I was looking for has come," or do you just say, "Well, let this one also serve. She is a servant; let her serve"?

Brother T.A.: I have understood something. She will not say, "No," but what she will say is, "Let her do it. I am not even so good." I don't know whether... It just hit me now that she will not fight with the person but it is her attitude towards her own self. She will say, "Well, thank God at least that she can do it because..." It is not an acceptance that is on the positive, but it comes out of "Well, what can I expect out of myself?"

Brother Zach: There is some woman who even said, Oh that God would take her so that a better woman would come and marry the man and serve the man. Do you think that was a servant? That is the epitome of pride, of self love. That means the person cannot learn, and is not willing to learn. But all that is coming through says that this is a problem area.

Sister S. E.: I have a terrible problem, Sir; I find out that physically I serve, but my heart is always quarrelling with my husband, always. I am always vexed inside at him, and it makes me, I feel so bad and against him inside. And I don't know what to do to myself to stop having an opinion. I wish I could just wake up and have no opinion. I think life will be better for me when that happens to me.

Brother Zach: That means God will change your personality.

A man is his heart.

Do you know what it means? You want to eliminate instead of dying. You want to avoid the Cross and have a resurrection. It says that you are a boss. A servant does not criticize.

From the heart, the servant does not criticise. The servant doesn't see faults.

You want things to go your way. Is that right?

Sister S.E.: At times I feel, maybe because the marriage is still young, at times I feel things should go in a particular way which I think should be correct, possibly my way, possibly the way I think we have been taught by our disciple-maker. But I find us going some other way which I know is not the correct way even if it is not my way, and I can't speak out; I can't really do anything about it. I just follow but my heart does not follow and then maybe because of my upbringing, I generally would not say anything. I will just keep quiet. Brother Theodore told me that I am sinning by doing that.

Brother Zach: You keep quiet but you are boiling inside.

Sister S.E.: Yes. Brother Theodore told me (because I have talked with him) that I was sinning if I see my husband going the wrong way and I do not tell him.

Brother Zach: Is it a matter of right or wrong or a matter of just opinions? If it is a matter of how his food should be served, how he should be received, how he should be treated; is it those types of things? Is that where the controversy is?

Sister S.E.: I don't know how to answer, Sir. But the controversy is in some of the decisions taken I just feel are not correct.

Brother Zach: You should say they are wrong.

Sister S.E.: Sometimes.

Brother Zach: Then you should speak out. Why boil inside?

Sister S.E.: Thank you.

Let us pray because most people are the slaves of self. Only God can show them that they are. Let us pray that people will accept the truth of where they are and do something about it.

8

JOSHUA: THE LEADER'S COMPANION

Exodus 24:1 Then he said to Moses, "Come up to the Lord, you and Aaron, Nadab and Abihu, and seventy of the elders of Israel. You are to worship at a distance, but Moses alone is to approach the Lord; the others must not come near. And the people may not come up with him." Moses went up with those people and Joshua accompanied him unnamed. He was not in the official delegation. Why did he go there? Because he was Moses' servant. Those of you who come from a place where there are chiefs, when they say, "This big man will come, this other big man will come, and this big man will come," the one who carries the chief's chair also enters when all those big people enter. He enters, not as an important person, but as the servant of the king. Therefore he hears everything and sees everything.

The servant has access to things that key officials do not have.

By being a nobody, he enters where those with identities might not be allowed.

I have prayed with Brother Yonke more than with any other person here because when he came around to do practical things, we ended up praying together. That is what the servant has. He is just in the right place in that minute which is free. He is given what others will not be given. Someday, Brother E will be here or in such similar places as a special servant. He has the spirit I was talking about in Theodore, in Yonke and.... he just wants to serve. He is fulfilled in serving. He begs to serve. When he found that I could let him give me a haircut, he was full of joy. He went and bought special equipment and keeps asking when he can give me the next haircut. I asked Brother L from Ebolowa to come and see me. By the time he came, I was very tired. Brother E said, "No, don't try to see Brother now," and he took him to his home, gave him food and got him to sleep there to wait to come in the morning.

9

A PREOCCUPATION WITH THE WELFARE OF ANOTHER

There were times when I had to go and do some work in the Department at night. Brother E would come and stay in the car while I worked, sometimes till 3 or 4 O'clock in the morning and take me back home without the slightest complaint, but just the joy of doing it. There are some people who make you know that you are troubling them. There was a day, the only person who was around was somebody who would drive me and consider that he was being disturbed. So I went by taxi. Why disturb a boss? No one wants to disturb a boss.

We prayed until late one night and we got to one brother's house. He had to go and struggle to look for something in the kitchen because we were very hungry. He dared not wake up Her Imperial Majesty, his wife. When I left, I prayed for him that God would give him grace to endure. I could not blame him. He must have suffered a lot to develop that kind of attitude. Everybody knows the soup he has eaten. So he could do that and go and sleep quietly because if he woke her, for the rest of the night, he would have it.

Just recently in the U.S., a man started a ministry and called it 'Zach Fomum Ministry'. When the wife found it out, he had to change it because the wife wanted her name on it. So the Ministry was renamed "A and B Ministry." A servant is a thing that you need to light a lamp in the day to see.

Joshua entered as a nobody because he was a servant. After the others had gone as far as they could go,

<u>Verse 12</u>

> *"The Lord said to Moses, 'Come up to me on the mountain and stay here, and I will give you the tablets of stone, with the law and commands I have written for their instruction.'"*

It was an instruction given to Moses, "Come up to me..., and I will give you,..."

<u>Verse 13</u> Blessed verse:

> *"Then Moses set out with Joshua his (servant),..."*

The servant has access to courts that others are disqualified from entering. All the leaders could not go up. God did not admit them. Then Moses set out with Joshua his (servant). Joshua didn't ask, "Why do I have to go incognito? Why did they not name me?"

<u>Verses 14-18</u> He said to the elders,

> *"Wait here for us until we come back to you. Aaron and Hur are with you, and anyone involved in a dispute can go to them. When Moses went up on the mountain, the cloud covered it, and the glory of the Lord settled on Mount Sinai. For six days the cloud covered the mountain, and on the seventh day the Lord called to Moses from within the cloud. To the Israelites the glory of the Lord looked like a*

consuming fire on top of the mountain. Then Moses entered the cloud as he went on up the mountain. And he stayed on the mountain forty days and forty nights."

Moses was on the mountain, Joshua was on the mountain. Moses was in the cloud, Joshua was in the cloud. And the Lord began to show the heavenly pattern: the art, the table, the lampstand, the tabernacle, the altar of burnt offerings, the courtyards, the oil for the lamps, the priestly garments, the ephods, the breastplates, all that!!! God was showing and talking. Moses was seeing. Moses was hearing. Joshua was hearing! In what capacity? As a servant. All of that up to Chapter 32:7.

Exodus 32:7-8a

"Then the Lord said to Moses, 'Go down, because your people, whom you brought up out of Egypt, have become corrupt. They have been quick to turn away from what I commanded them and have made themselves an idol cast in the shape of a calf.'"

Then there is the intercession of Moses. Joshua heard the intercession. He therefore knew how intercessions were done.

Exodus 32:14-16

"Then the Lord relented and did not bring on his people the disaster he had threatened. Moses turned and went down the mountain with the two tablets of the Testimony in his hands. They were inscribed on both sides, front and back. The tablets were the work of God; the writing was the writing of God, engraved on the tablets."

As they were coming down after having been there for 40 days, it was wonderful. Joshua is the only other person, apart from Moses, who had this deep experience.

<u>Exodus 32:17-18</u>

> *"When Joshua heard the noise of the people shouting, he said to Moses, 'There is the sound of war in the camp.' Moses replied: 'It is not the sound of victory, it is not the sound of defeat; it is the sound of singing that I hear.'*

Joshua attempted to discern the situation. He made a mistake, Moses corrected him, and thereby was training him in discernment. Joshua was not angry, saying, "Ah! Why did he not accept what I said? I will not speak again,"—what rotten proud hearts do—they cannot be corrected.

If you cannot be corrected, you are done for.

If you withdraw because you are corrected, and there are many ways of withdrawing,…

How do you react to correction?

Are you easy to be corrected?

Do you take corrections seriously?

That is the measure of a man.

That is the measure of a servant.

There are some people I have decided that I will not correct again because they have reacted badly each time they are corrected. I say, "Now God will handle this case."

Are you still open to correction?

Can you be corrected?

Or is your pride your undoing?

Do you have the type of character that if someone sees something wrong, he can easily tell you? Or will he have to ask himself many times, "Should I tell him? How will he react?" And finally say, "No, let me leave it to God"?

Can you be corrected over and over and over again? Or does the first correction make you start to boil and if there is another correction, the flames may burn the house down?

Have you got to be approached diplomatically?

Are you someone who says, "Ah! What you are saying is right but you have said it very hard?" That is a proud heart. That person does not deserve a second correction. It is a dishonest heart. He does not want to face what is wrong and he says, "Ah! But you said it very hard, you said it at the wrong time."

People who are concerned about how it was spoken, when it was spoken, have a near fatal spirit of the boss in them.

Those people who are difficult to correct have a very big problem – a big disease. They may get to a point where even God does not correct them any more. They may just go on until God smashes them finally, and then you wonder, "Why did God not warn the people?" They didn't have a disposition that could accept correction.

You should rate yourself: very very easy to correct, very easy to correct, easy to correct, a bit difficult to correct, difficult to correct, very difficult to correct, very very difficult to correct, impossible to correct.

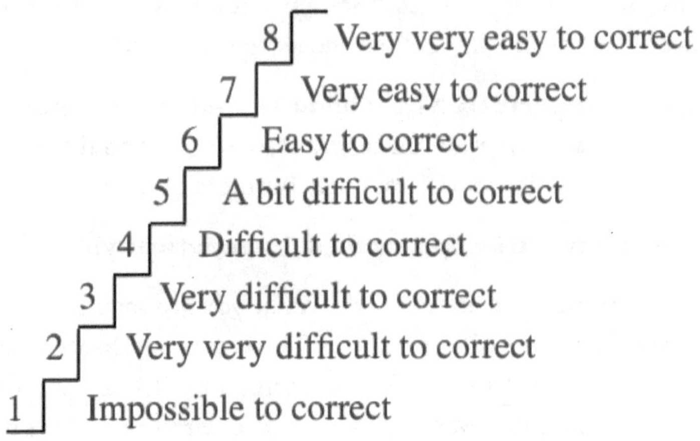

Now, fearing men is not one of my weaknesses but there are people whom I would grade here - impossible; therefore, from the experience of former corrections, I don't correct them again. I don't waste time.

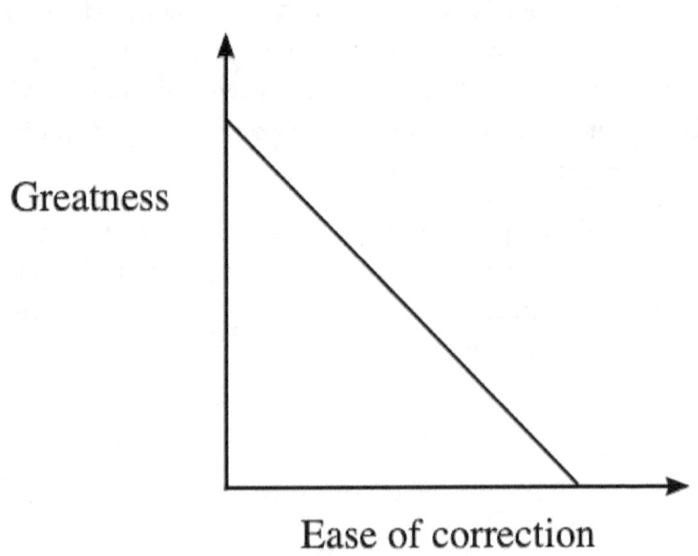

The more deceived a man is about his importance, the more difficult it is to correct him! And the more he can be deceived for years.

Greatness is directly proportional to the ease of correction.

The greater a man is, the easier it is to correct him. The smaller a person is, the more telling him that he is wrong is a dangerous thing. Please, I want you to know that these are very far-reaching things, things that determine whether a man's Ministry will grow or it will crumble. The person who is easy to correct, when he makes a mistake, he is corrected at once; so he makes progress. The person of whom you have to ask, "How do I tell him so that there is no war?" You leave him in his error until you can find a way or you forget the matter altogether. Now, where are you? We have given numbers, 1 to 8. Just call your number.

I want to say that this is something serious because it reflects how long you can continue in your error. If you are easy to correct, somebody will find the error and tell you, "This is not correct."

Put it this way: The people who are below you, evaluate their ease of correcting you because they may be the ones who see your back which you don't see, and who need to tell you, "Your back is dirty."

So, evaluate yourself in terms of your inferiors correcting you. If your juniors cannot correct you, your attitude to them needs correction.

Forget the ease with which your superiors will correct you because they have nothing to lose. Can your inferior come to you and say something is wrong? I was in some country, in fact, it was outside this continent. The pastor was having high blood pressure. He was recovering from depression, totally broken. I said, "What is the matter?" They said, "No one can go and tell him anything. A brother fell into a great sin. One year after the event, he had repented. But in that one year, he made four attempts so see the pastor and could not. He wrote four letters; there was no reply." And I asked, "Is there no senior person there who can take him to see the pastor?" They said there was nobody. No wonder he was dying. Now when you run away from the people, you are the only person, there is no access to you and there are no senior people who can come and tell you, "Please, let us look at this matter."

Question: Why does he still have a flock?

He started the Church, so he has that advantage of having started it. But the fact that there were no co-leaders who could go to say, "This brother wants to see you, this brother has a problem," I was surprised to see a man who had no one to whom he would listen.

When you are a leader without a second and seconds, when you are a leader who cannot listen to what they are saying, you are finished! In leadership, (and may the missionaries listen to this, please) there is the leader there, and there may be three or four people around him.

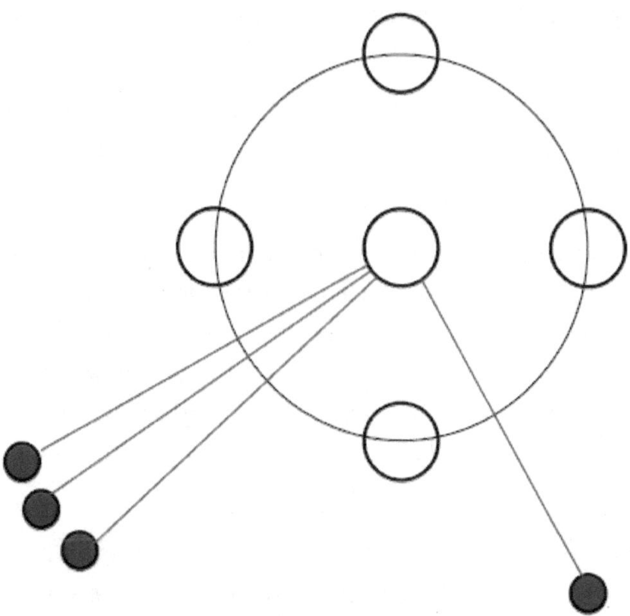

The Leader and his environment

If these people cannot talk with him easily about the way they see things, he will fail. He has failed already, because he has no team. If these people do not believe that you can listen to them, you are done for. Because, you see, following at that level cannot be separated from the fact that because they are weighing things before God, they can talk the things through. Unless there is some assurance that they can tell you that you made a mistake and you will laugh over it, or that if you are angry, when you discover it, you will repent,... If these people are people to whom you have never repented, you are ruined! Because, to put it in human terms, these are the king-makers. They are the ones who decide what you will become. If you do not spontaneously consult them because your knowledge is inadequate, — not out of formality but because you want to know from them what you do not know, because you want to check from them whether you are correct or not, if they must all keep quiet until the day you speak — your kingdom will not continue.

You have demolished it. To leave these people and ask some "Feng-feng-feng" (good-for-nothings) here who will always say, "Yes, Sa, Massa!" is to fail.

Once in Uganda, a brother preached a very bad message. Some of his supporters just went to him and said, "Massa, this is a fabulous message." I went there and got him and his supporters and said, "This was a bad message." It was just like those backbenchers in the British parliament who sat drinking tea and only when it was time for vote, they came and asked, "Which side is our party voting?"

To relate to the principal leader, to communicate with him without challenging him is the mark of an able second. He will bring in an invaluable contribution. But the person who goes to challenge him will be kicked out. Of course, the servant cannot challenge. The boss does; perhaps someone who wonders why God made that one the Number One and not him. To him, God did not see properly. **Missionaries, national leaders, do you have a team of people who can tell you you are wrong?**

One thing I don't understand, maybe I am too stupid, but from Yaounde, we send two missionaries - a man and a woman. Then they get there, and the man makes as if they sent one man plus a cook called "wife".

We attended the first government high school in anglophone Cameroon - Cameroon College of Arts, Science and Technology. We were in the second batch and it was a co-educational school. The girls got there and started to study. Then in the dining hall one fellow stood up and said, "The girls seem to have misunderstood why they were brought here. They think that they were brought here to get 'A' levels. No, that is not it. They were brought here to make the atmosphere conducive for the men to get their 'A' levels." He sat for four papers and had none, and the girls passed. So he was brought there to make the atmosphere conducive for the girls to get their 'A' levels.

On the mission field, the missionary is the Number One leader and the wife is the Number Two leader. Why? Because leadership is dependent upon maturity.

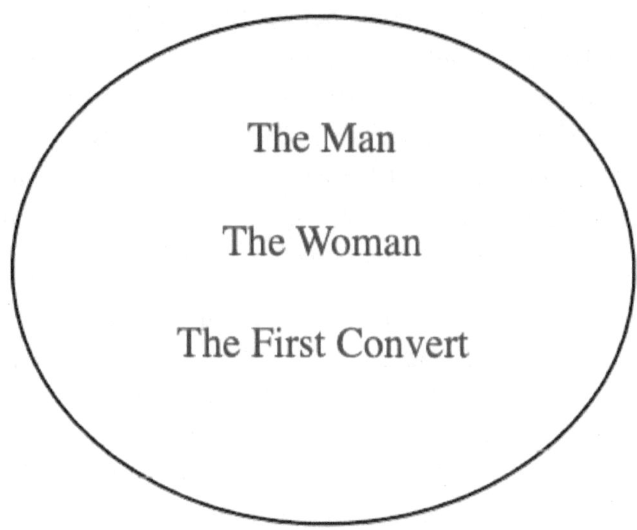

After that, they will have their first convert, the second, and so forth. They ought to immediately establish a leadership of three: the man, the woman and the first convert. That is the leadership team. He is their first convert; but as soon as possible, they should incorporate him into the leadership so that it doesn't remain a family affair. And as this one and the next one show some maturity, there will be the man, the woman, and one, two or three others. These are the leaders. But for a man to succeed to send out the woman from the beginning and just sit on these people and say, "Say that I am god," because the woman may tell him that he is not correct, is the sacrifice of the Church for personal pride. By virtue of her spiritual age and spiritual experience, she is the Number Two person. And if she says, "No," the decision must be suspended because something is wrong. Some missionaries went out without having become Yaounde Elders. In the Elders' team in Yaounde, if even just one person is not in agreement, the decision is suspended, even if the one person who does not agree is a young Elder that just came in.

We all come to harmony before the decision goes on. It means labouring but it gives us correctness. It means decisions are suspended. But it gives liberty for people to speak out. Now, if you have the wife who just says, "Yes Sa, Massa; yes Sa, Massa," too bad for you! When you will be entering the pit she will say, "Yes Sa, Massa; yes Sa, Massa." But she will stand outside. Women don't jump in so easily!

There was a brother in Yaounde who said God had called him to sell everything and go to the village. So they began to discuss everything. Finally, when he talked about selling the pots the woman stood up and said, "No, God has not spoken." They could sell the house but not the pots. That was the final test as to whether God had spoken or not.

You see, a man may not listen to his wife in Yaounde. The problem is light because there are very many leaders, 600 or more. And the eldership is 26 people. If the wife does not tell him that he is wrong, he will be told sooner or later because we speak freely. But on the mission field, it is a different thing. The wife may be the only person who can tell him, "You are wrong." In fact, often it is from the beginning because of her spiritual maturity, but also because of her experience about how things happen at home. Somebody may just say, "Ah! Since I don't know, maybe that is how it is done." But the wife knows that that is not how it is done. So listen, if you don't get your wife into the one who speaks and speaks freely, but you establish yourself as a "graffi chief" so that she must bow and say, "Mbeh! Mbeh! Cha-fon! Mbeh! Mbeh!" you are in trouble. You will go wrong very very often.

Most men use their head. Most women use their intuition.

Often the intuition is more correct than the head. But the spiritual man moves by the Spirit. And very few people have that standing. Even with radical consecration, it doesn't come overnight. Therefore, putting your logic and your wife's intuition together, and together praying for God's guidance, you will come to error-free decisions. So a missionary who does not listen to his wife, first of all, has ceased to be the wife's pastor. A shepherd who does not listen to the flock - what is he? A hireling. You may not agree, but listen. Discuss it. Find time to argue. Go by a lake, if there is one. Make some picnic lunch and go to the picnic to argue. Brother, it will save you and save us because I have found that in many of those cases, the wife was right; because it was the kind of thing that comes intuitively, and not by logic. If after you have discussed, she still says, "No," the decision must be suspended. We must be consulted. When a wife says, "No," and a man goes ahead without consulting us, in fact, he has resigned from the mission field because he is a sower of disorder. We don't send out single men or single women because we see the critical need of sending them two by two. If you think that it is just your wife that you took to the mission field, you have missed it. **We send out two missionaries.** And you missionaries, make sure you send me your report every month.

This is my report for August from Day 1 till Day 7 — periods of prayer, the actual time spent, the cumulative, with whom I prayed, the theme of prayer, then there is dynamic encounter with God, Bible reading, fasting, soul-winning, family devotion, prayer with my wife, writing the Gospel, Chemistry, sports, and it continues. For personal evaluation, you need all the facts. It will help you to know where you failed one month in order to catch up the next month. Any month where there are not 144 hours of prayer, I have failed the test because I am to spend 20% of my time in prayer. And that is 20% of a month, a month of 30 days. It is also so that there should be 72 hours of prayer alone and 72 with others. So when I compute like that, afterwards I compute how many hours I spent alone, so that to me, a normal ratio is that half of the time is spent alone. I consider the time spent with others important because if not, you begin to run away from prayer meetings to go and pray alone in order to blow up your prayer time. And, listen, there are levels of prayer where you can never arrive alone. And as you pray with people, your relationship with them is cemented. You disciple people through praying with them. At the end of the month I evaluate, I find out how many people I prayed with. And I record the topic of prayer. Let's just read some of them:

1ST OF THE MONTH:

- The missionaries
- The meeting before me
- My heart
- The need of miracles
- China

SECOND DAY:

- Brokenness in my heart
- Personal brokenness
- My separation from the common
- The sanctification of the Elders
- The Yaounde Elders and their wives
- The missionaries
- 15-minute retreat
- Thanksgiving
- Second 15-minute retreat
- Third 15-minute retreat
- Fourth 15-minute retreat
- America Ministry
- The Church in Yaounde
- The nation's government
- The Church in Yaounde.

Then I begin to see where am I failing. Now, you see, the 15-minute prayer retreats are the most all-comprehensive thing that you can have. In fact, when you pray those 15-minute retreats you have prayed for everything that is important to pray about. The book 'Retreats For Spiritual Progress,' should be a pocket book to be carried everywhere. I have photocopied the 15-minute retreats so that I go with them everywhere because I cannot follow them without the copy. I pray one point after another. I think about the retreat at noon - Pray for your Assembly. Pray for your spiritual leader. At least 75% of the days, I pray for Joe Mbafor because there is the prayer topic "Pray for your spiritual leader." Pray for 5 people who have not yet believed. Pray for the next 5 persons that have not believed. So the first 10 lecturers in the Department are being prayed for systematically because each day I concentrate on them. And so forth. The first retreat of the morning, which is the one which sometimes takes 45 minutes even though it is indicated to be 15 minutes: Thanksgiving for the night. Thanksgiving for a new day. Thanksgiving for good works pre-planned by the Lord. Second minute: Consecration to the Lord. Receiving the infilling with the Holy Spirit. Third minute: Asking for daily bread. Asking for other basic needs: transportation and so on. Fourth minute: placing your body, your life, your job, your finances, your feelings, your mind, your will under the blood for protection. By the time you finish there, 10 minutes have gone because even if you have a very modest list,... Praying for your job and all that will happen there. Then further praying for your job. Praying for a right attitude to all you will meet that day. All that until...item 11: Praying for your family members. Just lifting every family member to the Lord. Pray for your friend, your friends and all you love.

What I am saying is that I want, first of all, to tell people that I am accountable. And because I am accountable, I have the right to ask for accounts. When the reports come and we don't see that the man is praying with his wife, we shall know that there is divorce on the mission field, and we shall start praying for new missionaries to go and take their place. One cannot even understand. It is not like home where people are running to work, running to meetings, etc. They don't have the meetings we have in Yaounde. The Elders have eight meetings a week. Now, in the mission field, from 4 o'clock to 6, they can pray; 5 to 6, 7 to 8, right till evening, they have time to pray. Why don't they pray? Why don't you pray together? O.K., you will pray for us, you will pray together for our own sake. In fact, the programme of the day ought to have the fixed time for praying with the wife, in that case because they have their 24 hours controlled by themselves except the few hours for meetings. Go on prayer walks. Before you send your accounts to us, be accountable to each other. Wife, find out whether your husband is still praying. Husband, find out whether your wife is praying.

There was a brother somewhere on God's Planet Earth who did not bother about prayer. The wife used to lock herself very often in the nearby room and pray. Then when there was some problem in the house, the man said, "Yeah! Each time I look at your room there, it is dark now; you are sleeping. You are not praying; that is why there is this problem." Now, who is to pray? So the wife was the one to pray and he was the one to sleep.

Missionary wives, you have a right, by virtue of your appointment and ordination to the field, to discuss everything that pertains to the Work with your husband. Send us the budget signed by both parties. Send us the goal signed by both parties. Send us progress reports signed by both parties. Everybody say, "AMEN." But if you consider that what we are saying is wrong, say "NO!" Brethren, it is important, it is important.

Every error that one does in life is because one did not listen to somebody. God does nothing without warning His people, or it is because one heard God's voice and negotiated with his logic.

So Joshua was the companion of Moses on that mountain-top experience. And when it was time to look for a successor, there was only one man with that critical qualification. So Joshua was the obvious leader; there was no other person. The leader's companion!!

The leader's companion is the person who is just around, not the person who sees the leader by appointment.

We showed that Joshua was the leader of a tribe, but also a servant. It is again to say that being a servant is not for those who are not able, because if you are not able, how will you serve?

It is the ablest people who can be servants.

Anyone who thinks that his abilities are too many or his abilities are so great that he cannot be a servant, has got it totally wrong. Joshua was a leader of his tribe but also a servant of Moses.

If your greatness does not make you a servant, it is no greatness. It is greatness that needs to be corrected.

Joshua was a man of faith. He was one of the two spies who brought a favourable report. In fact, his relationship with Moses meant that he knew what God wanted. And regardless of what they saw, he brought God's evaluation of the situation. He brought Moses' opinion about the situation. When a man's heart is right with the leader, which is also a reflection of the correctness of that heart towards God, he knows what the person will think or what he thinks even without consultation, and executes it. Do you know the secret of Joshua being right? He must have asked there, "If Moses came here, what report would he give? If Moses came to spy the land, what report would he give?" And he gave the report that Moses would have given.

Corrupt hearts are always seeking for originals.

The person who is to be the next leader, if he is faced with a new situation, he will ask, "How would my leader evaluate this? How would he act in this situation?" And thus act. When he is sent to represent the leader, he will forget his own thoughts. He will say, "I am here to represent someone. How would he receive this? What answers would he give?" And that will decide his line of action. He wants to live the situation as if the leader was there. So Joshua went there and said, "How would Moses have reported this matter?" And that is what he reported. Brethren, that is what it means to have a correct heart. It flows from a right relationship.

Wrong decisions are not based upon wrong information. They are the overflow of a heart that is wrong.

You do not misrepresent a person because of limited information. It is the overflow of a wrong attitude towards him. "What would Papa have said in this situation? How would he have reacted?" That is the spirit of a loyal subordinate.

Brother Emmanuel co-ordinates the National Work. There is one Church where the people would say, "Ah! You are the one who is always telling Yaounde what is happening here!" where they accused one of the elders, saying: "You are the one who always tells Yaounde our things." It must mean that the things are questionable.

Faith's testimony: He believed God. He believed Moses. And he brought the report that God wanted. He brought the report that Moses wanted.

Then there is Faith's companion. Caleb was Joshua's companion. Caleb belonged to the Joshua company. Both of them belonged to the Moses company. And Moses belonged to the divine company. There was another one with the same spiritual condition. I see people having companions in fulfilling the office of a servant. It is two people serving, or a team of servants, so that if one person is not there, the others will do the thing. There was the Joshua and Caleb group. It is a thing that interests me. You know, when Anna was in the temple for all those years, Simeon belonged to the Anna company or Anna belonged to the Simeon company. They were two people of the glory, totally separated from the rest. They were two people with the divine vision.

Have you found your Caleb with whom to serve together?

There was the Joshua-Caleb company in the service of the Lord and in the service of Moses. They saw the things through the same eye. They came to the same conclusions. They took the right side until the people wanted to stone both of them. Have you a Caleb? Who is your Caleb?

Every Joshua needs a Caleb to stimulate you to righteousness in a confused world, so that both of you may see through the eye of faith and take a stand against those who do not see with faith.

<u>Verses 12-17</u> "Then the Lord said to Moses, 'Go up this mountain in the Abarim range and see the land I have given the Israelites. After you have seen it, you too will be gathered to your people, as your brother Aaron was, for when the community rebelled at the waters in the Desert of Zin, both of you disobeyed my command to honour me as holy before their eyes.' (These were the waters of Meribah Kadesh, in the Desert of Zin.) Moses said to the Lord, 'May the Lord, the God of the spirits of all mankind, appoint a man over this community to go out and come in before them, one who will lead them out and bring them in, so the Lord's people will not be like sheep without a shepherd. '"

He was not caught up with self-love and crying, "Oh, I am lost!" He was pleading with the Lord that someone else might be appointed to lead the Lord's people. He was preoccupied with the purpose of God and not with his own disqualification.

Verse 18 "So the Lord said to Moses, 'Take Joshua son of Nun, a man in whom is the spirit, and lay your hand on him.'"

Joshua was a man in whom the Spirit was.

Verses 19-20 "Have him stand before Eleazar the priest and the entire assembly and commission him in their presence. Give him some of your authority so the whole Israelite community will obey him." Hallelujah! He was to receive part of Moses' authority. "Give him some of your authority..." He didn't say, "Give him some of My authority," but "Give him some of your authority." It is fabulous; isn't it? God depending on man: "Give him some of your authority."

How important men are to God!

How important men are to men!

How tragic it is to undermine men!

Joshua was under authority! He was a servant!!! And, finally, he became the next leader.

Those who are at home are just as important as those who are on the mission field.

If you are not a missionary at home, you cannot be a missionary on the mission field. And the standards required of the missionaries must be those standards lived by those who are missionaries at home; so that there are not two standards required of the people.

If I am a poor husband at home, I will be a poor husband on the mission field. If I can't win souls at home, I won't win them on the mission field. When they put you in the plane and send you off, nothing has changed in you. You are just the same person. And as we are being changed here, the mission fields are also being changed, because the mission fields are the people who are there. And it is with gratitude to the Lord that we consider ourselves privileged to be allowed to so serve. I hope you are enjoying it as we are. Every new missionary couple going is sweet news. We want to assure the missionaries of our love.

Whitefield used to speak four times a day to five thousand people without a microphone. His was the loudest voice for God for all time. He was a tremendous man. One day he was preaching, and then a thunderstorm arose. Then he said, "You see the wrath of God warning you!" He was perhaps the greatest evangelist ever, although not in terms of showmanship. There were times when he would lie on the floor for seven days, waiting on God. Some people say that evangelists are not men of prayer. Such are superficial people who spoil the evangelistic ministry. If anything ever needed depth to be proclaimed, if anyone ever needed depth, is it not he who holds God in one hand and the sinner in the other? He is the centre of the greatest miracle - bringing God and man into vital communion. So, the evangelist is a man of fasting, a man of prayer, a man of radical holiness, who from the place of prayer or from the place of fasting brings God, and on the other hand brings the sinner, and brings them together in eternal union. So these people who have only their coats to show - don't confuse them with evangelists.

My host in the United States is from the School of World Missions. There they have the statistics that from what the big evangelists have reported from their campaigns around the world, 36 billion people have already been saved. The world has a population of 6 billion. So, six times the world population is already saved - very disturbing and distant from the truth, isn't it? It talks about the superficiality of the whole thing. We should pray that our evangelists should be men of profound depth; with many hours spent before the Lamb, day by day, men of profound prayer lives and men almost collapsing from fasting.

We are going to be fasting from 1st October to 9th November to decide the economic future of Cameroon. Each person will fast according to his capacity, from one to forty days. We are asking one thing from God: To prosper the economy of our nation; to prosper the spiritual atmosphere of our nation; that the Lord should grant to the Cameroonian believer an unusual hunger for God, an unusual hunger for holiness. 1st October to 9th November is 40 days. If you can take one day, you take it. If you can take two days, you take them.

The thing is that at the moment, most of the funds of the Work come from Cameroon. Last year, 96% of the funds came from Cameroon. The other nations are coming in significantly. Nigeria is going to alter the percentage this year significantly. Do you know what they gave me last time for Asia? They are investing much into India. They paid for my transport to come to this convention and they have paid for each of my trips to Lagos. That is a good-sized contribution.

In the plane I was travelling with the national Director of the Deeper Life Ministries in Cameroon. They were going for a convention in Lagos. Brother said, "You people have the big people." I told him, "God has nothing to do with how big people are. Naturally, the richer you are, the more needs you have. The more you have, the more your needs. It is a principle of placing all on the altar, that is the principle at work." And we shall keep going.

Socio-economically, Africa has remained poor because they kept receiving: "Britain, Germany, America, Holland,... give us." So that we developed specialist begging mentalities. One missionary even told us that the first words that come from an African child are: "Give me." It insulted whatever is left of the Africanist in me, and it is true. Africa has been trained to only go to beg. A Cameroonian pentecostal pastor, whom I know has no child, wrote to me and said he had nine children, and he gave their names. They sent me the form of a Cameroonian preacher, and he wrote that he walks from Edea to Yaounde with his dear wife. It is a distance of 160 km and there are buses and cars, with a train that come from there to Yaounde everyday. The days when people could walk from Edea to Yaounde are in the distant past, and it would have taken a week. It is just part of this beggarly mentality. That is why when you begin to beg, it is unending.

Our first missionary couple is already in the United States and there is another couple going to Atlanta. We must reverse this beggarly mentality and go to give them. Then we shall receive in superabundance.

Are you producing a giver-nation or a receiver-nation?

Are you producing a giver-Church or a receiver-Church?

Are you producing a Church that is preoccupied with its own needs or with the needs of the other Churches?

I would like to let you know that the Church in Yaounde, every month, gives :

30% of what comes in, straight into the Missionary Fund, and

30% straight into the General Ministry Fund - Gospel House.

In order to tell them not to boast, the Church in Lagos was born in this. Since they were born, they have given 60% of their funds to ZTF Ministries.

Brother J.T.M.: We have heard.

Brother Zach: But I was not saying this from a negative point of view. It is just that it is the right philosophy. Some day, they will give 65%, then give 70% and then 75%. In the past, I have said if I were a pastor, I would not rest until my Church gave 90% of its revenue to the Ministry of others. Then we would be a very blessed Church because the shortest way to blessing is to give, and the quickest way to poverty is to keep.

We thank you for your contribution in fasting. We thank you for your contribution in prayer. We thank you for your contribution in giving, and we thank Cotonou particularly for the contribution in human resources - our missionaries to Togo. We wait for the others because, finally, money is rare, but people are rarer.

Let me just say a word about the future of the School of Knowing and Serving God. We want to buy 200 hectares of land, i.e. 500 acres, as the home of the School of Knowing and Serving the Lord, because people will come from the 200 countries to be trained. Some will just come to be refreshed. We shall house not only the School of Knowing and Serving God there, but also the School of Fasting, the School of Prayer and the School of Walking by Faith. We do not expect people to come and read the Bible from morning till midnight. They might just become the Bible. In the morning, they will be taught. In the afternoon, they will work on projects - poultry, cattle, rabbits, goats, and fish farming as well as all other kinds of farming, inland fisheries and all these kinds of things. Then in the evening, they will pray, so that we shall produce missionaries who are related to practical life in reality and not just people who go and stand and tell people, "Believe in the Lord Jesus Christ!" God was the first Farmer and we cannot graduate from practical work!

A friend in the United States has asked that I should send someone whom he will keep for a year and train him free of charge in woodwork; so that by the time he comes back, he will send him with an engine saw. We are looking for the right person to send as part of the Ministry. He doesn't have to be a Cameroonian, because the Ministry is not a Cameroonian national affair. We don't confuse the two things at all. That is why we are not only looking for Cameroonians to go to the mission field. We are looking for people who are an integral part of the Ministry. The friend also said, because he belongs to a Drug Rehabilitation Centre, that if we wanted to develop rehabilitation centres for alcohol and drug addicts, he would be prepared to receive one person from us and train him to come back here and do that kind of work. He would train him at his own expense. I say this so that if the national leaders know the right people, they will inform us.

10

THE SECRET OF SUCCESS IN THE MINISTRY

"After the death of Moses the servant of the Lord, (the Lord said to Joshua son of Nun, Moses' aid):" <u>Joshua 1:1</u>

In a sense, the primary leader is the servant of the Lord and the others are his servants. It was not because he was the Number One man. It was not because God started with him. He was not called "servant" from the beginning. He went through the process step by step, serving Jethro, and so forth.

You can't start by serving God. Do you know Him?

I am not asking whether you are saved. You are very saved.

It is one thing for your sins to be forgiven. It is another thing to know God.

Part of my worry is that many people do not worry about the fact that they do not know God, and they are not actively seeking Him so that they will know Him. By the grace of God, we shall write the book entitled, "Seeking God," because:

There are many people seeking God's power but they are not seeking God. There are many people seeking God's blessings but they are not seeking God.

Three pretty girls entered a jewellery shop and the jeweller was very wealthy and very generous. He told them, "Ask anything you want in the shop and I'll give you."

Ah! One girl saw a very beautiful diamond. She wondered, "Can I ask for that?" Then she had the courage to ask for it. He told her, "Take it." Oh wonderful! She took it and she danced, danced and danced. The other girl saw some fabulous gold. The gold of Ophir. She hesitated and then she asked for it. The man said, "Take it." Oh! She took it and rejoiced. Then the third girl, timid, with shaky steps, walked towards him and said, "I want you." The man was single, so he married her and then she owned the shop.

God said to Levi, "You shall have no inheritance, no portion in their land. I am your Portion and I am your Inheritance." And in that act He made Levi the richest. Others have land, Levi has God. Finally, the others had land, Levi had cities. Levi had the meat that was already brought in, and the priests had what was already cooked.

My prayer is that you should stop looking for these things and seek God and, like that girl, when you have found God, you will have all these things. I am thinking about people who will take a long fast to invest it in seeking God, or invest a long prayer crusade in the seeking of God; people who will bring a sacrificial gift and say, "God, I place this gift on the altar and I ask that You give me Yourself."

The problem is that believers know too many words but too little action. Most people here have not had a personal appearance of God to them. Many know nothing about

Moses' experience when he said, "Lord, show me your glory." So that God had to take him, hide him in a rock and pass before him and show him all His goodness.

I would like the Yaounde Elders to repent because they have heard this truth about withdrawing to seek God that He might appear personally to you since 1981, for 15 years. I have given my testimony a number of times, when I went to Mont Fébé and told God that I would not come back until He appeared to me, and what happened. Brethren, you people have been very wicked to yourselves; none of you has come to ask me even to tell you a little more. Even those of you who are being discipled by me, I know most of you go on retreats, but I don't know anyone of you who said, "I am going to seek God."

One encounter with God can take a person 15 years ahead, because in one real encounter, the scales fall off and everything is different.

Listen, Brethren, when I was striving to sell the car we sold last year, Brother P.S. came and said, "But why is it that I don't know any bother about selling such things in order to give God? You have been bothering and bothering and bothering about selling this car in order to give God the money as supplementary giving. Why is it that I know no such desires?" The difference is not consecration because Brother P.S. is consecrated. The difference is that I was given a vision of hell and I was given a vision of heaven one year after that. It is as clear as if I saw it today - the agony of the lost and the ecstasy of the saints. One vision of what it means to be in hell, and even at your worst, you can never be the same. One vision of the ecstasy of the saints in heaven, and you are not the same. Most brethren here have not received ministry from angels, but they are satisfied.

Brethren, is it not surprising that after I came out of 7 days of waiting on the Lord early this year, having locked myself just to be in God's presence alone, the only person I know who set out to imitate me, one month after that, was Sister H.M. who locked herself up for 7 days? Some months after that, Sister C.M.B. locked herself up for 7 days. They might not have gone very far, but they have begun the practice that will lead to a breakthrough. The men around me surprise me by their horrible commitment to being originals. Brethren, the truth is that apart from a few exceptions, the people who are actively trying to imitate me are the sisters. It is an unholy contentment or an unholy "I-don't-care-ism." But I want to say that **God can be sought and God can be found.** And when you find Him, you want to seek Him some more.

This December, I shall lock myself up for 10 days. Next year, I shall lock myself up for 14 days. If the Lord tarries, in 1998, I shall lock myself up for 21 days. I shall do this increasingly, until the day when there will be 40 days that I have spent only beholding His face, undistracted by the face of man.

Spiritual experience is what is received in return for a price paid.

Why don't you say : "My Lord, I separate myself from all sin for ever and I give You my body in holiness so that it may be Yours for ever. In return, Oh Lord, show me Your glory," Or "In return, Oh Lord, give Yourself to me in full measure"?

"My Lord, I lay on Your altar all that I am. I lay on Your altar all that I have. Lord, in exchange, give me Yourself ." "My Lord and my God, I lay my all on the altar in this bleeding fast. Oh Lord, in return, give me Yourself, show me Your glory, give me Your glory."

"My Lord, and my God, I lay myself on the altar in bleeding prayer. My Lord, I will pray for 8 hours today, 9 hours tomorrow, 10 hours the day after and I shall keep going on until it is 24 hours a day or until I behold Your glory, until You show me Your glory, until You pass before me so that I might behold Your form."

"I love those who love Me, and those who seek Me, find Me." Everything depends upon the price paid.

Some people are so satisfied with His doings that they don't hunger for Him. They are so satisfied with His gifts that they say, "You can wait."

There is a deep worry in my heart. I rarely find those who want to know Him; those with successful Ministries but who are dissatisfied with these Ministries because they want Him and who say,

> *"Lord, You have shown me Your power, but show me Yourself.*
> *You have shown me Your goodness, but show me Yourself.*
> *You have blessed my works, but give me Yourself.*
> *You have given me good health, but I want the Healer.*
> *You have baptized me into the Holy Spirit, but I want the*
> *Baptizer.*
> *You have given me in abundance, but I want the Giver."*

Without encounters with God,

- something of the incentive to pay the ultimate price will be lacking;
- something of reckless sacrifice will be lacking;
- something of contentment in self-imposed poverty because of Him will be lacking.

After you have beheld His face, that which is beauty in the things of the world loses its power to make sense.

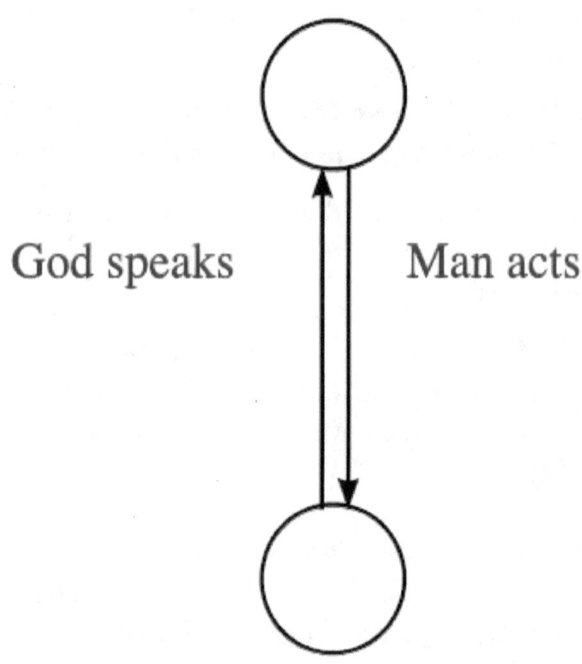

God speaks, man acts. God cannot speak and then after He has spoken, He acts. If He is to do that, then what are you there for?

God speaks. Man acts. Then things happen.

God speaks, man acts! Even if God kept speaking every minute for the next one billion years, if man did not act, nothing would happen. If you go to a young girl and say, "I love you; will you be my wife?" And she keeps quiet. If everyday you go there and she does not respond, will you go and sign the marriage certificate on the man's part and sign on the woman's part?

If God has spoken to you, He has done all that He should do. To be changed, you must act.

So, unless you come to terms with corresponding action, God's speaking will have been in vain. Brethren, you realize that when I speak, I speak with dates. When the dates are not clear, the seasons are settled, while I continue to seek God's mind about the dates. The thing is that many of you leave things in the air. Brethren, that is being dishonest. You have just heard of a bleeding fast. Have you asked yourself, "When can I carry out a bleeding fast in order to say to God, 'In response to this bleeding fast, give me Yourself'?" If you don't begin to contemplate the fast - the time, the length; how will you obey?

This is sheer corruption of heart not to ask: "When will I obey? How will I obey?" You have heard about prayer that lays all on the altar, and you have not begun to ask, "How will it be?" I have just begun to work out one such prayer that will result into 300 hours of battling with God:

- 1 hour the first day,
- 2 hours the second day,
- 3 hours the third day,
- 4 hours the fourth day,
- 5 hours the fifth day,
- 6 hours the sixth day,
- 7 hours of prayer the seventh day,
- 8 hours the eighth day,
- 9 hours the ninth day,
- 10 hours the tenth day,
- on the 11th day 11 hours of prayer,

- on the 12th day, 12 hours of prayer,
- on the 13th day, 13 hours of prayer,
- on the 14th day, 14 hours of prayer,
- on the 15th day, 15 hours of prayer,

until one is breaking on the 24th day when in total agony there are 24 hours of prayer, and God steps in to save you because you are almost finished, to show you His glory. It is this, I don't know why, not getting down to getting into action. What I began to say to myself is that the ten days of locking myself up will be the last days of praying of that kind. One of them will be the day of praying 24 hours, the next one 23 hours, 22 hours, 21 hours, 20 hours, 19 hours, 18 hours, 17 hours, 16 hours, 15 hours. Therefore, before I lock myself up, I shall have prayed up to 14 hours so that I go in for the end battle. Unless you are asking, "How am I going to work it out?" then you are being very dishonest, because nothing will happen.

I began to ask God, "Lord, when can I take the next fast for 40 days in order to have the next self-revelation of Yourself to me, so as to say, 'God, in response to this bleeding fast, give me Your bleeding Self,' ?" because the Lamb went to the throne with the scars of the nailprints. "Lord, in response to this bleeding fast, give me Your bleeding Self." The question is, "When will I put it in?"

I began to ask, "What can I bring to God as a significant gift and say to Him 'God, in answer to this bleeding gift, give me Your bleeding Self.'?" I began to throw it in my head. Then my heart began to warm up. If God would let someone buy the house we built earlier on in our lives, (it is the last thing we have on earth), then it would be laid before Him in exchange for Himself.

But it is the failure to work it out in practical terms that causes many believers never to move into experience. They don't know battles. And if you think that after God has spoken, God will come and do it for you, you are mistaken. Permit me to put it this way:

- It is God's duty to speak; it is man's duty to obey.
- It is God's duty to command; it is man's duty to act upon what He has said.

Unless what we are saying here is being translated into things that we are going to work on practically, we are wasting time.

Joshua 1:2 "Moses my servant is dead. Now then, you and all these people, get ready to cross the Jordan River into the land I am about to give them - to the Israelites." Spiritual leadership is not a man imagining his own things and doing them for God. We said God speaks and man acts.

Until God speaks, we can only wait.

After God speaks, woe to us if we don't act.

Until God speaks, woe to us if we act.

After God has spoken, woe to us if we don't act.

Until God speaks, what can we act upon?

After God has spoken, how dare we not act?

Until God speaks, if you work, you are acting in the flesh.

After God has spoken, if you don't act, you are resting in the flesh.

Some people are already in heaven. Nothing worries them, so they do nothing. They are just in unholy rest. One year after another, nothing happens. I want you to write down the major accomplishments of your life in the last 18 months, that is last year and this year. Write them down in your own note book.

1. --------------
2. --------------
3. --------------
4. --------------

In the last 18 months, behold my accomplishments:

Brother A.M.:

- In 1995, 30-day partial fast, October 1995.
- Started an Assembly in a new locality 3 kilometres from the centre of Meri.

Brother Zach: He planted a new Church, did a 30-day partial fast. That could have been done in two months, isn't that possible? Could you not have done this in two months, taking one month for your fast? *Brother A.M.*: It is possible, but when the field is very difficult, it is not the same thing.

Brother Zach: The work is good but small. It takes valiance to start an Assembly. We congratulate you, but do more in 18 months. Somebody can say he did ten months of partial fasts and planted five Assemblies.

Brother Firmino (Angola):-

- Two 40-day fasts,
- Two 30-day fasts,
- One 21-day fast.

Brother Zach: Let us all clap for him. And these are complete fasts. Now when you put a 30-day partial fast by the side of these, it is like a man carrying his giant rat and walking boastfully.

Brother Firmino:

- We have planted 11 House Churches.
- We have just built a Centre for our meetings, which holds 800 people.

Brother Zach: How many people are in the Assembly?

Brother Firmino: We are 600.

Brother Zach: In two years, they have passed from 120 to 600. You hear, Brother Martin?

Brother Firmino: We have raised 11 persons, 8 for evangelism, 3 for other services of the Church.

Brother Zach: This is what the fast produces. In 2 years, the Church goes from 120 to 600. Some people spend the year losing the people who were there. They are there to give away the flock. In 18 months, two 40-day fasts, two 30-day fasts, and one 21-day fast, not to talk about the numerous shorter fasts. That is spiritual aggressiveness! And it produces results. And when some people accomplish thirty day-partial fasts!

In fact, all the Douala Elders should stand up and repent for blocking Church growth in the nation. They have been hanging between 1 and 2000 for many years now. When the Church in Yaounde was around 2000, Douala was around 1000. Yaounde is approaching the 6000 mark. Douala is still hanging around 1000. And it is the nation's, biggest city. It is a tragedy. They should just admit that they are not committed, or what they are committed to needs to be known. You deceived yourselves that you could lead without great acts. No long fasts, no long prayer crusades, no bleeding gifts. Brother M. gives well to the Lord, but there is not one gift that could have caused hell to tremble. It has been a regular life.

A leader's life may be regular at a high level, but it is a regular life. **The truth is that leadership by regular living is folly.**

Listen, Brethren, Isaac was a good man but Isaac was not great. There were no great acts in Isaac's life.

Brother S.N. started with great acts, 30-day fasts... But it is all distant history. This man attacked the satanic prince of Douala until the prince had to hit him very hard one night and he totally crumbled. I had to come down and join the Elders for him to be restored. But he ought to have stood up and said, "O.K., next time you will have it." But he said, "Oh satanic prince, I am sorry to have stepped into your territory. From now on, I will not attack you again." And hell feasted. He did not say, "The Devil has attacked me, therefore I will now hit him twice as hard." Douala is, therefore, a city without great events. They love the Lord and they are serving Him as people in times of peace. There is no aggressiveness! There is no individual aggressiveness! There is little collective aggressiveness! There is no pressing on till breaking. May it be forever settled that

Without a great price paid, there are no great accomplishments.

There is lack of a holy determination! They are content. Maybe it is because they are perhaps the biggest real Assembly in the city. They are happy to be the top of the bottom. God does not compare you to the other Churches. He compares you to where you ought to have been.

The Douala leaders should repent of that spirit of indulgence and giant-rat hunting and for leading a stagnant church. It is a terrible thing because when you look at Yaounde, there was intensity. We had twelve weekend retreats, but they have become 24-hour retreats; so it is really 12 days and not 12 weekends.

Where are 40-day prayer crusades?

Where are 40-day fasts?

Where are 30-day fasts?

Where are heart-rending gifts?

Unless something happens, they will start to turn around with the numbers because their 24-hour prayer retreats once a month will not carry the Church to 10,000. It is a commitment to mediocrity.

And as for the missionaries, when I receive many of their reports, I kneel down and weep. They are like men bewitched. I ask, "What are they doing on the mission field?" I don't see exceptional fasting. I don't see exceptional praying. I don't see exceptional evangelism. No missionary has ever written to me and said, "This month, I led ten people to the Lord." No missionary has written to me and said, "This month I baptized four people, the fruit of my labours." And they hope to take nations by being very faithful regular people. I have not got one report from a missionary who prayed 200 hours a month. I ask, "What are they doing on the mission field? They are on holiday." Now, these are good men and they are doing work which by other standards will be considered exceptional. But when you know what they could do, you can only weep. When a missionary prays two hours a day, you can only weep. Why do you go to waste your life on the mission field? You could have stayed at home and done something better for yourself in this world. Are you bewitched to surrender the possibility of making a career in this world to go and be holy mediocres? Of all men, you deserve to be pitied. There is only one reason: laziness or ease. We said that the missionary should spend the time from 4 a.m. to noon with God.

Because the missionary is the lord of his time, from 4 o'clock till 12, it is 8 hours given to God; and he may not see anybody, he may do nothing until he has given God those 8 hours. And after that, he can then go to see people, to evangelise and to do the other things. But they have signed a pact with the Enemy not to obey. So they are not totally charged with the presence of God so that they could rain terror on the Enemy's kingdom. They are on holidays in a foreign land. Some do not even send reports. The thing is so bad that they cannot write it down. We have to pray because they could become Buddhists, because when a man has lost God completely, he can believe something else and still think that it is the pursuit of God. I can't understand it, Brethren.

I went to Makerere to get a Ph.D. There were days during which I was in the laboratory for 20 hours each day. The first new compound I synthesized, crystallized at 3.00 a.m. I danced in the laboratory alone. And then, when I started evangelism, for a period of two years, I was spending three to four evenings a week on the streets of Kampala evangelising for 3 to 4 hours each evening. And in those two years, I led 500 people to the Lord on the streets of Kampala. That was where I learnt evangelism. I was running after sinners. I can't see how a man goes to a place and after one or two years, there is no Church of 100 people. And these missionaries know what I didn't know then. I can't understand it. If they spent the time from 4.00 a.m. to midday with God, if they have meetings for two or three days, the afternoons or evenings should be on the streets, where the sinners are. What do you do with the time, people? What do you do with the time? If a missionary led only one person to the Lord a week, by his own effort alone, a man could have a Church of at least 100 people in one year and for a man who goes out three or four times a week, normally he will led two or three people. He spends the morning praying it through and puts two, three or four hours on the streets. It is a scandalous shock. Have you asked yourself why you are on the mission field? Some of you gave up good worldly positions to go to the mission field, to go and sink! I can't understand it. It is just because of an unwillingness to be aggressive.

Listen, Brethren, to a report of the first year of our work in Yaounde, because we went there as missionaries. In fact, I had got it ready. In fact, I meant to send it out to you people. I couldn't speak French. We were having 8 meetings a week. At least, I was at 8 meetings a week, excluding the All-nights, and the All-night was born with three of us: Prisca, Jean Ndongmo and myself. And I had the burden that you people don't have. I had to teach at the University. I had to supply all the money of the Work from the beginning. We had meetings in six quarters in the first year. By some strange grace of God, I called them Assemblies. There was one in Olezoa, one in Tsinga, and the rest in other places. And they have become Assemblies today. Whatever were my faults, and there were many, I put in my whole self, I put in every ounce of my energy. And, Brethren, I did not know what you people know now; I had not even been baptized in water, although I had been baptized in the Holy Spirit.

This time in the United States, I was busy every minute. Because the meetings were few, I decided to pray and to read the Word. And in three weeks I read 500 chapters. Yet there was much travelling by road. One day I had to travel nine hours from one place to the next. Brethren, we are not in for a joke! And when it is joking at leadership level it is tragic.

The results produced are proportional to the investment in time.

Souls are won in proportion to how much time is spent in evangelism.

How many days a week are you on the streets? How many hours a week are you on the streets evangelising? Or have you become an administrator of nothing? For a missionary to go and sit down as a pastor is extreme folly. **The missionary is a Church-planter.**

Many of you have settled as dangerous pastors. Maybe the title is confusing you. You are in charge of a national Work. Therefore, get back to the Pauline methods! Some of you think that you have to build places for the people to meet in. That is the pastor's job! That is not your job. Where did Paul build meeting places?

Brother Fiogbe, listen, where did Paul build meeting places for the people? That is how to settle to be a pastor and begin to carry the burdens of a local Church, and that is how to lose the nation!

You are not a local pastor, Sir!

You are not a local pastor, Madam!

You are pioneer men to take a nation for God!

If the people are truly converted, it is their duty to find their meeting place. You are there to give them some counsel. The problem is that you are doing a missionary Work, producing missionary churches.

Missionary churches depend on the headquarters for money and supplies. That is the worst thing that a man can take to a nation.

This month the missionary couple is going to London, another missionary couple is going to Zambia, and another missionary couple is going to Niger. The reality is that there is no money in Yaounde for that. By the time we were leaving Yaounde, we had half of the amount it will take. Some miracle has to take place between now and the end of the month for them to be able to go. Consequently, we cannot abandon New Testament patterns. That is a question that you need to ask:

Are the missionary methods you use, biblical or yours?

When Paul went along on the first missionary journey, apart from preaching the Word, did he give anything? Did he become a social centre to provide for the needs of the people? No! He gave them God and he left Him to them to provide all the other things for them. Of course, if a man wants to be a pastor (and you cannot have an itinerant pastor), then he settles in a place, he leads people to the Lord, he builds a hall, and he ensures that the number keeps growing. He is a pastor but not the missionary. And that is not the national leader.

The national leader is a person who goes to places, leads sinners to the Lord, brings them together, helps them to grow, and allows them to decide where they will meet and how they will meet. Then he will carry the spiritual burden. He will carry no practical burdens. We say it again: He will carry the spiritual burden - the formation of Christ within, the walk in holiness, basic doctrine - baptism in water, baptism in the Holy Spirit and so forth. But when he starts looking for plots to build for them, he has derailed, he has abandoned the nation to become a local pastor. When that happens, we need to send a missionary there because the first one has derailed and settled as a local pastor.

The burdens for the practical things must be left for the people.

When a man goes to the Mission field and says, "I am looking for a big house where I will hold the meetings," from the word, "Go," he has missed it and he may never get back. He must look for a very small house. After he has led four or five people to the Lord, it must be such that very soon there is a problem - where to meet. And the pastor must ask the people, "Where are we going to meet? Your Church is born, I am just here to help you; now where are the meetings to be held?" And let the people themselves look for an answer. They should propose an answer to him, then he may help them to discern. But he carries no burden of it because when you carry the burden of buildings, you cannot carry the burden of Christ.

That is where the Elders in Douala ended up in the Enemy's pocket: They were carrying the burden of the building in Bonaberi. They were, first of all, carrying the burden of the plot that they lost. Then they started carrying the burden of the building at the Power House. Then they were carrying the burden of building so many rooms in Power House Number Two. Then they began to carry the burden of the plot at Omnisport, and then the burden of building the meeting place at Omnisport. And they didn't ask, "What is happening to the people?"

When a missionary, who is a primary leader in a nation, allows himself the luxury of being sidetracked into providing buildings, he has decided to settle as a pastor. And the people will now depend on him for everything: "My house is leaking, Pastor, do something." "I have no rents, Mr. Pastor." "My child cannot go to school." You have now converted a spiritual leader into a social worker. O.K., he will do the social work, but the nation will be lost. Sometimes, it is as if they fear being forgotten: "Let me go there and teach because they may forget me." If you cannot trust others, you can't be a leader.

Six months after Brother Joe Mbafor believed, when we were going to hold the Bamenda Crusade for Christ, I left the flock in Yaounde in his hands. And he has continued and has taken care of the flock since then.

When you think that the people must become angels before they are left to lead, you should ask yourself, "When did you become an angel?" When a missionary settles as a pastor, first of all, he will be frustrated because he will be looking here and looking all over. The pastor just looks at one place. And even in the locality, a pastor who is bothering about buildings is a pastor gone wrong. That is the work of deacons!! How a missionary can pose as the one to whom people go for money, I don't understand it. From the time they believe, if he is an honest man, he is to teach them to give for his needs. If he does that, there will be a breakthrough. They will know, "This is our man. We are keeping this man in this country. He belongs to us, we belong to him." And then the work will be indigenous. It will not be a foreign work. And the people will put their head there because they will know that if they don't, nobody will do it. And if they don't want to do it, let it not be done. So the wise missionary wants to become the responsibility of the local Church as soon as possible. Twenty years from then, he will be glad that he did that.

In the first year in Yaounde, we were giving money for the evangelism that the New Life For All was carrying out in Ngaoundere and Maroua and in those areas. And when the Americans offered to help, I said "No." We would have become America-dependent.

Listen, Brethren, the person who does not allow people to struggle on their own has produced people who will be dependent. And if they are dependent in material things, they will be dependent in spiritual matters. They will not labour to lay hold on God. They will always wait for somebody to come and tell them what to do.

Most of the time, help is disastrous.

It ruins initiative and destroys the vision.

What a man suffers to acquire, he appreciates it. We say again,

The missionary bears the burden of lost souls; and then when people believe, the burden of the formation of Christ within.

Structures and social issues - he leaves them to the deacons or he leaves them with the local leaders. Missionary methods - biblical ones or our own?

Listen, if you see that you have not done something you ought to have done, what I do is I thank God that I am going to do better. There is a word they call DISCOURAGE-MENT; it doesn't exist in my life. Discouragement is in the dictionary; leave it there. If I see what I ought to have done which I didn't do, I say, "Now, good, I am going to do it." In fact, it is pride, to say, "How could a wonderful person like me make a mistake?" You are not important. We are all learners in the School of Jesus. So when you realize a mistake, when you are shown a mistake, it should be a point of rejoicing, "I am going to do better." We are here to set the pattern for doing better. Don't let self-love overthrow and destroy you, because discouragement is just saying, "My self-love has been touched."

It is rare to find someone succeed who never failed. And if you have never failed, you have never attempted really great things.

If you go hunting giant-rats, the chances of failing are very limited.

In Bafoussam, one brother who is in the army, prayed saying, "Lord, show us the way to lion-country!" The Lord is showing us the way to lion-country. We are a privileged people. Let us give Him a clap.

When I started to preach in Uganda, Dr. Peter Charles, who was an older brother in the Lord but not a preacher, used to follow me. After I had finished preaching, he would give me a list of my errors, sometimes three pages long. He once said, "In the first twenty minutes, nobody knew where you started from nor where you were going to. You were just confusing everybody." That is how I was brought up. And he did that for two years at his own cost. I was younger than him physically, I was younger than him in the Lord, but he said he felt that I was going to be of consequence. His criticisms were painful but effective. Praise the Lord!

We hope that the Ministry of the Word is tearing down giant-rat projects; and that in your meditation you are pulling down all those giant-rat projects.

Fasting is for destroying the Enemy fundamentally.

When the Lord was fasting, He met the devil. Apart from the angels that came and strengthened him, there was nothing mentioned about God. The devil came! A person who does not go on long fasts does not take the devil to task.

Long fasts are for smashing the Enemy. They are for warfare and for the release of spiritual power. But prayer is for building the Kingdom of God. Prayer is for personal transformation and the transformation of others.

The Apostle Paul says, "My little children for whom I am again in the labours of childbirth" - that is prayer - "until Christ be formed in you." So, you will have to build a strong weapon of prayer. If not, your fasting will smash the Enemy and bring the people in, but when you look at their character you will be very sorry, because it is with the weapon of prayer that Christ is formed in the believer. Therefore, fasting, fasting, fasting, fasting, then prayer, prayer, prayer, prayer. One leg represents prayer and a man who just goes on one leg is handicapped. A man who only fasts is also handicapped. The man with long fasts should also become a man of long prayer crusades - a man of long seasons of prayer - so that he takes the Devil to task and knocks him out. Fasting should precede prayer. You knock out the Enemy with fasting, and then with prayer you build the Kingdom. So, normally, the year should start with a fast to get the Devil out of the programme and out of the way. After that, prayer should come in to build. Actually, a man should do more praying than fasting. If a man does two 40-day fasts, he should do three 40-day prayer crusades. I will tell you why. The 40-day fasts knock out the Enemy. But the matter of the formation of Christ within, of building Christ into the believer, is a herculean task because the people can be saved and they are there, but when you look at them you are totally angry. We began to war in Yaounde because of the love of the world that is infiltrating into the Church. And the Devil's purpose is to establish a continuum so that you don't know where the Church ends and where the world begins; and it is not that wearing of a head scarf that tells people that you have left the world. You know some of these "foulards" that are seen in Onitsha - such very big things that seem to be saying, "I swear to God." That is not separation from the world. Separation from the world is not external, although it may have external manifestations. It is fundamentally an inward, holy attachment to the Lamb. Make sure that every fast is followed by a prayer crusade. Better still, make it one fast, two prayer crusades, then another fast, and two prayer crusades. Then you will knock out the Devil and establish the Kingdom of God.

In this whole matter, we have to distinguish between a spiritual man and a spiritual leader. A spiritual man is a man who is after God, running after God: "Should no one go with me, I still will follow."

A spiritual leader is a person who carries a mass of people with him.

At the extreme of it, one brother expressed it in Uganda, putting it in these extreme words, "I am not saved without my neighbour." Somebody can begin to go on retreats just out of self-love. He can fast out of self-love, just so that they will say, "Oh Massa! You don fast oh! You pass we!" = "Wonderful! You have really fasted! You surpass us!" Of course, any fast or crusade that is rooted in self has no consequence before God. In fact, it will win only stripes from the Lord. It is the worst abomination to fast for self, to give for self or to pray for self!

A spiritual leader says, "Where are my people?"

After a man has done great exploits, he must come and take the people along on great exploits.

If Brother A does three 40-day fasts, this is 120 days of fasting and he is almost totally broken. If Brother A gets 100 people to do 3-day fasts, there are 300 days of fasting. If he gets 100 people to do 7-day fasts, it is 700 days of fasting. If he gets 100 people to do a 10-day fast, he has 1000 days of fasting. If he gets 1000 people to do a 10-day fast, he has 10,000 days of fasting.

A1: 3 X 40 = 120 days of fasting.

A2: 100 X 10 = 1000 days of fasting.

100 X 100 = 10,000 days of fasting.

A2: is the spiritual leader.

A1: is the spiritist - "Should no one go with me, I still will follow." This is selfishness, especially when it comes from a leader. He has resigned from leadership. He is now pursuing self-love. About the leader, the questions is:

How many people did you carry with you to great heights? The leader is preoccupied with the people he is carrying to great heights.

If a leader wants to go into a fast alone, he should first resign. Can you imagine 1000 people doing a 21-day fast? It is 21,000 days of fasting. Brethren, you know that the Devil fears numbers. In the final overthrow of the satanic prince of Yaounde even babies fasted.

The Devil asks: "How long is the fast?"

Then he asks: "How many of them are fasting?"

The Devil asks: "How many of them are there?"

When they say, "One man is coming," the Devil says, "I've handled his kind." The Devil asks: "How long is the fast and how many of them are there?"

The power released in a fast or prayer crusade is directly proportional to the number of people involved, every other thing being equal.

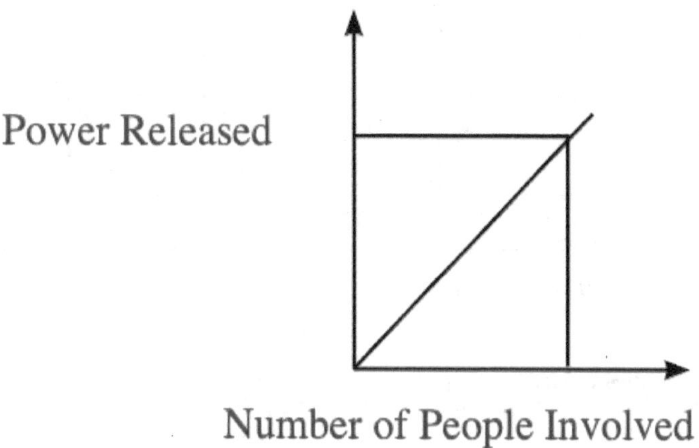

Power Released Proportional to Number of People Involved

So a leader gets the whole team involved in the battle; so that the whole team might share the reward. The leader is always asking: "How can I get the whole team to share the reward? And not: "How can I get the reward alone?"

How can I get the whole team to be involved in the battle and therefore share in the reward?

The challenge of leadership is the power to mobilise all the people.

To mobilise yourself alone is cheap. Mobilising oneself alone is hunting giant-rats.

Greatness is proportional to the number of people mobilised. Greatness in spiritual leadership is directly proportional to the power to mobilise people.

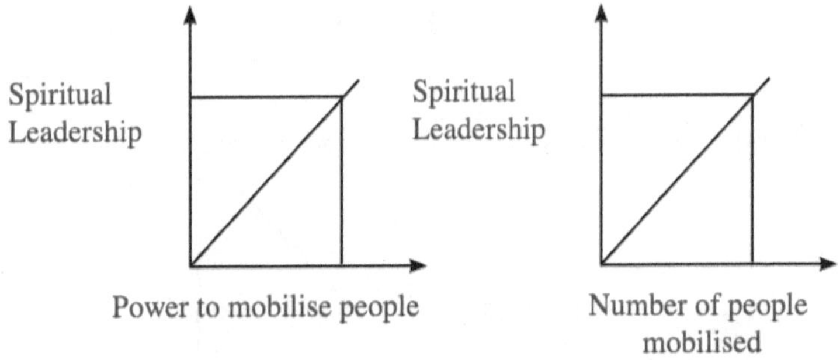

Spiritual Leadership Proportional to Power to Mobilise People and
to Number of People Mobilised

The power will lead to people, which also is again saying: Spiritual leadership is proportional to the number of people mobilised.

So, a leader without a team is actually no leader.

Brethren, may God write these words on your hearts. Caleb was one of the successful spies, but an individual overcomer. He said, "Give me this mountain." He was looking only for one mountain. He said, "They promised it to me. I am 85 and still strong enough to go to war." He didn't look at Israel. He said, "Give me this mountain. It was promised to me." He was a righteous man, a man with a different heart who fully followed the Lord, but he had no vision for the people. If they had made him the leader, it would have been catastrophic.

The leader focuses on the people: "How can I mobilise all the people?"

It is better to mobilise all the people to do a 10-day fast rather than that you alone do a 40-day fast. As you do your 40-day fast, the people will be spectators. They will not be one with you in paying the price. It will remain your vision and your burden.

We don't only want seekers of God. We want the leader of seekers of God.

I had some friends in East Africa. They were engaged. The sister did something that touched whatever was left of Adam in the brother, to the fullest measure. You know what she did? "Oh, look at that Brother, he is __". And that blew the man up completely.

Then she added more salt to it. She was 25, he was 26. She said, "But this whole matter of marrying boys,... A man of 40 would know where he is going to." I think God allowed those statements so as to deal with this man's self-love at the roots. This happened on Tuesday. They used to fast on Wednesday and pray for their coming marriage. They used to go to the college chapel and pray together. That Wednesday, when the Brother went, he knelt down and started praying. The Sister came and knelt by him. Then when he turned and looked and saw that it was her, he left and went into the vestry, locked himself there and made noise for two hours. Then in the evening, he told me the story. I told him that he was not praying to God. He was praying to himself. The Bible says that the Pharisee was praying to himself. But there is something of the Pharisee in each one of us, a "holier than thou" attitude. "Don't kneel by me and pray," forgetting the Bible that says, "First go and be reconciled to your brother before you come and pray." Somebody says, "Your head is big." You say, "O.K. I will not see him again." That is reaction and not conviction. Believers act by conviction, not by reaction.

Most marriages are ruined by reactions. In the U.S, a big quarrel arose between a husband and wife and the matter came up to me. When visitors came, the woman gave herself to serving and serving the visitors. When they left and she turned to serve her husband, the man would not accept the service, saying, "I am the one who is served after all the people you are interested in are gone." I was amazed by the man's infancy. We can easily discern that which came by reaction. Obviously, because God who is All-supreme receives gifts, although He is the greatest Giver, no one can separate himself from gifts and be in God's position. This morning in the reading of the Word, I was struck afresh.

Exodus 34:20b "No one is to appear before Me empty-handed." So God is commanding you and everyone else to give. The missionary must command the people to give to him. If not, his pride is the ruin of his Ministry. That is the way to bless the people. We thank God that by the instrumentality of our Ministry, people have transferred one billion two hundred million francs to heaven. If we had said that we were going to do it all alone, even if we were billionaires, we would still stand in the way of God. To react because some people abuse it is not maturity. From the time people believe, they are to be commanded to give to God and to those who feed them.

Galatians 6:6 "Anyone who receives instruction in the word must share all good things with his instructor."

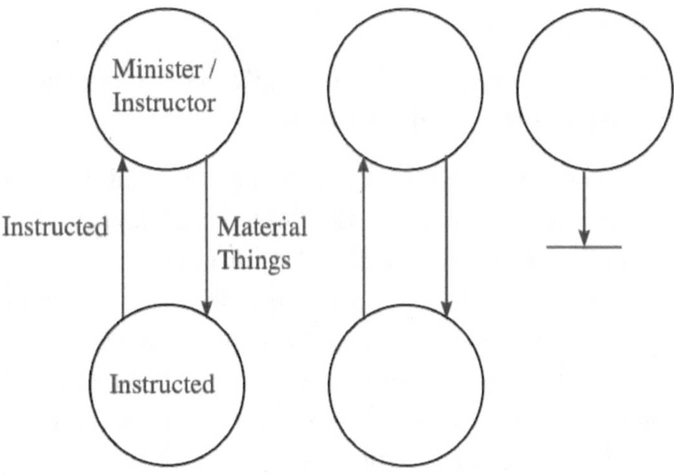

Giving to one's minister

The minister sows the Word. The people are to sow good material things. If a man sows the Word and refuses that they should sow all good things into him, so that you now have a barrier between them, what will happen the next time is that the Word will bounce and not reach the people. They will hear but they will not be transformed. Why? Because there is a block. In order that there may be no block, when the man has sown the Word, he must allow the other person to sow the seed of material things. I want to tell you, when you see people who are not sowing materially into their minister, they are also not growing. There is a problem (and the solution is that) they should not only give to God, but also to the instructor.

Brother J.D.D. and I made a mistake in Douala. My share in it was that I agreed with what he did. Brother M. would not be away from the Church today had Brother J.D.D. accepted the car that he gave him, even though it was not in good condition. From the time that the car was rejected, everything began to go wrong.

People put themselves in their gifts and when the gifts are rejected, they feel rejected.

Listen, when the Lord Jesus Christ came, He did not arrange that they would be sending Him funds from heaven month by month or quarterly or annually. He didn't say, "I'll just ask My Father and My Father will perform a miracle of coins dropping." Imagine the frustration of those women if that had happened. They would not have known and loved Him. Their joy was to minister to His needs and to His disciples' needs, and that gave meaning to their wealth.

If you are going to be a faithful teacher, you will teach the people to give to you. If not, you are not proclaiming the whole counsel of God. And if you don't accept the gifts, your pride will catch up with you because when you teach, the Word will begin to bounce back.

When the person gave to you, it created room for he himself to receive. Since he could not give to you, there was no room for him to receive. And some people here are fundamentally selfish. They give only to God. To them, there are no human beings. Do you give to human beings? Do you give to the ministers of the Gospel? You receive instruction Sunday by Sunday, week by week; then you see the teacher and smile. The Bible did not say, "Smile at the teacher." It said, "Share all good things." You have a good shirt; get the teacher's own. You have a good tie; you get one for the teacher. You have a good car; you get one for the teacher. You live in a good house; you get the teacher to live in a good house. When they give the teacher a good house, he should not run and go to live in a ramshackle house in mud saying he is being poor for God.

By God's grace, next year I shall spend a month in the U.S. One man there has committed himself to fly me for that one month. His plane is called, "On Eagle Wings." He is blocking that one month to fly me so that I may save time. You go by plane; you get your instructor to go by plane!

Brother Zach: Brother J.G, tell me what the laughter is about, so that I can share it with you.

Brother J.G.: ..because I was saying that you are going to the other extreme.

Brother Zach: Where is the other extreme?

Brother J. G.: Well, you would be the dumping place for the gifts of the people.

Brother Zach: How can you be a dumping place? O.K., when they give you the gifts, bring them to me if you don't know what to do with them.

Brother Joe Mbafor: We've killed it already in Yaounde.

Brother Zach: Oh! but we'll resuscitate it. The people are happy when they give. Also, the people are always eating at the Elders' houses. One day Sister P. gave breakfast to 37 people, and it wasn't a special occasion.

We are telling the missionaries, "Tell the people to give." We are telling them, "Have an indigenous Work." We are telling the people, "Be supported on the spot." And at the same time we are saying the missionary must be proud enough to receive no gifts. That is a contradiction. If a missionary gets the people to take over all his expenses as soon as possible, it will advance the

Work. It will be their Work instead of a foreign Work. Take, for example, a man goes to America and decides that he will be going on foot. First of all, it will not work. Without a car in America, you are finished. To go to Church, and for just everything, you need a car,... To say, "Well, I am so consecrated; I won't have a telephone," is missing the whole purpose of sacrifice. It is punishing yourself, and making punishing yourself a sacrifice for God. If they bring food here, and you say, "Go and give it to the Indians. I will not eat. They should pack and parcel that food and send it by post to India!" I still want to say:

Gifts bond people.

God is a giver-God and a receiver-God.

God is a giving God and a receiving God.

Who can outdo God in His wealth?

Who can outdo God in giving?

But that same God says, "No man shall appear before Me empty-handed" - for their own good. The question is, "Whose interest?" We must admit that finally it is in our own interest when we say, "No." After that we feel some inner satisfaction that comes from the flesh. Jesus did not say, "You women, don't bring Me your gifts. My Father will give Me everything." I know there is greed but the answer to greed is not to keep away from gifts. Rather, it is to receive them and perhaps invest them in the needs of others.

The problem is accumulating things, not receiving things. If you are accumulating things, you are in trouble.

When we were in Belgium, a brother brought me a number of shirts and some ties. He is a brother with whom we had virtually no relationship. He had fallen deeply into sin and was seeking to be restored, and he was restored. When he brought me those gifts, I knew to refuse them would be to push him back into the depressed condition. I received them warmly and gladly, and six brethren have benefited from these — six brethren who have no opportunity to go to Belgium; and even if they went there, perhaps nobody would give them anything.

The leader is in a position to receive for the people. If his consecration has set him free from things, he is rich for the people. He receives so that he may give to people who will not on their own be able to be beneficiaries.

Besides just facing the fact that the leader has needs, **leadership is a spending position.**

Yes, leadership is a spending position. Every leader knows that he would be wealthier if he were not a leader. Of course, if his heart is right, he needs to receive to continue in leadership. Because when people bring their gifts, you look up and say, "God bless you,..."

I will never forget a brother who is one of the leaders now in the Work. He failed his exams in the second year in Yaounde University and came to my office, totally broken. Everything was dark. He had no money to pay for his room and no money to go and tell his father about the catastrophe. I gave him 25,000 CFA francs. Now he is a provincial leader. It was a 25,000 francs gift that made history. Praying for him and blessing him would not have solved his problem, he might have continued in the depression.

The Lord has ordained that those who preach the Gospel should live by the Gospel. And the Lord has ordained that those who minister the Word should receive all good things from those who are ministered to. And because this is not obeyed, the Lord is hindered.

What have you done for the person who led you to the Lord? Where is the mark of your gratitude to the person who has been instrumental in blessing you spiritually? Where is your gift to your House Church leader, to the leaders of the Church in the city, to the national leaders? You are not the poorer for giving.

When a man just sees God, he gives to God and only to God without seeing men! He will soon go to heaven to see God. He does not need to live with human beings. But that is not what the Bible teaches.

11

A CORRECTIVE COMMENT

In public praying one or two sentences are enough.

- If you pray one minute, people pray with you;
- the second minute, they pray for you;
- the third minute, they pray against you.

And when you are saying what people are not even hearing and you expect that they will say, "Amen," only liars will say, "Amen." How can you say, "Amen ," to what you did not hear? If a man is saying, "Curse God, in the name of Jesus," and you just hear: "in the name of Jesus," and say "Amen!"

Once in Uganda, when I.A. wanted to attack Tanzania, I went to a Nurses' Fellowship. One sister stood up to pray, "Oh, may the Tanzanian army come to nought." I didn't allow her to pray the second sentence. I stood up and I stopped the praying. Why should the Tanzanian army come to nought; because a mad man is attacking? What of the believers in that army? When there is war, have you found out on what side

Jesus is? I am told that in the World War I, nations met, and were praying that God should help them to win; the other nations met and they were praying that they would win. Who was God to hear? When there was war between China and Japan, Watchman Nee was in Britain and, being the godly man that he was, he stood up and prayed, saying, "God, we do not pray for Japan, we do not pray for China. Oh! We pray for the interests of Your Son in Japan and in China." He had risen beyond national politics. He saw the interests of the Lamb. Some people pray, "Oh, may our team win." They might soon end up like the pastor who was the pastor of a football club and practised sorcery for the football team. Are you excited when your nation wins? What did it win? Twenty-two fools running after compressed air and greater fools watching in excitement. All the excitement is because compressed air has passed through two poles, and it is a world event; and you can go privately and pass the same compressed air through the same poles 1001 times. Has anything happened in the spiritual realm? People say, "Ahhh!!! Yeah!!! They have scored!!!" compressed air has passed between two poles. And they make that the fame of a nation. And they declare a public holiday. In Nigeria, they did it twice. In Cameroon they did it once. That is the victory of compressed air. And the man who sent the ball through the poles is a hero. He may be the worst thief in the nation. He may be morally bankrupt. May we see through the eyes of the Lord! May what excites us be reconsidered!

<u>Joshua 1:2a</u> "Moses my servant is dead. Now then you and all these people,...all these people,..." you and all these people! - That is the leader. You and all the people! You and the whole flock — the flock that is there and the flock that is to be added: You and all. The call of God is an all-inclusive call.

"You and <u>all</u> these people." Please mark those words... <u>all</u> these people!!"

Not "You and the valiant men."

Not "You and the doers of great deeds."

Not "You and the obedient ones."

Not "You and the consecrated ones."

Not "You and the serious ones."

Not "You and the fasting ones."

Not "You and the praying ones." But,

"You and all these people."

May God write that on your hearts! "You and all the people." Without one of the people, you have failed.

When a man dares to think that he can do without one sheep, his folly has reached the extreme.

"There were ninety and nine that safely lay

In the shelter of the fold;

But one was out on the hills away,

Away from the gates of gold."

The ninety and nine sheep, are they not enough?

The shepherd's reply is, "I'm looking for that one."

The ninety and nine, are they not enough?

The 599, are they not enough, Pastor Firmino?

Pastor Joe Mbafor, the 5999, are they not enough?

And so forth. The answer of the shepherd is, "I am looking for that one."

You and <u>all</u> these people! That is God's charge to the leader. Listen, Brethren, when the one sheep went astray, the Bible says that he left the 99 in the open country to go and look for the lost sheep.

<u>Luke 15:4</u> "Suppose one of you have a hundred sheep and loses one of them. Does he not leave the ninety-nine in the open country and go after the lost sheep until he finds it?" In fact, some other versions say in the wilderness. I was studying this. The Greek says, "in the wilderness." It is just that to many people, the wilderness doesn't mean anything. That is why they put open country. He did not leave the 99 in secure ground. He risked the 99 for the one. Oh yes, he risked the 99 for the one!!

The shepherd risks the 99 for the one. He left the ninety and nine in open country. You and <u>all</u> these people. Oh we have an all-inclusive God. If a man's heart is not broken that one sheep of the flock is not there, he is not a pastor, he is not a shepherd. He may be a very good leader, but he is a good hireling. We recommend the book, *"Leading A House Church."* It is really *"The Shepherd And The Flock"* - that is the more popular title of it. We are photocopying some copies to get them ready before the book is published. The photocopied and bound copy will cost 2,500 CFA francs. It is a book that a shepherd ought to have as soon as possible.

The ninety and nine, are they not enough? The shepherd's answer is: "I am looking for that one."

Do you know what the Lord has put into looking for you?

I am shocked by some people's hardness of heart that is just content to see the sheep fall away, provided something remains. And there are some missionaries who lack the power to keep the flock. In one of the countries, after two years, not one person who was on the first list of thirty was in the Church. I said, "This is a disaster." Always a new list! It is like carrying water in a basket with holes. Nothing is left. When you trace it, it is something wrong in the heart. When a man is: "Me one! Me and God," if he has zero capacity to bond, he is just somebody on whom the people just bounce and go away, bounce and go away, bounce and go away. He has a wicked capacity to hold himself back. Such a man will, first of all, hold himself back from his wife. He can't give himself to his wife, he can't give himself to his children, and he can't give himself to his friends. Finally, he can't give himself to the flock. He cannot keep the flock. Or he is a man who knows how to act in an emergency. If you have a problem, he gives you attention. Then he is finished with you. And he goes to the other person who has a problem. He touches people. He touches the needy but when you have no more problem, he is finished with you. It is a problem in the heart. They do not want to pay the price of continually giving themselves to the same person. Their work can therefore not bear lasting fruit. They know how to act only in an emergency. The Lord says, "You and <u>all</u> these people." They are unbroken people. Because they are unbroken, they can be in a heap of stones; because in a heap of stones each stone maintains its individuality. In a building, people are to lose their individuality. They are reshaped to fit in with the others.

May God convict you of the sickness of your heart and the selfishness of your life, and of the fact that you have resisted the Holy Spirit; so that you are not smashed! You cannot fit in.

I know that any person who leads the flock in which people only come and go, in his personal life, he does not know how to keep relationships. He is ever starting and breaking them! What a sick being! I am not saying that such a person cannot have a Ministry and have some success. But he may be succeeding with 1000, whereas he could have been succeeding with a million - lacking the power for sustained investments in one person, then two people, and so on.

I am increasingly worried about the number of people who have no friends. They belong to everybody, which means that they belong to nobody. I am increasingly worried by people who have not even a single covenant relationship. I am worried by the number of people who are always starting relationships but none matures. It is a prophecy of a poor shepherd. There needs to be very very deep repentance about the wickedness of allowing the sheep to perish because people are maintaining their individuality.

How many people did you once lead?

How many are you leading now?

When a leader of multitudes becomes a leader of a few and he doesn't confront the fact that he has lost God, then he is not only sick, he is blind! God has put him aside. And it is almost always because of pride, because every proud man is a damaged man.

When you settle in your heart that you can do without one of the flock, God may also decide that He can do without you.

He is the Chief Shepherd. May the Holy Spirit convict the hirelings here!

Have your prayer crusades been for the flock?

Have your fasts been so that none of them will perish?

In 1995, I prayed through the lists of everybody who was in the Church in Yaounde, name by name. And I have the file. I also prayed for as many names as got to me from the Work. That is why I want accurate records. When I went to the U.S., I went with the list of everybody in the Church in Yaounde. I didn't finish praying through the list. I shall be continuing in India. And if I had the list from Douala, if I had the list of all the Churches in all the nations, there would be prophetic prayer for each person - tearing down all that must be torn down, and building all that must be built. But some people only send me the lists of those who are very strong. Who told them that they themselves were very strong? Who made you a judge of the strength of others? This betrays the corruption and pride of your heart! Some of those you reject are holier than you at least in one aspect. At least they are humbler, and God has a place for the humble and no place for the proud of heart. May God convict you of the Pharisee spirit! "Oh! I fast twice a week, I tithe. I am not like this publican. I don't want this publican in my Church." Some of us seem to have forgotten the depths from which He picked us.

<u>Joshua 1:3</u> "I will give you every place where you set your foot,." "I will give you every place where you set foot on!" So you do not stand stagnant and then He gives you. "I will give you every place where you set your foot!" It was a call to march ahead. "I will give you every place where you set foot on!" God is committed to people who are moving with Him in His direction! "I will give you every place where you set your foot!" If you set foot on 5 metres, He will give you 5 metres. If you set foot on 50, He will give you 50. If you set foot on 5000, He will give you 5000. If 500,000, then 500,000 - "I will give you every place you set foot on!" Oh, you have to stand up and walk and press on and set your foot.

God says, "I will give you every place where your foot sets on." Some people say, "God, give us, then after that, we shall walk on it." God says, "Set foot on, then I will give you." If I were a national leader, I would put a 40-day fast into every province as my way of setting foot on it. Then I would say, "God, give me, I have paid the price."

I say to all who are involved in the conquest of big cities that you have to pay the price of a long fast and a long prayer crusade into each of the zones of the city. If not, forget it because those are nations. Lagos is a nation. The city of Lagos is a nation: 6-7 million people. You should be able to say to God, "God, I have paid the price for this city, I have paid the price for this zone, I have paid the price for this province, or I have paid the price for this Sub-Division or whatever word is used for the unit which the nation is divided into. God says, "I will give you every place where you set foot on!" You say, "I place my foot here in the Name of the Lord." It is not just by accident that you are passing and you touch it. Where you set foot on is a determined choice and a determined action, placing the foot by choice to possess. So, it is not just some disorderly fasting. It is a fast to possess this province or this district or this division." It is a fast or a prayer crusade to possess an area. When a spiritual leader is not an imperialist, when he is a spiritual houseboy or a hunter of giant-rats, there is trouble because behind him may be lion-hunters. As he possesses, then the others can come and take their zones. But when you find a national leader who has now become the pastor of a Church in a suburb and he says, "Let's praise God,"

WHAT OF THE NATION?

What of the unoccupied provinces?

What of the unoccupied divisions?

What of the unoccupied sub-divisions?

If you are a provincial leader or a national leader worthy of your salt, you don't boast about the provinces you have taken. You are burdened about those that you have not yet taken, because God will ask them of you. The limits are not decided by God. The limits are not determined by God.

God has left it to us to determine the limits!

Oh, my dear Brethren! God has left it to us to determine the limits! How frightful! How magnificent!

The limits are not set in heaven. God has left it to men to determine whether people go to heaven or to hell. God has left it to men to determine whether believers will be perfect or they will be imperfect.

God has left it to men to decide whether believers will be sanctified or they will remain in the flesh.

God has left it to Brother Tim Obiaga and the rest to determine whether there will be a Church of 100 people or 1000 people or 10,000 people or one million people in the city of Lagos.

God has left it to man! How great! I asked God, "How many books should I write in my life?" He said, "Write the number you want." I read that Wesley had written, translated or produced 400 books. What he wrote, what he translated from others, what others wrote and he produced came up to 400 books. So I said, "God, I will write 500," and He said, "Amen." We have written 74. God has left it to man to decide! Oh! God has left it to Brother Fiogbe to decide. Yes, God has left the things with Brother Bossoun to decide.

He has left it with Brother Maurice to decide.

Yes, He has left it with Brother Parfait to decide.

He has left it with Brother Joseph Gado to decide.

He has left it with Brother Ndasi to decide what happens to Britain.

He has left it with Brother David Atogho to decide.

He has left it with Brother Paul Foka to decide.

He has left it with Sister Gemma, to decide.

God says, "I will give you every place where you set your foot!" "I will give you every person you birth through prayer!" "Christ will be formed in every person through whom you further birth the formation of Christ through prayer!"

No travail, no births! Births are directly proportional to the travail, to the labours.

The Lord said, (Verse 4) "Your territory will extend from the desert to Lebanon, and from the great river, the Euphrates - all the Hittite country - to the Great Sea on the west." God gave them everything. Oh! that we might confront the limitlessness of God's offers. Listen, Brethren, if we were not prepared to follow the Lord, we could have just stayed with Cameroon Ministry. We could have even just established the one Church in Yaounde and said, "The nation belongs to God." The 249 other Churches would not exist. We could have said, "We are a poor country in a crisis; how do you start sending missionaries? It will be impossible to support them." Fifteen missionary couples have gone out since 1994. Next Sunday, three new couples will be sent out. In November and December, three others will be sent out. And as we asked, next year eighteen will go. One day, there will be 10,000 couples in 200 countries. Has it been because the economy has changed? No! In a sense, in the visible nothing has changed. If anything, they have got worse. But we do not move according to what is in the visible. Anybody who moves according to what is in the visible will not move. The average Nigerian's salary is not enough for food. Yet they live and give sacrificially to God. Hallelujah! Each one according to his vision. Each one according to his capacity to risk for God. It has to be: "I have risked all." I don't just want people who leave all, but people who risk all for a limitless territory whose borders and boundary marks are where the curse is found. The limits of our territory are where the curse no longer exists. When you get to where there is no longer the curse, you have reached the limit. When you get to where there are no sons of Adam, you have got to the limit. But wherever the curse is found, there we must extend, there we must set foot on. Every missionary should be dreaming about the day when he will overflow to the neighbouring countries, and join us in Yaounde.

When I was an Africanist, my big dream was to build a big army and conquer all these small countries and produce one Africa, but the vision is now bigger than Africa, because the colonialism of sin and the neo-colonialism of self is not an African problem; it is a planetary problem. Please, arise, first of all, in your heart from your giant-rat vision and see with the eyes of God. So that when you are in Zambia, by prayer, you extend your hand to go right to North Africa. So that when you are in Benin, you stretch your hand right to Senegal where we shall have missionaries next year; so that if one night is for praying for Benin, the next night is for praying for the rest of the world. If one night is for praying for Lagos, the next night must be for praying for Nigeria, Africa and Planet Earth. "I will give you every place where you set your foot."

<u>Verse 5</u>. "No one will be able to stand up against you all the days of your life. As I was with Moses, so I will be with you; I will never leave you nor forsake you."

Hallelujah! "No one will be able to stand up against you all the days of your life." They will come but they will fall! They will not be able to stand. That means, they will not be able to have victory. They will come, but they will not stand. No one and no principality will be able to withstand! No demon will be able to withstand! Hallelujah! All obstacles in the battle of the Lord are surmountable! Fighting at God's command, fighting for the glory of the Lamb, fighting with the weapons that God has given us, all obstacles are surmountable!

In the battles of God, all obstacles are surmountable:

- the obstacle of my character!
- the obstacle of my failures!
- the obstacles of the Enemy!

All obstacles in the battles of our God!

All obstacles are surmountable!

And all obstacles shall be surmounted!

Song:

> *We are able to go on and take the country,*
> *To possess the land from Jordan to the sea,*
> *Though the giants may be on our way to hinder,*
> *God has surely granted victory!*
>
> ***Chorus:***
> ***We are on the victory side (3 X) with God,***
> ***We are on the victory side (3 X) with God.***

We are able to go on and take Lagos,
To possess the land from Ekpe to Badagrey —,
Though the giants may be on our way to hinder,
God has surely granted victory!

We are able to go on and take Nigeria,
To possess the land from Sokoto to Port Harcourt,
Though the giants may be on our way to hinder,
God has surely granted victory!

We are ale to go on and take Africa,
To possess the land from Cairo to Cape Town,
Though the giants may be on our way to hinder,
God has surely granted victory!

All obstacles are not only surmountable, all obstacles shall be surmounted! Let us say,

All obstacles shall be surmounted!

With our God on our side, we shall surmount all obstacles.

Mountains shall melt like wax!

SONG:

I am a victor all the time,
I am a success and not a failure.
I am a winner, not a loser,
I am the head and not the tail.

He's a mighty Man of battle
El Shaddai.
Glory to Your Name
Jehovah
Glory

Winner Oh! Oh! Oh! Winner! (2 X)
Jesus, You don win Oh! Winner!
Jesus, You go win forever, Winner!

I am a winner in the Lord Jesus (2 X)

Not only will mountains melt like wax. If it is Red Seas, as we raise forth the rod of God, the wind of God shall come and create a way in the Red Sea. Roads shall be created in Red Seas. We shall not tremble before Red Seas. We shall just raise the rod of God in prayer, and the wind of God shall come and we shall walk through the sea. All obstacles shall be surmounted - be they mountains or rivers or lakes - all obstacles shall be surmounted. Victory is inevitable. In fact, we are condemned to victory.

What it means is that each person just has to enlarge the area where he will put his foot on. Pray the biggest and wildest possible prayers, but each one according to your faith. You see, Brethren, going fully assured that victory is inevitable makes all the difference.

I am not going to try. I am going to succeed.

You are not trying. You are going to succeed.

1. Your success on the mission field is guaranteed.
2. Your success in taking the nation is guaranteed.
3. Your success in taking the city is guaranteed.
4. Your success in planting new House Churches is guaranteed.
5. Your success in raising leaders is guaranteed.
6. Your success in raising a team is guaranteed.
7. And your needs shall be provided. And all the needs of the work shall be provided.

Can you believe it, Brethren? We found out that since we started, just in Gospel House in Yaounde, we have invested one billion two hundred million CFA francs into the Work. That is the amount we have spent from Gospel House. In the first year, we had less than a million. It is the story of God supplying the needs. And when you confront the fact that 99% of this came from Cameroon! I think this year we shall have 5% from the other nations. And the portion from the other nations is growing as the Work is growing. The interesting thing is this: the Missionary Fund is a separate fund. Even with the introduction of the Missionary Fund, Gospel House still has about the same money it had in the past, or more. There is the God that provides. When we got this figure from our archives, we were surprised. And the figure will rise increasingly from now on because in the first year it was less than a million, then it went to one million, and so on, as the consecration increases and the number of believers who catch the vision increases. Send us your contribution, even if it is very small. Remember that the winner was the widow who put in two coins.

A famous Nigerian said, "When you give, you are on top and the receiver puts his hand under yours." So he will always be giving and being on top. The taker is under. You know, each time you are giving, somebody has to go under to receive. That is imperialism. That is how to conquer people. Above all, we win their hearts to the Lord Jesus Christ. I am very persuaded. You see, we have a team praying for the funds. Every month about 25 of them take a 7-day complete fast, to fast for the funds. At least a hundred of them meet to pray.

We can trust our God. The missionaries should be at peace. The Lord's hand is not shortened. Their needs will be supplied. I expect every missionary to eat well because it is better to eat well than to be treated from diseases that come from malnutrition. Even if you were to double your food money, it would cost us less than complicated medical bills. I don't want to hear that you are boiling rice and eating it with red oil. I am not saying, "Don't use red oil." Don't misunderstand me. Put some meat or some fish inside. Let it be good to look at and good in the mouth. I went somewhere and the missionaries were lying on their mattress on the floor. I rebuked them because I sleep on a comfortable bed. If some serpent came into the house, let it go under the bed, but let it not go on the missionary.

We use money in a consecrated way, but we meet all the needs because that is how our God is.

If we are rigorous, it is out of love to meet the needs of many more. It is not that our God wants people to live in hardship. We don't send you to be John the Baptist. His era has passed. We started from there. We are in the era of the Lamb. If an unbeliever invites you to come and eat, go and eat, but don't eat until the man is frightened. Eat from a position of authority. Before or after that, preach to him. You are his boss. Wherever you go, you receive the hospitality as a boss because you represent the Most High. Command people to serve you. Do everything to fulfil your Ministry. "I will never leave you nor forsake you!" God is saying, "I will never seal the heavens against you. I will not let your cry go unheard. I will not let your efforts be frustrated." But you see, if the missionary goes and he and his wife become Mohamed Ali and George Foreman, which will be God's side? God is compelled to leave them because He cannot go on the woman's side or on the man's side. But if they are together and proclaim it to God, and ask and labour in prayer together, mountains will melt like wax, Red Seas will open. And as we are going to see very soon, the Jordan will give way.

Be strong and courageous. Be physically strong. Every missionary — the missionaries abroad, and the missionaries at home — must have a programme for exercise. If not, when you are 90 you will be looking for somebody to lead you.

Two years ago, in the United States, somebody came to see me. I was visiting the son. He was 92 years old. He drove 60 miles to come and see me, driving his wife who was 86. And we talked till 8.00 p.m. and he drove her away — at 92.

Go jogging! If there is no room and no place, jog on your corridor. But at all cost, exercise. Be strong physically. Build a strong physical body. When the fast is over, eat well. If you can consume vegetables, good for you. Grow some. Build a healthy body, be strong. Murder rocks as you walk. Have the kind of body that when you step on a rock, the rock goes to bits. Fight against old age. If a woman is 60 and she cannot be mistaken for a girl, she has not kept herself well. Don't become a grandmother at 25. Keep a fresh look; especially freshness of character, because there are some people who by character, are old at 18. They are like grandmothers. They have frowned until the whole face is wrinkles. The sponta- neous laughter flowing from youthfulness - they know nothing about. They carry all the cares of the world. The slightest thing is a problem to them: the burden of the flock, the burden of the children, the burden of the husband... Then they sing, "It's not an easy road..." Their faces make them look like holy horses. Even if she is as young and pretty as anything, when she looks like that, she is already in the terminal stages. The husband has to ask for extreme grace to spend one minute with her. She has this and that complaint! Some say, "My foot is paining", then: "My back is paining," then: "My leg is paining," then, "Oh my head!"... Then, "The plates are broken, the cups are broken, the children are trou- blesome." Oh the power of an innocent smile!

I think my highest moment in the University of Yaounde was when one of the very old professors called me and said, "Fomum, you are moving in this place with the joy of an infant. Don't you know that there are problems here?" With the fulness of the Lord, we must have that which makes the world forget its problems. Now, some people need maybe some spiritual plastic surgery, to give them a new face look but it has to happen in the heart. Some people, I don't know when they last laughed heartily. When the song was going and it was time to dance, I found some people's legs too heavy. They lack the power to forget themselves. They have made themselves the centre of the universe, carrying all the cares of the world. "Oh! This one is backsliding, this one..., the other one has gone away." If the person has backslidden and you are going to look for him, if you are joyful, you have greater hope than if you are miserable. If they tell me that some frowning person is coming, I'll be tempted to say, "Lock the door doubly."

Be strong and young. Now, when you see the possibility of conquering a nation and you are God's instrument, you come alive.

As long as the nation remains to be conquered, I must be young.

And don't dress like a retired preacher. First of all, because a retired preacher is a man who has left God. That is the only way to retire from preaching. Look at yourself in the mirror. Do you still like what you see? Are people pleasantly surprised that you look nice when they meet you? You are preaching a serious message. They say, "That pastor - fear him." So people think that it is somebody who is already 110, who is already tired of life, and that is why he is asking people not to enjoy themselves. When they meet you, are they surprised by the joy, by the radiance? Do your eyes sparkle with hope and a great job that is being accomplished? Be strong.

When I was 48, I passed through France. The immigration officer followed me and said, "I would do anything to be as young as you when I am 48. I told him, "Have Jesus." That was all I could say, I went into the plane. Wherever you go, look like the overcomer, like the person who is in control. You have nothing to apologise for. Your Father owns everything. You go to the government office, your Father is the Lord there. You don't go there like a dog that has been defeated, that has to put its tail between its legs... The nation belongs to your Father. The earth is the Lord's and the fulness thereof. And you are heir to the throne. You are the crowned prince. You walk with the confidence of the Lord, knowing whom you believe.

<u>Verse 6a</u> "Be strong and courageous."

Be courageous. What does courage mean? It means, first of all, faith to attempt great things for God - faith to think the thoughts of God - and then faith to attempt great things for God. Faith to start a 40-day fast: If you stop on the twentieth day, you have not failed. That is as far as you have gone for that time. Next time, you will make it.

The first time I withdrew for a long fast, after two weeks my gums were bleeding. I thought I was going to die. I stopped the fast and some sisters mocked me very well. But the same people did not praise me the next year when I did it. There are some people who only mock; they don't know how to praise. But I am glad that they mocked because they made me determine more firmly that I would go through. One particular sister said, "Everything that people do not do, they blame it on the Devil." Listen, leadership is a very dangerous place.

If you are not ready to hear all kinds of things, forget about leadership. Anyone who thinks that leaders are only praised is totally mistaken. Somebody who has not done a 3-day fast will blame you for stopping at 21 days. That is leadership.

Be strong and courageous. I want to say this: **No failure is final.**

If you stop on the fourteenth day, you have not failed. That is as far as you could go that time. Next time, if you stop at 21 days, you have not failed. That is as far as you could go that time. If the next time you don't make it beyond 28 days, you have not failed. The next time you will be there!!

I do not know how to cry over spilt milk. When I fail to do something, I start doing the next one with all my might. It is pride to go and sit down and say, "Ohhhhhhh!!!" After all, I am just a weak vessel made strong by the Lord. I don't have the time to go and sit and cry when there are many other things to do. If I fail in a fast, I start a prayer crusade. If I fail in a prayer crusade, I start to write a book. If I fail in writing a book, I leave it and start preaching the Gospel. I keep the flag of Jesus always flying. Don't have a self-pity party. If there is a problem with one river, you jump into the next river. The Bible says that rivers of living waters will flow from us. "Rivers," not "a river." So if there is a problem with one river, you just jump to the next river and keep going. By the time you come back to it, the river will be ready for work. The leader flows, flies in the victory of the Lord. The leader must always be victorious. If not, he is proud, and pride is the worst sin. Don't enter your bed, turn your back and look at the wall and say that nobody should see you because you broke a fast too early. If somebody wants to talk, call him and let him show you his greater fasts than yours. More than that, let him show you how many hours he prayed for you to go through that fast. If he did not pray, he should be the one to repent, not you. The leader leads from a position of unceasing victory, always courageous in his God. There is not just one project! So if one project has a problem, you turn to the next project and succeed at it. If there is a problem walking on land, you go by sea. If there is a problem on the sea and the land, you go by air. And by the time you land, the earth and the sea will be ready. Sometimes God stops the things so that you may tackle the project that is ready. No self-pity parties. Be courageous. Determine that you will succeed. Accept every obstacle as temporary. If you plan Church growth, if you plan to triple and you only increase by 50%, don't have a self-pity party. Have a praise service to praise God for the 50% increase. And then you will reaffirm yourself to move further. Because if you are discouraged, what should happen to the people? If you are the husband and the children come to meet you, and you are on the ground, crying, "Ohhh! Ohhh! Ohhh!" Then your wife will come and get near you and start crying "Ohhh! Ohhh! Ohhh!" Then very soon you will have a weeping family. Listen,

The leader is always victorious.

He says, "O.K., this thing has not worked. Now, what can I get to work, and work so well that I might encourage myself in the Lord from there?" Be very courageous. When everything seems not to be going, look for the ray of light and rejoice in it.

I read about two people who were locked up in a prison. One looked at the wall of the prison, so ugly, so dirty and so bad, and he was very discouraged. But the other one lifted up his eyes and saw the moon shining, and he was rejoicing. Their circumstances were the same outwardly, but their inward circumstances were different. The other one was gazing at the wall. The other one was gazing at the moon.

What is your gaze on?

The Lamb is on the throne. We don't fix our gaze on Calvary; we look through Calvary and we fix our eyes on the throne. And we will soon be on the throne with Him.

Take the world, I have my Jesus, (2 X)

Oh you'd better take the world, I have my Jesus. (2 X)

Take your failures, I have success, (2 X)

Oh you'd better take your failures, I have success. (2 X)

Take your failures, I am a success, (2 X)

Oh you'd better take your failures, I am a success. (2 X)

Take your failures, I am a winner, (2 X)

Oh you'd better take your failures, I am a winner. (2 X)

Take your failures, Jesus is Winner, (2 X)

Oh you'd better take your failures, Jesus is Winner. (2 X)

<u>Verse 6</u> "Be strong and courageous, (because you will lead these people to inherit the land I swore to their forefathers to give them.)"

<u>Verse 7</u> "Be strong and very courageous. (Be careful to obey all the law my servant Moses gave you; do not turn from it to the right or to the left, that you may be successful wherever you go.)"

<u>Verse 9</u> "Have I not commanded you? Be strong and courageous. Do not be terrified; do not be discouraged, for the Lord your God will be with you wherever you go."

A three-fold call: Be strong and courageous. Actually the thing is this: When a man gives up hope, all is finished. Have you set what could be considered near-impossible plans? If you don't have such plans, you have chicken plans, they are not worth pursuing.

If your goals are such that without divine intervention, failure is guaranteed, those are the right goals.

The right goals are those goals that if God does not intervene, you will fail so hopelessly that you will be very sorry for yourself.

Anything that you can accomplish without God's miraculous intervention is not good enough. When you set goals that you can accomplish without God's miraculous intervention, those goals are too small.

So set goals such that if God does not intervene, you will fail so terribly that you will be sorry for yourself.

When I see the goals of some people, it is as if a giant rat should come and accomplish them. The goals are written from a safety point of view, such that they will accomplish them effortlessly. There is no room for saying, "Oh God, help me or I will fail." If on my own I can do a thing, I will aim at doing the thing three-fold, then God must come in or my failure is guaranteed. The goals must be such that all of yourself will have to be sacrificed for them to be accomplished. The goals must be such that you will know that if you hold anything back from them, you have lost all. The goals must force your all out of your hands.

I shared the other day about our money from TESSA which just matured. TESSA means Tax Exempt Special Savings Account. In a sense, I have no choice but to give the money to God. If I hold it back, the Missionary Enterprise will collapse for this month and next month, because even just the sum of money to convince the British government to give us the visa for our missionaries, that must be presented to them as a guarantee, is the money for four missionary couples. If you feel the price is too much, who sent you? You sent yourself, so pay the price.

The thing is that we really don't have choices, if we are sincere with the goals that God has allowed us to set for ourselves. The goals just say all must go and there is no regret because of the joy of seeing the goal accomplished. Do you have giant rat goals? One reason why it was said, "Be courageous; be very courageous; be courageous," from the beginning is because many people start and then they go back. They are discouraged. There is a point when plain logic just says, "Don't be foolish. You aimed too high." It is at that moment that the Bible says, "Be very courageous." "Be courageous," is no longer enough. It is now, "You must be very courageous." And then towards the end, the Devil does not like finished projects. Many people stop before the winning point. That is where the Word of God again comes and says, "Be strong and courageous," meaning: "Be strong and courageous to finish it!" I had never seen this until this morning.

We need encouragement from the beginning.

We need double encouragement in the heart of the challenge, when the barriers are enormous with discouragement from left and right. The people who stood with you have left. Then they begin to ask you, "Are you sure you heard God?" Then to finish, you know there are people who write letters but they don't finish, and they don't post them. Their joy is that they have written the letter. But without posting it, nothing has happened. The Word of God again says, "Be strong and courageous." "Be strong and courageous to start." "Be strong and very courageous to continue," and, "Be strong and very courageous to finish the task," because the winning point is not towards the end but at the end. I am told that at the Olympics towards the winning point, the Kenyan girl just jumped. It is the jump that made her win.

Until you touch the winning point, the medal is not in your pocket, and the Enemy does not want you to reach the winning point. The Enemy does not want you to have the medal in your pocket. Be strong and very courageous to finish your project. Even if you have lost the year, you can start now and, with the help of God, see the impossible happen.

You can't be very strong unless you see very clearly what you can do.

Courage is pulled out by the great objective that is to be achieved.

Until the goal is clarified, and it is massive calling for divine intervention, it is useless. What is courage for? How can you tell people going nowhere, "Be strong and very courageous"? It is a massive goal which in its own self says, "Give up your all." With such a goal, then the words, "Be strong and very courageous," find a place in the heart to germinate. Oh, you must have very massive goals that call for your all and after your all, it will not be enough. So that there must be divine intervention. So you place your all on the altar and then call the fire of God. Until your all is on the altar, on what will the fire of God fall? Many people expect the fire of God to fall on an empty altar. God is waiting for the sacrifice on the altar: Clear objectives — that it will need God's intervention for success. Then the man calls on God because if he didn't call on God, his failure would be horrible. And he presses on until he smashes the barriers and brings down the power of God. If not, you are going nowhere in particular. We thank God that since it has become clear to us what we must do in the Ministry, we are pressing on. What we saw vaguely has become clearer. We will succeed. We don't need the Devil's permission to succeed. We have received the Lord's commission and that is enough.

Listen, Brethren, it is very necessary to clarify what your contribution to World Conquest must be. In the U.S., I clarified and put in writing what I must contribute: 45 points. There are things that only I must do and there are things that as a leader, I must ensure that the others do. And I have zeroed it to 2045 when we should be handing the Work to the Lord complete. When I did it, it became obvious to me that every day was critically important. I must read my Bible 200 times. I wrote the number of Daily Dynamic Encounters I must have, the number of 40-day fasts, the number of 40-day prayer crusades. Now, I have changed them according to the light I have now. The number of 400-hour prayer crusades; because if somebody says he has a 40-day prayer crusade, praying 3 hours a day, that is a joke. Those who came this morning found that I was not ready. I was working on strategies. One of the strategies is 33 historic days of praying 426 historic hours, as follows:

7, 7, 7,
8, 8, 8,
10, 10, 10, 10,
11, 11, 11, 11,
12, 12, 12, 12,

then

13,
14,
15,
16,
17,
18,
19,
20,
21,
22,
23,
24.

Now, this is combining persistence and intensity. When you pray 10 hours every day for 40 days, you are being persistent, but there is no increase in intensity. I have been given an assignment to go to China and in five days pray 100 hours. I have postponed the journey because I need to train. When I shall have accomplished this programme, I shall be ready to go, because you cannot train on the battlefield. That is why I am postponing the trip to china until I can pray 19 hours one day, the next day 20 hours, the next day 21 hours, the next day 22 hours... Brethren, it is like preparing for a concert - you spend countless hours preparing for maybe one or two hours of action. These 100 hours are the hours of acting. As part of the preparation, I intend to be able to pray 12 hours a day in tongues, so that I will pray 12 hours in tongues and 12 hours with words on the final day, before I leave.

The other strategy is to pray 420 hours in 36 days. In 40 days, 480 hours. In 42 days, 510 hours. In 43 days, 525 hours. 535 hours in 43 days is the super adult dose.

Adult dose : 42 days, 510 hours.

The fighters range: 40 days, 480 hours.

Then the gentleman's: 420 hours in 36 days.

Listen, Brethren, it means that you come out of the prayer crusade thin. People seem to get only out of fasts thin. You get out of this prayer crusade thin. It is like this:

- 7 hours the first day,
- the next 2 days, 8 hours a day,
- the next 3 days, 9 hours a day,
- the next 4 days, 10 hours a day,
- the next 5 days, 11 hours, each day,
- the next 6 days, 12 hours, each day, and so forth.

You come from there thin. In that way, it will really be crusading. You start and then you tighten up; as you go on, more time is required in the place of prayer.

Listen, let us not make crusades into jokes. A fasting crusade of 40 days and a prayer crusade of 40 days, are life and death issues. You could die in a 40-day prayer or a fasting crusade. After 35 days, you have entered the death range, because you could effectively die. At that point your body is too weak to provide the blood supply to your brain. And we do not tell people to jump there with much folly. I also want to say, by the grace of God, I don't know anyone who died during the fast. But I know people who died after breaking fasts.

I was told of a Nigerian pastor who took a 10-day fast and broke it with "eba - garri", the type they cook for us here. He took a good "eba" meal as he was breaking his fast, and passed into his Saviour's hands. Those of you who have read the book,

"The Ministry of Fasting" know that Brother E.E. is alive today by God's grace. Mrs S.K., who was not in our Ministry, took a fast. Three days after she broke it, she went to be with God.

That is why the book: "The Ministry of Fasting" must be available. There is no book like it in the world with such practical information. You will not die in the fast. The Lord did not die. So people should not make 40-day prayer crusades jokes. If somebody tells me of a 40-day prayer crusade of 5 hours a day, I just say, "This man is in for a joke." There are people who normally pray 5 hours a day. The minimum number of hours for a crusade is 8 hours! Don't be deceived! To run away from the pressure that makes it a crusade is a joke. Those of you in Yaounde know that when we have a 40-day prayer crusade, virtually everything is suspended because it is night after night! If we had said 5 hours a day, just come at 7 p.m, at midnight you go, it would have been a joke. There is the persistence. There is also the intensity. It is aggressiveness. Aggressiveness means that you take it by force, because the Kingdom of God is proclaimed and men of violence take it by force.

- You take the fast by force.
- You take the prayer crusade by force.
- You pluck things from God's hands by force.
- You impose things on cities by force.
- You impose things on nations by force.
- You impose things on regions by force.
- You impose Churches on districts by force.
- You impose Churches on tribes by force.
- You impose hunger on the people without hunger.

Oh, national leaders, you impose hunger on people without hunger. Pastors, you impose hunger on people who are satisfied without eating.

Spiritual imperialism is imposing hunger on those without hunger. Spiritual aggressiveness is imposing thirst on those who are not thirsty. It means that you ignore the person's condition and you ignore the person's contribution. Aggressiveness means that you ignore the person's contribution. We say that again: In spiritual aggressiveness, you ignore the contribution of the person. You act as if all depended upon what you do. You consider that the person is a dry bone and that all will depend upon what you do and on what you will do. In spiritual aggressiveness, you consider that the person will contribute nothing, and that all depends upon you; that is one way of looking at it. Another way of looking at spiritual aggressiveness is to consider that the person will resist actively; and, therefore, you must overcome his resistance and impose what you have to impose upon him. That is the second phase — that the person will resist. Therefore you must overthrow his resistance, and then give him what you must.

I told you about that man I wanted to evangelise in Kampala. He asked me whether I was a saved man. I said, "Yes." He said then he didn't want to listen to me. I said he would hear me. Then he started to run away and I started to run after him. I started to run after him. Those were the days when I was mad. But I am going to become even more mad. I am going back to the streets of Yaounde! I kept jogging after him. That is why you must jog - because some sinners will be running away, and you will have to run after them. I knew that in time, he would be tired. After he was tired, he started to walk. I started to preach as if I was preaching to 5000 people. I was preaching with all my might, aloud and following and following and following. After I had preached for long, he was hungry. He stopped and told me he wanted to listen. Man! I blasted! I preached! When he was totally absorbed, I gave him my address and I ran away. My joy was great the next day when he found my room in the university, having spent two hours looking for it. That is aggressiveness!

In Yaounde we must be 10,000, whether the Devil likes it or not. We shall go to the streets! If it means carrying the sinners on our shoulders, we shall carry them on our shoulders! And we shall give them Jesus.

I shall go to the streets. That is where I started. And you shall go to the streets, out there where the sinners are. You shall go to the streets in season and out of season!

You shall speak to those who want to hear and those who don't want to hear. You shall gather all of them, and you shall carry them on your back, into the arms of the Saviour. That is aggressiveness. Aggressiveness is taking that which resists.

I talked about the first level of aggressiveness: dealing with those who are indifferent, taking that which is indifferent, taking those who contribute nothing.

Second level: taking those who resist, who say, "Don't take me."

The final level of aggressiveness is taking those who attack you. They don't only resist but, they attack you.

    3 Those who attack
  2 Those who resist
  1 Those who are indifferent/ who contribute nothing

Levels of aggressiveness

In the resistance level, we were going from door to door in Makerere University, witnessing. We went in pairs, a brother and a sister. Because the evangelism that day was centred in the Women's Hall, we got into one girl's room. She politely said, "Welcome." Then she said, "What can I do for you?" We said we had come to proclaim the Gospel of Jesus. She opened the door and said, "Get out of here!" I have never been so summarily ousted. And only a woman could have done it. No man has ever said anything near that. We went away like dogs (with our tails between our legs). Brother Martin was nearly killed by a sister's husband in Douala. Brother, tell us what happened.

Brother Martin: The thing is that the man had the wife terribly beaten and the wife came to our home. She kept her things in our home and she went back home. So the man had her again well-beaten, and took her to our home. I was in the room because we were already sleeping. So when he entered, it was my wife who went out first. And he asked whether she was not married. She said she was married. By that time, I was already coming out. He only pulled out his knife. I don't know how I dived and found myself outside. So I broke the fence of our compound and ran away. The following day, people were saying that a thief came in, and asking whether we heard that there was a thief, but they didn't know I was the "thief." The man had wanted to take his gun but he took the knife. And then when he went home, he came back again.

Brother Zach: With a gun?

Brother Martin: I don't know whether it was a gun because when he came back, I had come back, and when he saw me, we started running again. But the funny thing is that he was chasing an enemy he did not know, because the following day we met in the airport and greeted each other. Brother Zach was coming down and his director was also coming. So we were all in the airport. I greeted him and discussed with him, because he was dealing with my Company, but he didn't know the man he was dealing with.

Aggressiveness means conquering those who attack you with guns and cutlasses. Anybody who says, "They have a cutlass and a gun here; so I give this up," is not aggressive. The spirit of the aggressor says, "There will be victory at any cost."

To the aggressor, no door is closed.

To the aggressor, the door to no heart is closed.

When people say, "The people here are hard," I just say, "These people are not aggressors." Which land is not tough?

I believe with all my heart that every nation and every tribe can be taken for our God. I also believe with all my heart that every big city and every small city shall be taken for our God; that we shall impose the Kingdom of God in the hearts of men and that we shall conquer, because Jesus has conquered. The Enemy must give way.

Don't waste anyone's time telling him about your difficulties.

All difficulties are surmountable.

What you are trying to tell the person is that you have not paid the price. Should he come and pay it for you? Don't go and tell somebody that your marriage is not working.

It takes two people to make a marriage not work.

One man alone cannot cause a marriage not to work because nobody is ever 100% wrong.

A sister once said to me, "You always say that I am the one who is wrong, and not my husband. This time I will act like this so that they will know that even if he is right, he is only 99% right, and 1% wrong. I want to draw the people's attention to his 1% fault." It was a full dose of Adamism, but she was proclaiming a truth.

It takes two to quarrel.

If one person speaks and the other one doesn't speak, soon the person will stop speaking. If they knock you to the ground and you don't rise up and they knock you on the ground, and you don't raise up your head, they will not continue knocking. They might even think you are dead. And the Enemy has gone away many times thinking that the people were dead, whereas it was a strategy. If there is a problem between the two of you, at least you are contributing 1%. Get rid of that 1% and then God will step in. God is not stepping in because it is still a combined fault. When it is just the problem of one person, God will intervene very urgently. If God has not intervened, it is because the person who is less wrong is contributing something. If the door is not yet opened, it is because the person who is less wrong is contributing something. If the door is not yet opened, it is because I have not paid all the price I should pay. If the door is not yet opened, it is because I have not handled all the doors that are already open. And why should God open more? You must own up and say, "If I am not having what I should have from my partner, it is because I am standing in the way somewhere." Where are you standing in the way?

Let me digress for a few minutes.

Are you married, and your husband has lost interest in you?

You look at yourself in the mirror and you still look nice. But have you become a man in a gown, more combative than a lioness? Outside, you look like a lamb but inside, you are not a lioness, you are a lion. The man knocks and knocks his head. Inside, you are a total man, maybe you are one and a half times a man. Homosexuality is forbidden.

If inside you are a man, how can this man love another man?

Your arguments are sharp and strong and just,... Everything is so indisputable. You can argue more than a Queen's Counsellor. The man has to sit and arrange his arguments before he comes to you. Outside, you look like a woman, but inside, you are two men - strong to a fault. Impossible to convince. So he stays off. Before he does one thing you have given him "Pang! pang!" A lioness in a gown! Men can't marry another man. I want to tell you - the physical appearance can deteriorate. A man will not be very shocked; but it is this lion that is inside (maybe it was asleep, but now it is awake), that is most difficult to contain.

If with passing time you are not becoming increasingly more tender, you will lose your man.

There will be no divorce, but there will be separation. The marriage will be broken because you are a hard smart woman who smashes a man and brings his ideas and everything to nought. The man comes home with trembling feet. Outside, you look weak but to move you from your position, you need ten bulldozing caterpillars. Where you have stood, alpha and omega have spoken. Unless inwardly you become increasingly soft and tender and increasingly malleable, you have sued for divorce.

There will be no physical divorce. You will keep the marriage certificate. But you have wounded the relationship. Something I didn't know for long, I now know very well. It is not beautiful women that men are looking for. They are looking for a soft woman. Sometimes in the world they say, "Why does this man go and look for a hopeless girl? Why does he not look for a beautiful woman?" He is looking for a soft and tender woman, not a beautiful hard netherstone! She can be as tiny as a broomstick, but Man!

Three days ago, one brother told us he looked at the woman and she was very small, so he said, "I will hold her like this to follow me." He has had the shock of his life. It was absolutely impossible. Her strength is inversely proportional to her size. She has not changed one bit, but the strength to crush the man has gone up many times.

Men are not looking for beautiful women. They are looking for soft and tender ones.

I don't know why I am even saying that but there must be a reason. It could be that there are many men here who are overpowered, or that there are a number of sisters here just like what I've been describing.

If what I am receiving in my heart is correct, there are many women here who need to repent for being men in women's clothing. I have a research project going on. I have a questionnaire among unbelievers who commit immorality. Unbelievers don't think that it is a bad thing, so I am having the answers back. It is from that research that I was shocked to discover that they did not go running after beautiful women. They were looking for soft, tender women. And that for that softness and that tenderness they were prepared to pay any price. They were looking for a woman who danced to their tune effortlessly, a woman who made them feel, when they came, that the king of the universe had come. That is the secret to adultery. If that is what is happening in the world, I extrapolate and say that in the Church, that is what the men are looking for, but they can no longer go and commit adultery because the Cross has stood in the way. But it doesn't prevent them from looking for a tender, soft and sweet woman in place of an aggressor. I needed those answers in order to write one of the books: "A Solution To Marital Problems." I am extrapolating them to get to know what is happening even among believers. If this is a description of you, then you know at once why your marriage never got to where it could have got. You might have managed to draw a bit of juice out of it, a teaspoon instead of a jug. Because the results startled me, I want the sisters to know that that may be where their problem is.

The last thing I want to say about it is this, that it is put on. Some sisters who are most tender with me, grind their husbands. So it is deliberate. It is as if when they are coming to me, they keep the lion at home. When they get there, they release it. Those of you who are involved in marriage counselling know what I am talking about. It is wilful. It is deliberate. That is why it is a very grievous fault against God. God shall hold you responsible for your marriage that did not reach the height it ought to have reached because of the lioness that you kept in your heart.

12

GUARANTEEING SUCCESS

The Divine Perspective

<u>Joshua</u> 1:9c

"For the Lord your God will be with you wherever you go."

<u>Verse</u> 5c

"I will be with you; I will never leave you nor forsake you."

God gave Himself, His companionship, to guarantee Joshua's success.

I am your Inheritance.

I am your Portion.

God gives Himself to guarantee success.

I will be with you.

I will be there.

I will be in the conflicts.

I will be the Captain.

I will be the Commander.

I will lead.

I will guide.

That is why, Brethren, it becomes critically important to know God the Captain so intimately that you know when He is moving and when He is not moving: to know the mind of God.

And God gave Joshua His Word.

<u>Verse 8</u>

> *"Do not let this Book of the Law depart from your mouth; meditate on it day and night, so that you may be careful to do everything written in it. Then you will be prosperous and successful."*

The Bible is the mind of God.

Now, you see here, God gave Himself, then He gave His Word, to tell you that:

- **You cannot separate the knowledge of God from the knowledge of His Word.**
- **You cannot separate the knowledge of a man from a knowledge of his writings.**

If I am absent and a page in a book is lost, and there is no way to find it on earth, go, let Theodore complete it. He is the one person on earth who will get as close as possible to what I thought. He is the one who has studied the books more than anyone else. He also knows them more than anybody else.

Without a knowledge of the Word, knowledge of God is not possible.

Those people who don't know God's Word, but go and say, "God, reveal Yourself to me," God will hide Himself from them.

The first thing needed is a profound marriage to the Word of God. He said, "This book of the law shall not depart from your mouth." So you are to:

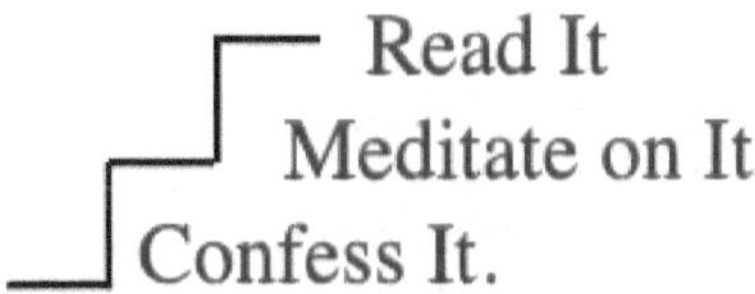

Not departing from the mouth is this state of confessing it. You read, you mediate, and you confess It.

"This book of the law shall not depart from your mouth." It shall not depart from your confession.

- You are to confess the Book!
- You are not to confess your feelings!
- You are not to confess what you see!
- You are to confess the Book!

What do we say? You are to read the Book. Meditate It. And confess what the Book says. You are to read It, receive revelation through the meditation, and confess the revelation. Read It, meditate It and confess It.

Many people confess the weather. Many people confess their feelings. So they are confessing change. They say, "Oh! Now it is raining. Now the sun is shining." Listen!

I think about this missionary to Burkina Faso. He talks about his fiancée in the most superlative terms. He talks about his failures, but about her, everything is correct, correct and correct. Anyway, he is still overtaken, and he sees things through a fog. But I am going to put him to task so that he continues to confess what he is confessing now. The confessions shall not change.

Lovers have a lot of faith. That faith shall be maintained.

They shall continue to confess it.

> *"Darling, you can count on me*
> *Till the sun dries up the sea;*
> *Until then I'll always be devoted to you."*

That is what you said. You shall continue to say it. You said, "Oh! This is the sweetest face on earth." You shall continue to say it.

You said, "Oh! This man is the most charming person on Planet Earth." You shall continue to say it.

You said, "Oh! There will never be another you." You shall continue to say it!!

You said, "Oh! Darling, I love you so, as an evergreen tree." As an evergreen tree! Now, look at that tree. It is evergreen. Don't change.

God has set what we are to confess and it does not change.

What you confessed, keep confessing it, if it is a good confession. You read It, you meditate upon It and you confess It. Say, "I will read It. I will meditate upon It. I will confess It. The Book guarantees my success. I will read It. I will meditate on my success. And I will confess my success. In the midst of the greatest defeat, I will confess my success. In the midst of betrayal, I will confess my success.

Listen! When Judas entered Gethsemane, the Lord said, "Friend." What a confession! The Lord had made all 12 of them His friends. And the betrayer was coming with the lots, and the Lord confessed the friendship. Hallelujah! Oh! that is triumph! The Lord confessed what He had confessed before. The acts of Judas did not make Him change His mind. "It is written," so you read It. You meditate upon It. You read It, you meditate upon It so that it possesses, soaks, saturates, possesses your heart and flows out through your lips in confessions. I have a file I call "The Great Confessions Of My Life," where I write Scriptures that I confess.

By His stripes I was healed.

By that one offering, I have been sanctified, I had been sanctified, and I am sanctified, I had been perfected, and I am made perfect.

I confess the "It is written" of God. You read It, you meditate upon It, and then you confess It.

There was a slight uncertainty about the number of times I had read the Bible, particularly the number of times I read It in Uganda. And in order not to make an error, I decided to forget all those and start counting from the time I had this NIV Bible. There will be 200 readings, four times a year. This year I am rather late because I am still on the second reading. As an author, I shall have to soak myself unceasingly in the Word, so that when I confront any truth all the truths of the Scriptures are immediately obvious.

Brethren, I am worried about believers who don't read the Bible or who read it too little. What do they read? Missionaries, what do you read? How can you explain the fact that you spend too little time reading the Word? When you send your accounts, you will account for your reading of the Word. If you do not read It, how will you meditate upon It? How will you confess what you don't know? When I was a student in Uganda, each time I set my experiments, I sat there reading the Word. I read and read and read the Word. I read the Word! I read It with the aggressiveness of a learner.

If you read ten chapters a day, you will read the Bible three times a year. Some of you read like the snail: "In—the—be—gin—ning." Then you rest. "God—cre—at—ed," then you sleep a bit. Then you wake up.

I want you to get married to the Bible, that is your first husband. I want you to read It, to read It, and read It until if it were possible for It to come out of your head, It would be coming out. I want you to read It in such a way that if someone quoted a verse, you would say what Book it is in.

Somewhere on Planet Earth, they asked somebody to write the tribes of Israel. He wrote, "The Jebusites, the Amalekites,..." They asked for the apostles, somebody put Reuben, Apostle Reuben! I thought the person was from one of these African countries where there are so many apostles.

You read and you study It. If they asked you,

"what is the message of Haggai?" You ought to give it.

"What is the message of Malachi?" You give it.

You don't only read, you marry yourself to It, you know It, you know It in and out!

"What is the message of Jonah?" You give it.

"What is the significance of Jonah to the saint today?" You know it.

What is the message of Nahum?

What is the significance of Nahum to us today?

What is the message of Jude?

What is it saying to the believer today?

What is the message of 1 Peter?

What does it mean to us?

You are to know it so thoroughly that if they took away your Bible, you would still preach to yourself seven messages a week. You read It and read It and read It! You study It and study It and study It!

Every believer should know the message of every book of the Bible:

- What is the message of Genesis?
- What is the message of Exodus?
- What is the message of Leviticus?
- What is Leviticus about?
- What does Leviticus say to the saints now?
- What does Leviticus help us to understand?
- What is the message of Numbers?
- What is the message of Deuteronomy? And so forth.

You read the Word. Then you meditate on It.

You take It, you read It and you ask God for revelation. You read It little by little, waiting and crying out to God that the message may come from there and be stamped on your heart; and you confess It: "This message, this Word."

Your strength depends upon your relationship with the Book.

Your courage depends upon your relationship to the Book.

Strength without the Book is natural strength and it will fail. Courage without the Book is natural courage. It will fail.

The courage that flows forth from the Book, from the God of the Book, from the Holy Spirit of the Book, is that which will stand all the tests.

Do you study the Bible or do you speculate? For Bible reading, I don't recommend Study Bibles because people are distracted from the Word to begin to look at commentaries. And I am not telling you not to use commentaries. I am not telling you not to use Study Bibles. If you are studying the Bible, you use a Study Bible. But when you are reading the Bible, get a plain Bible where you get the comment of nobody, so that you will be unbiased as you come into the presence of the Word.

It shall not depart from thy lips.

Where is the Word on your lips?

Many of us are speaking about what is happening around. What is on our lips is what is happening around. What is on our lips is not what is in the Book. What is on the lips of many is what their husbands are doing. It is not what is in the Book. What is on the lips of some is what their wives do. And one thing I have found is that though men may rebuke their wives, they will not go and complain about them outside. Even when it is not going, they keep quiet. But women jump, "Chhh! Chhh! Chhh!" (telling stories). I can understand a woman opening up to one person who can get both of them together, who has authority to bring both of them to task. But it is: "Chhh! Chhh! Chhh!" such that she complains even to unmarried people.

There was a leader somewhere in the Republic of Cameroon, with adult children. He had a problem with his wife. And the wife went and got some young man who was just engaged, to come and solve the problem. The man's Adam was tested beyond measure because to give theories about what a marriage should be and to go through the marriage experience are two different things. When a married man talks, his words have been tempered by experience. He will not make impossible demands. The unmarried person has untempered idealism; it has not been through fire. And people who have untempered idealism; when that idealism fails, they become the very opposite of what they were saying. A man who says, "Anybody who steals a franc shall be shot," may afterwards become a man who steals billions.

I was almost like those untempered idealists. In High school, during my backsliding, I thought that education would solve Africa's problems. I was very convinced that what we needed was to educate every African, and then the problem would be solved. And I believed that Nkrumahnism was the key to it. If I had not come back to the Lord before the event, it would have been very bad. There was a Nkrumahnist movement at the university. At midnight, when they were shouting from Conakry: "Imperialism! Neo-colonialism!" And all the other "isms," I went to a small university college. About a third of the men came out and lined up at midnight with sticks, all dressed like freedom fighters; so convinced were they. Then there was this fellow who had a big picture of Nkrumah. It was said that he had gone often to Conakry and seen Nkrumah. So when he was passing with the picture the students with the sticks of the freedom fighters would be saluting. My shock came when they said this student had stolen the money of the students' club of which he was the treasurer. I thank God that the Lord had come in because untempered idealism can lead people to very opposite positions, such that you cannot reconcile them. That is why people leave monasteries and become prostitutes. People leave monasteries and their vows of poverty, and become the mightiest lovers of money.

There was a man, Jesus of Oyimbo, who preached extreme capitalism, that Jesus had come this time to enjoy. The first time He came and suffered. I hear people are still waiting for Him years after He has died.

A man must soak himself in the Word and he must meditate upon the Word so that the Word transforms him. It is not how many times the Word is read but what marks It leaves. Each time you read through, let It leave permanent marks on you, and you will be a confessor of what you read.

So when the Enemy was there, Joshua was to confess the Word: "I will be with you; I will never leave you..." So when the Enemy was there, he was to confess, "The land of the enemy is my land." So when a furious enemy was coming, he was to confess, "We are going to possess the land." He was to confess the Word, to courageously confess the Word when everything else was saying, "Forget it." When the circumstances say that the victory is lost, you are to confess the Word! This Book of the law shall not depart from your mouth. That was referring to the Old Testament Scriptures. In fact, this Book of the law was the first five books of Moses. That was what the man was to digest. And we have more than that today.

To guarantee success, God has given us His Word and He has given us Himself. He has given us Himself to

explore increasingly and in ever-increasing depth. He has given us His Word as a deep ocean to exploit Its depth, Its breadth, and Its Height, and never come to an end because the Word is limitless in Its depth.

Some books of the Bible, I have read at least fifty times. I don't think there is any I have read less than thirty times. But sometimes I read and come to places which are as if I were reading them for the first time. Take, for example, what I was sharing with you, that "He who believes in Me, rivers of living water shall flow..." It is only this time that the "s" has dawned on me. It had been "river" in my understanding all along. But now, knowing that there are rivers, what possibilities!

The more you read It, the more you need to read It.

The more you discover revelations, the more you need revelations.

After knowing, you will know it is just the chipping of an iceberg. It is the work of the Holy Spirit. Its profoundness is beyond total grasp.

We bless the Name of the Holy Spirit, the Supreme Author of Scripture.

We bless the Lord Jesus Christ to whom all Scripture points.

We bless God who has given us all the treasures of heaven.

The Word was be read. The Word was to be studied. It was to be meditated upon. It was to become revelation. And It was to be confessed and proclaimed.

You may get some ideas and, as you pray them through, they are only in your head but not in your heart. Don't act until your heart agrees.

We are not led by the ideas in our heads.

We must be led by what is in our hearts.

Let me illustrate this: Our publishers wanted to bring many books to Lagos, but the thing was not clicking. The logic was correct but the rhema was wrong. A number of cartons were prepared for Cotonou. Finally, all the books had to be left behind because, in the final analysis, it was a matter of either the books coming and the people remaining or vice versa, because the books and the people could not come in the two buses that were available. But five minutes after they left, we got the fax from Cotonou asking for three titles in two cartons. We brought those. That was what Cotonou needed and the message was got within five minutes after their departure; when they were still within Yaounde. It caused some brethren to tremble. I gave the fax to Christian Publishing House. They got the three titles Cotonou wanted in two cartons. After they had packed the two cartons, the people started packing a small carton again. Obviously, Cotonou knew what books they needed and that was what their fax demanded. The imaginations of Yaounde versus the real needs of Cotonou! It comes to something that I am anxious that the saints understand. Too many believers are led by their heads, by logic, by the soul and not by the Spirit. Every mistake I have made in my life has been because I used my head and not my heart. Brethren,

We are not called to walk by our heads.

The G.Ts are in Northern Nigeria. We tried to get them into Liberia but it wouldn't work. The very moment when they offered to be missionaries, I said they were to join Theodore in Nigeria. That's the first thing I said. It was the flowing forth of the Spirit. Afterwards, we tried to work out logic. We bless the Lord that He didn't let logic triumph. It would have been tragic. By His grace, He brought us back to what was the mind of the Spirit. Listen, Brethren,

That which is from the Holy Spirit, as you pray about it, things settle more and more. There is more and more peace. There is more and more harmony. There is more and more inner joy. It seems as if the wings of the Dove - the Holy Spirit - are totally spread out.

There are other things, as you pray about them they don't seem to be able to settle. The thing does not seem to settle inside. The more you pray, the more you doubt; but when you come back to logic, the logic seems correct. But the more you pray, the more uncertain you are. The first piece of advice I want to give believers in such a case is first to postpone action, even if there have been public proclamations. It is not holding. Don't rush ahead with your head and carry it out.

Time is a great servant of the Lord, as Watchman Nee said.

In time, things will be clarified.

We are dealing with the God we have come to know as the Father of our Lord and Saviour Jesus Christ. If it is a matter of sin, of course, you just stop it. But there are many things in which it is not a matter of sin. Therefore if you don't obey immediately, there is nothing at stake.

Give more time until the harmony inside is consolidated, until the peace has become permanent, until the doubts have gone away. If the more you pray about it, the more doubts you have, forget it.

When I think about the first girl Brother A.M. wanted to get married to, the man would not have been going to the mission field today with that girl. And she would have crushed him to nothing; she is a real lioness. And when she is a lioness before she comes into your house, by the time she comes in, you will be outside, begging to come in. When I think back, I tremble. If he had married that girl, he might have backslidden. But he waited and that affair evaporated. And God brought the right girl into his life. And they are in an adventure with God.

Don't go by your head. Don't even go by your commitments.

You have spoken, and even if there are barriers, you just take a pole vault and you jump over, saying, "I must keep to my word."

Is it more important to keep the Word of the Holy Spirit or your own word? If a word has to drop, whose will — the word of the Holy Spirit or your own word?

The other day, I was reading Oswald Chambers. He says,

People who do not want to be considered unstable will miss the Holy Spirit's guidance very often in their lives, because, as he said, sometimes He says, "Go forward," and then the next minute He says, "Go backwards;" and consistent people do not know how to advance and come back. They will just keep going on.

Are you jealous for the voice of the Holy Spirit or for the voice of your flesh? Do you have an inclination to defend your reputation?

Then you have a lot of trouble with God.

When the whole of your being does not come to unity in the act, the best thing is to wait, because even a good thing done with doubts is sin, it does not flow

forth from faith. If you are sincere, in time God will make things clear.

So, if you have meditated and you confess, and the confession does not catch fire, wait. The questions to ask are:

Am I jealous for the glory of the Lord or for my own glory?

Am I anxious to be consistent before God or before man?

When we think of those who were moving with the Cloud, from Egypt to Canaan, nothing could have tested the flesh in man as that trip, because they would get somewhere and the Cloud would just stand for one day.

Then the next day, the Cloud would start moving and they too would start moving. They would get somewhere and the Cloud would stand for one week, one month, or even one year. Can you imagine what it would have meant to some people? Somewhere a friend of mine said, "When people were cooking their best food, the Cloud started moving." I told him, "No, they just had manna to cook; so there was no best anything about it."

There must be a holy jealousy for the glory of the Lord, and a holy spite for our own reputation.

They were to move.

Joshua 1:10-13 So Joshua ordered the officers of the people: "Go through the camp and tell the people, 'Get your supplies ready. Three days from now you will cross the Jordan here to go in and take possession of the land the Lord your God is giving for your own.'" But to the Reubenites, the Gadites and the half-tribe of Manasseh, Joshua said, "Remember the command that Moses the servant of the Lord gave you: 'The

Lord your God is giving you rest and has granted you this land.'"

They were given land east of the Jordan:

Jordan River

Canaan | Promise land

The Reubenites, the Gadites and Manasseh settled on the wrong side of the Jordan. In the original promise all of them were to be west of the Jordan. But when they got there, they saw the pasture land and said, "We have found our inheritance here. We will not go over."

They chose, and God gave them.

They chose to settle east of the Jordan. They knew that God's original purpose was that they should all settle west of the Jordan. Oh! but they looked around and they saw the massive grazing lands. And they decided. They found their own inheritance by personal choice east of the Jordan. And they decided and said, "We shall go and help the other people to settle, but we shall come back here."

They were moved by what they could see.

Of course, Moses gave them their choice. And they settled on the wrong side of the Jordan. God blessed them on the wrong side of the Jordan.

A friend of mine was telling me of a young couple that has come to grips with the fact that they got married outside God's will. How to manage the east of the Jordan is a hard job. You can do your best but it can never work. Now, let me change my shoes, as people who marry the wrong partners. Do you know the interesting thing? It is that they are pointing to different directions. The goals are different. Their hearts are in different directions. You can do all. And the whole of your life, you are trying to turn the thing. After a lot of prayer, you may come a bit closer together, but immediately you leave it,... Put in a 40-day prayer crusade of 400 hours. After that, you may think that things are really going. But you will begin to feel the strain again just when you stop praying. You have ruined a crucial aspect of your life.

It is not very easy for someone else to know the agony that another person has. I had some friends, who were engaged, and they were walking at the moment of the worst crisis in their relationship. As they were walking, troubled and in agony, one brother looked at them from a distance and said, "What perfect lovers!" He came and told me; so when my friends came, I told them. The man shook his head and said, "That's the assessment of a fool. He does not know the agony that I am undergoing."

Listen, Reuben is the one who went into his father's couch, and lost it there. Gad is the son of Zilpah the woman with whom Reuben slept. You remember when Jacob put the right hand on Ephraim and put the left hand on Manasseh. Do you know why? Because with prophetic vision he found that this man Manasseh would land on the wrong side. That was why he put his hands like that. Ephraim passed to the Promised Land and this man stayed on the wrong side. Some of you just bless! You bless according to your nose: "Navigation à vue." You just see with human sight. Because of prophetic sight Jacob saw that Manasseh would not cross into the Promised Land. And these two and a half tribes were the first ones to go on exile long before the other ones.

Oh! when something is wrong in the heart of a man, in ten, twenty generations, you still see it.

When something is wrong in a man's consecration, when you marry a woman with a divided heart, you see it in your children. Listen,

Your divided heart is the greatest wickedness you can do to your children.

You have cemented their history, and most of them will always be divided at heart. One or two may get out of the ordinary, but from a divided heart, the trend is towards division of heart. You know, these people stayed 400 years in Egypt from the time Reuben did this thing. This settling was about 400 years afterwards. And these events are determinant. Can you be so wicked to your progeny? Can you be so wicked? The seed you are sowing will be harvested in 400 years. You are there to help others to settle on the right side while you go and settle on the wrong side of the Jordan.

Have you weighed the person spiritually?

Have you investigated the person's progeny to find out?

If you want to marry a girl, look at what the father was with regards to God; look at what her grandfather was. If they were solid men after God, take the woman with all your joy. Even if they were unbelievers, there are unbelievers who are disciplined and honest and with integrity, and there are unbelievers who are fundamentally crooks. Look at the boy's history. Where does he come from? If the parents were Christians, was it a steadfast, undeviated love for the Lord? Or did they say, "God, You are good. Satan, you are not bad either"? If you marry the daughter of a sorcerer, even if he is a sorcerer who goes to Church, you will have it. It is a frightful thing. By the time children are born, a lot is already settled.

My host in the United States is a godly man. He adopted two children. The older of them was adopted maybe at two months and the other a few days after delivery. The daughter has three children with three irresponsible men. He has now had to adopt the three grandchildren. It has nothing to do with him. It has nothing to do with his wife. They are consecrated people. They brought up these two children in a godly home from the ages of two months and a few days respectively. They sent them to Miami Christian School, where they paid four times the fees that are paid in public schools. The son, at 31, just came out of prison. He was imprisoned in 1994 for the first time. He was almost crushing his adoptive mother, such that she had to call for the police. Neither of the children would turn to God. They came from mothers who did not want the children, so they offered them for adoption. They could not have been mothers of integrity. Neither of the children was born in wedlock. Fools rush where angels fear to tread.

Don't quarrel with your wife. She is just an extension of her mother, and you closed your eyes as you chose her. Don't blame your husband. He is just a continuation of his father or a continuation of his mother. The thing is that the children will decide either to be their mothers or their fathers. As someone said,

In genetic inheritance, nature sides with hidden flaws.

If there are two parents, A and B, one strong and the other weak, the children will take the weakness. Nature sides with hidden flaws. And it is true. If we are going to be honest, and from your experience, you will agree. But we have also been given the authority to alter spiritual genetics. The thing that worries me is that I don't know people who have gone on 40-day fasts and 40-day prayer crusades to alter the tragic negative spiritual genetics that they inherited, and have a new beginning. Everything is taken for granted.

Have you confronted what is wrong in your family background

- in their attitude to God?
- in their attitude to truth?
- in their attitude to commitment?
- in their attitude to loyalty?

Look at your brothers and your sisters and you know the weakness that is in your family. Don't deal with it and you will pass it on.

A sister in Yaounde was more stubborn than an ass. I asked her, "What is wrong with you?" She told me in French, "Ça vient de loin" = (it comes from the distant past.) She found herself behaving exactly like her great grandmother and she was an impossible woman; not that her mother is possible either. We had a schoolmate; he is now a medical doctor in New York. He used to do things that were very strange. One day, he told us, "They told me my grandfather was 20% mad, and my father 10% mad. I am controlled by the 5% madness." And when you look at him, you will not doubt it. There was a 5% madness factor there amidst academic performance.

The two and a half tribes settled east of the Jordan. They were confirming events that took place more than 400 years before, because the 430 years in Egypt, plus the 40 years in the desert, plus the time before they went to Egypt. Let me say it for the last time:

Look at your brothers and sisters and you will immediately know what is wrong with your family line. Look at your wife's brothers and sisters; are they bent towards God? And when they believe, do they put in their best? Or when they believe, it is like this: in/out, in/out? Look carefully, because that is what the person is putting into your children. So that you might know how to destroy it before. You may not have enough time to study the parents, they may not even be alive. But just look at the brothers and the sisters of your partner, and you know the hidden flaws that are being injected into your children. Look at your own brothers; within the context of the revelation that they have received, are they true? Is there hunger for more and more of God? I am not asking for perfection, but I am asking for an increasing twist towards God. Then you can be at peace. If you love your children, you will invest in destroying these negative genes that have become their unfortunate lot. I am not a biological geneticist but I have come to begin to study spiritual genetics.

And spiritual genetics is even more accurate than natural genetics.

We may not come to these matters again even in the coming years, but know that I have spoken to you.

Not to try to destroy the negative genes aggressively, just being indulgent, could be saying that you are continuing your family line that is indulgent over eternal issues. If not, how can you explain the fact that you have never risen up into a 40-day fast, a 40-day prayer crusade or even 21 days within the limits of your strength, to wrestle just to shatter what you see gripping and bringing your relatives to nought, coming from a family where nobody seems to be on fire for God, and nobody seems to be radically consecrated? They are all negotiators, and you also just negotiate by continuing in indulgence. It is striking!

Joshua 1:1b "...The Lord said to Joshua son of Nun..."

Joshua 2:1 "Then Joshua son of Nun..."

Joshua 2:23b "...Joshua, son of Nun!"

The verses are saying, "Immediately you look at Joshua, look at the father." The two of them are there: ...Joshua, and Nun!!

The Christian life can be divided into three parts:

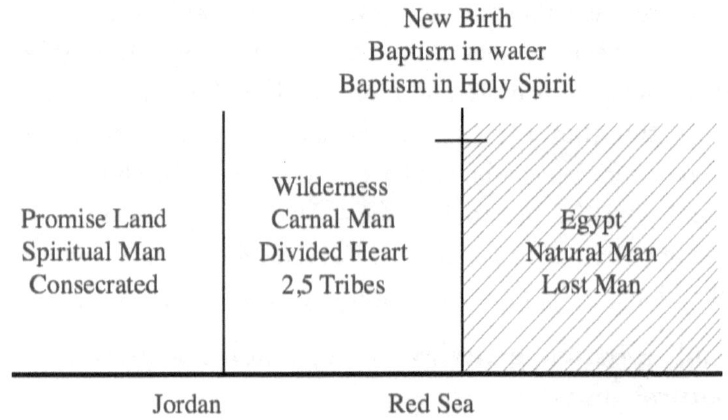

This is Egypt - You confront the Cross. This is the Red Sea. And this is the wilderness. And this is the Jordan. (I want to take it the other way). That is the Red Sea. This is Egypt. The Red Sea. The Jordan. The Promised Land. These people settled here, the two and a half tribes, east of the Jordan. This is the wilderness.

This is what it means to be a carnal believer.

This is what it means to be a natural man.

This is what it means to be a spiritual man.

This is what it means to be lost - Egypt.

Here, this is the divided heart.

Here is the consecrated heart.

One mark of the divided heart is that there is no hunger to do great things for God.

The period in a man's life when there are no great things for God is the period of the divided heart. He is settling in the land of abundance, where there are no labours, missing God's best, on the wrong side of the Jordan. Now, we have written extensively on the wrong side (of the Jordan) in the book: "Leadership According To The Pattern Of Moses."

The Red Sea, that was the dividing line beyond which the Egyptians could not go. Yes. This is the Spirit-filled life, but it is not the baptism in the Holy Spirit because people are baptized here. They were baptized in Moses, in the Cloud and in the sea. One thing that characterizes this period is a lack of full satisfaction in the Lord. They will always look to Egypt. "We had this in Egypt!" Always wanting things! Wherever they pass they buy!

I want to challenge our co-workers. In the last ten years, what have you seen me bring from America? The first time I brought the fax machine for the Ministry. This time I brought the fax machine for the Ministry, and I brought some books. What did you see me bring for myself? What did you see me bring for my family? A brother told me, "Let's go and shop, let me buy you some things." I told him, "No!"

The buying spirit is the wilderness spirit.

The buying spirit is the overflow of the wilderness heart, it is the overflow of dissatisfaction that thinks that things can satisfy the emptiness of the heart.

The buying spirit is a wilderness spirit. There is no contentment. And the reality is that some things are even more expensive abroad than they are here - anybody who has done shopping knows. And wilderness people, each time you are travelling they say, "Buy me this!" They give you dangerous long lists!

Do you have a wilderness heart?

Have you begun to look at the things of this world with spite?

Have they lost their power to satisfy?

If you were told you were not to buy anything for the next ten years, would it affect your joy? That is what your children will be like. What a pity!

Just as those two and a half tribes settled on the wrong side of the Jordan, there are some brethren who have never moved from the divided heart to the consecrated heart. They can get to the border of the Promised Land, but the final break with the love of the world, they will not let it happen. They may come even right to the limit, but they will move far back. A wilderness heart - a divided heart!

There are many people who will not be helped by crusades; even a thousand 40-day fasts will not do anything to them. Without a final "No" to the world, even a thousand 40-day fasts will not do anything to them. There is a final "No" to the world, and a final "Yes" to Jesus that they have not said. And even if they carry out 40-day prayer crusades, the heart will still be divided because years ago, they abandoned their first love for the Lord. Some people shook their town at their conversion and their baptism. But somewhere along the line, they said: "No" to Jesus, "No" to the Lordship of Jesus, and "Yes" to the world. They are not bad people. They do many good things. But the heart has been divided for years.

These two and a half tribes were prepared to go over and fight the battles and take the risks, and get their brothers settled, provided they came back. Oh Brethren, listen, I am not a natural pessimist. In fact, I am an optimist. But I see very few divided hearts becoming consecrated. What it will take to shatter the grounds, to shatter the links with the world, and go in for a pure walk with Jesus is too much. They are prepared for some temporary modifications. But to cut the tap root is too much. There are people whom I have known to be divided at heart for 15 years. They have moved far ahead, but they will not jump to victory. Their world would break. Their world would shatter. And each one of them knows what the issue is. Putting in many long fasts and many long prayer crusades on a divided heart will not do anything.

Without radical separation from the love of the world, without radical separation from the love of the things of the world, without a final "Yes" to Jesus, long fasts, long prayer crusades and big gifts to God are the concretisation of sandy soil for a foundation.

The Lord Jesus says, "I do not want your fasts. I do not want your prayer crusades. I want your heart." And many would rather fast for very many days, and very many weeks, than give Him their hearts.

"My daughter, give Me your heart," says the Lord.

"My son, give Me your heart," says the Lord. And you know where the problem is.

<u>Matthew 6:22-23</u>: "The eye is the lamp of the body. If your eyes are good, your whole body will be full of light. But if your eyes are bad, your whole body will be full of darkness. If then the light within you is darkness, how great is that darkness!"

I just got light on the meaning of that in the U.S. When you withdrew to the mountain top, when you went on a special retreat, at that special weekend, or during your meditation, God showed you what He wanted, and you saw it clearly. It demanded harsh renunciations, radical abandonments and a new welding. When you came back from the mountain, you negotiated - either to forget it completely or to offer something partial. By that act you caused the light that was in you to become darkness. And from that day you are not the same. Inwardly there is decay. You try to gather things together, to launch all over. But you find out that there is no take-off. The light in you became darkness. God told you to go and humble yourself and to repent, to humble yourself and own up the pride of your heart, or the wickedness of your heart, or the sin of your life, to go on your knees, to expose what you have been hiding, and you said, "No." And the light became darkness. Now you can't see any more. Everything is blurred.

You can no longer distinguish between the voice of God and the voice of man.

You can no longer distinguish between the voice of God and your own voice.

It is all so foggy. You can no longer see. Your eyes are bad now. Your body is full of darkness. The light within you is now darkness because of deliberate disobedience. You broke your covenant with God. You broke your vow to God. Like

Samson, in breaking your vow, you allowed your hair to be trimmed. And you go about thinking that you are the same man. You are no longer the same man. You have made your choice.

I mentioned that I put one believer on a prayer programme 15 years ago. That believer said, "No, it is too much," and lost 15 years. When the believer said, "It is too much," God said, "It is alright," and I said, "It is alright." Fifteen years have been lost. When you look at it from eternity, the horror cannot be understood. If a person has 100 years to live, let us take that eternity is 1,000,000,000,000,000 years, which is just joking.

It is 15/100 x 1,000,000,000,000,000 years that are lost.

Or let us take it that the believer lives for 100 years, and that he believed at 20. So he lost the 20 years in unbelief. So God gives the believer 100 years on earth to build this number of eternity years, and he wastes 20 years.

It is 20/100 x 1,000,000,000,000,000 years that are lost.

People lose that and then go around as if nothing has happened.

A brother in our Ministry was interested in a certain sister about 15 years ago, and the Lord told him, "No." He insisted. The Lord said, "No." He went from Yaounde right to Kumba and from Kumba right to Tombel to see the girl. As he sat in the sitting room and the girl was in the kitchen, the Holy Spirit said, "No," three times. He crossed from the sitting room, met the girl in the kitchen, and proposed. The girl said, "No," and he lost God for the next nine years. For nine years, there was no communion between him and God. He took a ten-day fast every year, but it was empty. It was after nine years that God spoke to him again. When the light in you becomes darkness, how great the darkness is!

Listen, Brethren, Abraham lost 75 years of his life in unbelief. He was 75 years old when the Lord called him. After 10 years in the land without a child, at the insinuation of his wife, he took Hagar and went in to her. Eventually Ishmael was born. That event took place when he was 85. And the heavens were sealed. For the next 14 years, God did not speak to him. The last time God spoke to Abraham, it was just before he was 85. And the next time God spoke to Abraham was when he was 99. And when God spoke to him that time, it was a rebuke. "Walk thou before Me and be perfect!" The heavens were sealed for 14 years while he flirted with Ishmael: "My strength! My child!" From the age of 85 until 99 were 14 years during which God was silent. What a tragedy! Abraham lived to be 175. He lost 75 years before he believed. So he had 100 years to serve the Lord. And, like this person I was talking about, he lost another 14 years. It will take eternity for people to realize what they lost. The problem is that some people have had no revelation of eternity.

In 1967, I had a revelation of eternity. I was frightened by the magnitude of eternity, and I wrote the article: "The Magnitude Of Eternity." If you have a revelation of the magnitude of eternity, you will see how woeful any loss of time in time is. How can you comprehend eternity? If you were given a teaspoon, and you were told to use this teaspoon to carry water from the Atlantic Ocean and go on foot and throw it in the Sahara Desert in Algeria and come back and take the next, eternity is the length of time that it would take for you to empty the Atlantic Ocean with a teaspoon - taking it one teaspoon at a time and dropping it in Algeria and coming back, going on foot. And you have only a hundred years to prepare for it.

One day lost is already a horror. But believers are wicked enough to spend 14 years, 15 years in a divided condition of heart. They are prepared to walk around without the testimony of the Holy Spirit that they have obeyed God in everything that God has demanded. They are prepared to walk around and preach without the testimony of the Holy Spirit that they have obeyed God in everything. They are prepared to do all that. And it is all a waste because, without the testimony of the Holy Spirit that a man has rendered total obedience to God in all that God has shown him, the person is wasting his time.

Where you are now, what is the testimony of the Holy Spirit?

Have you obeyed God?

Are there issues of outstanding obedience that have been in suspense for years? Then God is also in suspense for years.

"Walk thou before Me and be perfect!"

And if God could be silent to His friend Abraham, what of those who have not even wooed Him to have His friendship, infatuated with what this world has to offer? Oh! that God might give to His children a revelation of the magnitude of eternity. As I was saying, with too many believers, there is just no spiritual experience. There are no encounters with God! No wonder there is very little incentive to obey. They don't know their loss. They can also not apprehend the gain. If they did, the god "self" would be overthrown. This night they ought to overthrow it just as Gideon overthrew the idol that night. But they will not humble themselves. They want to maintain their dignity. And God lets them go to build mansions, castles in the wilderness - the wilderness of pride, the wilderness of self-love. "(But) if (then) the light within you is darkness, how great is that darkness!" Could the truth be that in your experience, with increasing time, God seems farther and farther away? It is as if God had left you to navigate alone.

Before my father made me his friend, he could say: "Tanee," and "Tanee" could be: "You are in trouble" or "You are honoured," because "Tanee" could be: "My father" because his father's name was "Tanee;" or "Tanee," "My troubler." To the onlooker, it was just "Tanee" but between him and me, we knew which "Tanee" meant what. When people have lost God the two "Tanees" become the same. Is that what has happened to you? Maybe it was not one crisis event, but just one small thing after another, little by little, until you are now facing the opposite direction. You didn't go away from God in one swift act, but as the hymn writer says,

"By many deeds of shame, we learn that love grows cold."

And between lovers it is hardly ever one event. One disobedience and then another one! One act of self-will! And the flame is extinguished. But I also know that on the way back, a man comes to a point when he confronts the issues. God brings a man face to face with the issues and demands an overthrow of all of the world, all of the love of the world and all of the love of the things of the world. Again, many people negotiate and then it is settled.

Before they could enter the Promised Land, they had to cross the Jordan. Immediately they crossed the Jordan, they were in foreign land, the Promised Land; so it was like: "Cross the Jordan and fall in the hands of the enemy," or "Cross the Jordan and land in the victory of our God." There were instructions.

<u>Joshua 3:5</u> "Joshua told the people, 'Consecrate yourselves, for tomorrow the Lord will do amazing things among you.'"

Let us comment a bit about the Levitical priests and the ark of God. Who were the priests? They were of the tribe of Levi. The original purpose of God was that the whole nation of Israel would be a nation of overcomers. God had intended to have a nation of overcomers.

<u>Exodus 19:5-6</u> "Now if you obey me fully and keep my covenant, then out of all nations you will be my treasured possession. Although the whole earth is mine, you will be for me a kingdom of priests and a holy nation. (These are the words you are to speak to the Israelites)."

A kingdom of priests! Oh! The whole nation a kingdom of priests. I think we treated this topic in "The Way Of The Overcomers." It was intended that the whole nation would be a kingdom of priests. But when Moses came from the mountain and the golden calf had been made, Moses said, "Who is on God's side? Come to me." They had all sinned. All of them could have run to him. He would have continued to have a nation of overcomers. But only the Levites moved towards him. The others chose not to come to God. That was how the nation of overcomers now became a tribe; that was how instead of a nation of priests, it now became a tribe of priests. The Levites who moved forward became the special tribe. They took God's side. But God did not leave it there, because

All consecration has to be tested!!

God does not just accept the words of man, because some people don't know what they are saying. All consecration is tested! So when they moved forward to indicate that they were on God's side, Moses said each one was to take his sword, go kill his father, his mother, his son, friend and the rest — all those who had sinned and had not taken God's side. Do you know what he was trying to say? He was saying that

The overcomers are people who have learned freedom from natural emotions.

Because your father had not taken God's side, you were to kill him; or your son, your mother or whoever. If he had just said, "Go and kill others," there would have been no problem. You were to obey God at the cost of your wife, at the cost of your husband, at the cost of your brother,... and they did it. They shattered natural emotions that they might build a holy relationship with God. As it is in the Revised Standard Version, Moses said to them "This day you have ordained yourselves at personal cost for the service of the Lord."

At personal cost, not at general cost. Each one at the price of his father, his mother, his son. You have ordained yourselves at (personal) cost!

Exodus 32:26 "So he stood at the entrance to the camp and said, 'Whoever is for the Lord, come to me.' And all the Levites rallied to him." It is wonderful. A whole tribe rallied to him. It is also horrible - eleven tribes disobeyed. Not even one person from the rest of the tribes obeyed. And not one person from Levi held back. Oh God! It is possible to have a Church of overcomers. All the sons of Levi turned to him. So the whole Church can turn to God in radical consecration, in radical holiness. The whole Church can enter into the perfection of God. One must not always have mixtures. But where do we have a college of consecrated Elders, with none of them divided at heart? Oh! I see the great possibilities. "(And) all the Levites rallied to him."

Oh Eternal Father!! Oh! The possibility that the whole Church could be brought to the perfection of God brings new hope to my heart.

Oh but the tragedy of the lost opportunity to ALL the rest! Of all the rest - not one of them moved forward.

Do you know that you represent a thousand people that will come from your progeny - from your children, your grandchildren and your great grandchildren?

Maybe you represent 100,000 people; and because of not moving forward in obedience to God, none of them can come to the fulness of God. So you stand here maybe as a representative of a million people. And when you move ahead, you move the one million people into the fulness of God. And when you play games, when you hold back, a million people are blocked.

How far-reaching the decisions of individuals are!

Exodus 32:26b-27 And all the Levites rallied to him. Then he said to them, "This is what the Lord, the God of Israel says: 'Each man strap a sword to his side. Go back and forth through the camp from one end to the other, each killing his brother and friend and neighbour.'"

That is what God said. Each one killing his brother! Each one killing his friend! Each one killing his brother! The natural was being totally tested.

And when you choose your wife instead of God, you are not worthy of Him.

When you choose your friend instead of Him, you are not worthy of Him.

When you choose your son or your daughter instead of Him, you are not worthy of Him.

They were confronting the radical condition for discipleship. The Lord Jesus said, "If anyone comes to me and does not hate his father and mother, his wife and children, his brothers and sisters - yes, even his own life - he cannot be my disciple" (Luke 14:26).

The Levites did as Moses commanded. At the human level, it looked horrible. At the divine level, it was wonderful. God had got people who could obey Him in everything. And Moses said, "Today you have ordained yourselves for the service of the Lord, each one at the cost of..."

You have ordained yourselves! Self-ordained priests! Today you have ordained yourselves!

The service of the Lord is for self-ordained priests.

You ordained yourself. And Moses said, "Today you have ordained yourselves for the service of the Lord, each one at the cost of his son and of his brother that he may bestow a blessing upon you this day."

Ordination is at cost. Self-ordination is at personal cost!

Men can lay hands on you, but ultimately, only you can ordain yourself. And it is always at great cost, at total cost.

If you go nowhere, it is because you did not ordain yourself at great cost. If you are going round, round and round in circles, it is because in the deceitfulness of your heart, you thought that you could make it without the indispensable sacrifice.

When did you ordain yourself? And at what cost was it?

There are leaders who know only the ordination of man. They do not know personal ordination. Therefore they do not know the ordination of God because the ordination of God follows self-ordination at personal cost.

The ordination of God is preceded by self-ordination at personal cost.

My dear Brother, my dear Sister, when was your own ordination? And at what cost was it? Let me ask you again, and I ask you in the Name of the Lord:

Are you a caricature in the Ministry, without personal ordination and at personal cost?

How long will you deceive yourself? It is very easy to see that in a group of people who say they are ordained, some lack the marks of ordination. The outward show took place for all of them, but because there was no personal ordination, there was no ordination.

<u>1 Corinthians 10:1-5a</u> "For I do not want you to be ignorant of the fact, brothers, that our forefathers were <u>all</u> under the cloud and that they <u>all</u> passed through the sea. They were <u>all</u> baptized into Moses in the cloud and in the sea. They <u>all</u> ate the same spiritual food and drank the same spiritual drink; for they drank from the spiritual rock that accompanied them, and that rock was Christ. Nevertheless, God was not pleased with most of them."

All! But with most of them, God was not pleased. You could have a college of bishops, all of whom received the laying on of hands, and had prophecies from God, but because the gifts and the calling of God are without repentance,

Anyone who thinks that special gifts necessarily mean that he is consecrated is totally deceived.

You could have a heterogeneous college, a mixture of the ordained and the non-ordained, a mixed leadership, the ordained and the non-ordained.

Are you the one causing trouble in the leadership because you are not ordained, because you do not know self-ordination?

And because you are there, the whole Church cannot enter into the victory of God; because if the leaders are not united in their consecration, there is no possibility that the whole Church can enter into the victory of God.

Are you that wicked man, that wicked woman, because of whom the victory is lost?

Achan alone caused the victory to be lost. May God search your heart through! May you be honest! And I am sorry for the superficial, because they can never even understand anything in depth any more. They quickly jump to the conclusion that they are consecrated. They have never really faced the light of God. It is now all darkness, darkness, darkness.

It was intended that at the end of this Course, the Voice of heaven would say, "I have this person 100%. There is not one area that is unsettled. All is settled," and that the people would say, "God, You know that in all the domains, I have yielded in the full range of it."

So it is self-ordination at personal total cost. Not just at cost, but at personal cost. Not just at personal cost, at personal total cost. Bear those words in mind:

13

PERSONAL TOTAL COST

First, personal ordination at personal total cost to the service of the Lord.

And when you go away without that testimony, you may never have it again, because the ringing call at this level may never happen again. And after you have disobeyed or negotiated, whatever comes afterward will be easier to resist, and God will never speak again. And God will never even give you His best again.

Brethren, come with me to Exodus 13:17-18a

"When Pharaoh let the people go, God did not lead them on the road through the Philistine country, though that was shorter. For God said, 'If they face war, they might change their minds and return to Egypt.' So God led the people around by the desert road toward the Red Sea."

Do you see one thing, Brethren?

What God gives a man before he begins to choose, is already according to what God sees in his heart.

The best route was through the Philistine country. If God had had a totally obedient people, prepared to totally believe Him, He would have led them through the Philistine country. God said, "If they go here and face war, they will go back to Egypt." God could not trust them. He could not count on them. So God said, "Let Me give them what they can handle. I will lead them through the Red Sea. I will avoid the Philistine country." Because of what God saw in their hearts, He gave up the best. He didn't even present it to them. He led them in the path of the second best. They saw miracles on this second best road. Oh, but it was still the second best. Along this second best road, they lost 40 years.

Do you know what your resistance has led God to give you as His will?

So you say it is the will of God. Yes, it is God's second best because God saw in your heart that you were not prepared for the best. I want to ask you,

- **Do you have the type of heart to which God can propose His best?**
- **What is your record in obedience?**

Brethren, even along this second best, they refused. When they spied the land, they refused to walk into it. They now entered in the third best of God. God did not propose the best to them because He knew what was in their hearts; and even what He proposed to them, they lost it through self-love. Listen, Brethren, it is possible to miss that from the beginning:

- because of a persistent sticking to something that God says you should let go,
- because of a persistent desire to own something of which God says "No,"
- because of a refusal to humble yourself,
- because of the refusal to be a servant indeed,
- because of the spirit of a boss,
- because of the love of food,
- because of the love of sleep,
- because of the pride of life,
- because of the desire to be popular,
- because of the desire to be accepted,
- because of the desire to be honoured.

Is this God's last chance that He is giving you that you might be led along the Philistine country?

Do you have the heart with which God can call you to His best?

Do you have the type of heart with which God can make of you His permanent prisoner?

Do you have the type of heart of which God can demand the severest?

When C.T. Studd was separated from his wife for 13 years in order to take the Gospel to the Belgian Congo, God could not have made such a proposal to him if he did not have that kind of heart and if he had failed the test of giving away the money — £29,00.00 in those days. He signed one cheque for £5,000.00 to Moody for his evangelism. He signed another cheque for £5,000.00 and gave it to Booth (the Salvation Army leader) for evangelism, and so forth. Oh, if C.T. Studd had failed the test of going to the mission field, abandoning cricket at its height to go to China, abandoning the desire to be a cricket star, and burying it! And then in China, he entered into this inheritance - £29,000.00 - incalculable wealth for today. And then at 53 he had to come to the Belgian Congo without his wife because she was in a health condition in which she could not go with him. So they were separated for 13 years. During those 13 years, they saw each other only for two weeks when she visited him.

I want to talk to the missionaries. I hope you have read "Champion of God." Missionaries, if you have never read "Champion of God.", read it. C.T. Studd lived in utter simplicity. He had a round hut and that was all. His bed, his table and everything he had was there and he was the head of the mission. He worked extremely hard. Even at 60, he was working 17 to 18 hours a day. When he was translating the Bible, he had no time to stop and eat. He just put food there and occasionally he would take a spoon and put in his mouth and continue.

And all these lazy men on the mission field with the blood of men upon them! At 60, C.T. Studd was working 17 to 18 hours a day. What about you? Many people tell me that they are "full-time," but they are doing less than a third of the work that I am doing. And I have a senior position at the university. I wish I could sit with some of the "full-time" people and let us compare our accounts. I don't understand it. It is wickedness at the extreme. "Full-time" idleness in the Name of the Crucified. The provincial leader of the South West Province is a very disciplined man and works very hard. The only problem is that since he became "full-time," he has never attained the records in performance as when he was working. I have all his monthly accounts. I look at the records before he was full-time and I look at them now and I bemoan the whole matter of calling oneself "full-time." I bemoan it. I weep. Why do we not have one workaholic missionary? I am waiting for one "full-time" person to cause Zach Fomum to rethink. The best of them are working at the level they would have been working if they were doing some job. Others are working less. Full-time with two or three hours of prayer and one hour of meditation, and that is all for some days! Then they spend the rest of the time chatting. I do not understand it. I am waiting for one full-time man who will tell me, "Zach Fomum, I consistently give God 16 hours a day for prayer, for Bible reading and for evangelism." I am waiting for that. C.T. Studd was different.

François Xavier worked an average of 21 hours a day as a missionary, and did in his lifetime what it takes ten lives to do. In fact, when I read about him, I modified my goals. I thought at the apex, I would get to 20 hours. I must get to 22 hours. May God convict you of total wickedness of heart - for being on holiday on the mission field! Those of you who are going to the Mission field, don't go to be a curse to those people. If you give God less than 16 hours a day, you are being a curse because if you were putting 8 hours into earning your bread, you would still give God 8 hours. And "full-time" just means that you should now give the 8 hours you would have been investing into earning your bread to have 8+8 = 16.

He lived in utter simplicity because he did not want to create a difference between himself and the people he was reaching out to. He lived at their level. The other missionaries almost carried out a mutiny against him. They said he had made the conditions unnecessarily hard. But those conditions were written in the life he lived. Had he sought the way of comfort, the World Evangelisation Crusade would never have come forth.

Will God use indulgent people to birth great movements?

Will God use indulgent people to take nations in a mighty way?

Will God use indulgent people to shake cities and bring a new day?

Will God use indulgent people to leave footmarks on the sand of time?

In 13 years this man and his wife saw each other for two weeks. He could have chosen to be with his wife, stayed in Britain and let the Congo perish. It would not just have been the Congo. It would have been the 80 nations in which World Evangelisation Crusade missionaries are functioning today for the glory of God. He did not love his life. "He though dead speaketh." He turned his back to fame and a cricket career. He gave away all the money so that on their wedding day they had only $5.00 because what he left for his wife, the wife also took it and gave it to God. He asked, "What was the rich young ruler told to do?"

He did what the rich young ruler failed to do and rose to the heights that the rich young ruler abandoned.

He turned his back to the comforts of home, his wife and his children. And on the mission field he was totally ruthless with himself.

Will our missionaries give us a C.T. Studd of our generation?

Are you allowing the opportunities just to slide by because of some indulgence with food, with money, with pleasure, with comfort and all the rest?

There is the hall of fame in heaven, and the possibility of being enrolled there, and the possibility of losing it permanently, because you are clinging to something that you cannot really keep.

You are trying to gain something that you cannot really keep.

Oh, C.T. Studd was the man to whom God could say, "Leave cricket." C.T. Studd was the man to whom God could whisper in his heart, as he read the Scriptures, "Give away £29,000.00. Leave nothing for yourself."

Do you know that the possibilities of rising to total greatness are just before you?

His greatest work was done after 53 when he came to Africa. Even his wife thought he was not well. Even his wife thought that he had missed it all. Nobody would back him. He had so many diseases in his body that they said he was a museum of diseases and nobody would support him; but he went. And as he was going down the Nile, in order to get to the Congo, the Lord said to him:

"This journey is not only for the Congo. It is for the whole unevangelised world."

First of all, it was the Heart Of Africa Mission, then it was the World Evangelisation Crusade. If he had relaxed there as a buffoon on the mission field, if he had lived at ease, and transferred Britain to the heart of the Congo, he would have been forgotten. Such men who are pregnant with comfort, pregnant with ease and pregnant with the world, can only give birth to the love of the world. If he had said, "Oh! I am an old man. I need 12 hours of sleep!" He worked for seventeen-eighteen hours a day at 60. What about you?

The distinguishing mark is not gifts. It is hard work! It is not talents. It is hard work.

The Apostle Paul was not more gifted than the others. He did not have more power than the others. But he said, "I worked harder than them all! And as one untimely born," born when the time was over. In human language he became the king of the New Testament. What set him apart? Hard work.

All of you know that Sister E.K. is the most distinguished woman in the Work in so many domains. Last year she prayed an average of 7 hours 14 minutes a day, plus all the other things that she does.

It is not superior gifts. It is extremity in hard work.

I have no problem about seeing her because I see her every-day. And there is no problem about it because if I have to be available at 2.00 O'clock in the morning, she will be there; but she always carries along her work. So if she is waiting for one, two, three or four hours, she is working, whether it is writing prayer topics or writing the summary of my month. She is distinguished by one thing and by one thing only - hard work.

And God has given to every man 24 hours a day. There are not people with 28 hours. May the Holy Spirit convict you of wasting the only thing that cannot be regained!

Time lost is lost eternally.

God can bless you so that in one day you make a million Naira. But God will not bless you with another 24 hours from anywhere. What you have lost, you have lost for ever.

Time is the most perishable gift.

When you have squandered a minute, it is squandered. If we look into the horizons of the future, people shall position themselves according to how hard they worked. I leave it for you to think and rethink.

There must come a day, and may that day be today, when you ordain yourself to extreme hard work. I hear about some nonsense they talk of in America about being "burnt out." In French they call it "surmenage" or "épuisement" or that type of word. What are they talking about?

The best people who work hard use 2% of their brains.

Lazy people sit down and they are overworked. Of what? I tell people all those things are sins. All those complaints are sin.

Why did Francis Xavier not burn out? Why did John Wesley not burn out? He burned on until 86. And at 84 he was still walking 12 miles to go and proclaim the message of the Crucified. And he rode about 250,000 miles on horseback a year. And on the horseback he was reading the Bible, and other books. He wrote books but he was also a mighty devourer of books. He read and read and read. Do you know Murray who lived at the close of the last century? He wrote 240 books and they are all top quality books, and he was the director of a mission. While others were sleeping he was pressing into the heights. He was really an apostle, involved in Church planting, but the best description for him is — the apostle with a pen.

Have you read "Deliverance From The Sin Of Laziness," and "The Art Of Working Hard" ? Everybody needs it. It is a "must" reading for all Africans, many of whom are rich and lazy. We are sitting on diamonds, but we are poor to the core. Brother J.G. went to the Far East. Here is what he says:

Brother J.G.: It was in South Korea. It was with the firm Daewoo. They were people who were working very hard. They had many computers, but in spite of that they worked extremely hard. If I am not mistaken, they were working from 7.00 a.m. to 6.00 p.m. And one day, we were just chatting, in their conversation they mentioned that some time ago they were just a nation of orphans, always begging. But now, everybody knows that they are among the four nations that are called the four new tiger nations. We can't go into details but they are really high up, and if we were to discuss shipbuilding, they should be among the top rank; they are the first. They are probably the first nation now in oil rigging.

And some people want more and more holidays, more and more rest. May angels block the way when we want to carry out the madness of sending somebody who is not extremely hardworking to the mission field. And, Brethren, I have tried to work hard and I am still working on improving. There are people who have lived around me and have rubbed shoulders intimately with me for 20 years, but have hardened their hearts to learning anything about hard work, such that just there where my strength seems to lie, there is none of it in their lives.

We have just determined the structure of a compound. It is an unusually interesting structure. It could be the most interesting structure of my whole career. By the time we got the structure, the student who was at the bench and who did the basic work in the laboratory had been dismissed from all universities in Cameroon. At the Master's degree and at the first year of the Doctorate he was right at the top of his class. We have to look for another student to repeat the work so that we may get the details. By the time he was dismissed we had read his doctoral thesis for the first time and we had corrected it. We had read it for the second time and he had corrected it. And it was ready for defense. Then he was given some papers to mark because doctoral students are involved in marking. A girl had 03 out of 80. He just added a top to the zero, changed it to 63 and made her the best student in the class. And he did that to three students and denied it, but all the evidence was there. In our group, because we are committed believers, we have impact there; so that even the enemies of the Gospel hide their enmity. But this man was a bold proclaimer of Satan. He spoke the greatest evil against God. He was dismissed from all the universities of Cameroon.

Your sins will find you out. After 60 years of laziness, you will face the facts.

General Booth sent his daughter, I don't remember whether she was 19 or 23, but she was still very young, to go and start the Salvation Army in France, in the Devil's own territory. She hired a garage and started the meetings there. And she succeeded. If our missionaries don't succeed in Britain, they have only themselves to blame. First of all, they are two, and they are baptized in the Holy Spirit. She wasn't. And they are going to Britain, not France. I have been to maybe thirty countries, but I have never stepped foot on a more godless place than France. Even the Wednesday partial fast is an uphill task. I went to Paris in 1982 and went to the centre of the market. I was trying to shop. Then three people came to suggest magic to me, magic things from three different people, one after another. And I was looking around, looking for a shop with cheap things. Then I just saw women in houses, at the doors, inviting hopeless men who were passing. I wondered how many fools trying to buy things just landed there and entered into the booth of death. As I stood there stupefied, I saw a tall man, and then a woman came and she took him in. And I saw afresh what is written in Proverbs 7. The man was going to the lake of fire. France has never known a great revival, but we must succeed in France. We are looking for a missionary to go to France. He must be prepared to separate himself from his wife for three years because it may take three years for them to allow the wife to enter. If "Darling, darling" is more important to you than God, if you don't have the C.T. Studd spirit, don't go because you have already failed.

In France, not everybody will do as a missionary. In fact, if some of the present missionaries go to France, the Devil will pocket them and put them on display — and make a public show of them. A man who cannot see a naked beautiful woman and be untouched will just go there and lose the whole time until the Devil takes him home.

Testimony from Brother T.O.: That same 1982, I was in Paris and for some reason all the hotels were occupied. After a long search, I got a hotel in a certain quarter. What I didn't realise was that it was the Red Light Area. In all the cities of the world, that quarter exists, which is called the Red Light Area. So I checked into the hotel. I was there for exactly five minutes when I realised I just had to leave. I wasn't even a believer yet. Fortunately, I met a man I knew, and I slept with him that night and that was how I was saved from the Red Light Zone.

In talking about going to have a prayer crusade in China, the Chinese girl who directed me to the hotel to which I should go in Shin Jing, told me, "The only problem is that you can hear knocks at the door, and when you open, it will be a woman begging to be allowed in." Already, last time when we were in China, when we were going at night to this place where we were to meet, there were girls who would run outside and say, "Come, come, come, come." These were young girls in their teens. I said to myself, "The type of missionaries that will be sent here,…"

To what extent do you know indifference to the appearance of women?

We shall need men of a sterner stuff. We just need a wall-breaker, a man who breaks barriers, a man who storms until the thing opens. When I look at the reports that come in, many of the missionaries have lost what they had. The fiery nature seems to have gone. They have given up the big dream. I am thinking of a man who says, "O.k., the door has to pass through here. This wall will collapse," and gets the wall to collapse. And, Brethren, to go to a European country, we cannot just send a strong man married to a spiritual house girl. It will take two violent people to break through. It is not enough to have a bulldozer. You must have a bulldozing man and a bulldozing woman. It must be a violent man and a violent woman!

You know, in one of those books about the past communist world, they were insulting the Lord Jesus Christ publicly during a communist rally. There was a man of God there with his wife. The woman said, "Stand up and wipe that mud from Jesus' face. Stand up and say that it's a lie, it's wrong, they are lying." The man said, "If I stand and say it, you will not have a husband." She said, "I prefer to be single than to be married to a coward!" And he stood up and spoke and was locked up! I like that kind of women. Oh! That was Wurmbrand. Oh! May we have many of them - women who prefer to have husbands in prison rather than have a coward sitting by them. The worst thing that can happen to a woman is that she has a coward sitting by her, who does everything to run away from imprisonment, who denies Jesus in order to be with his wife. Oh for women who would say, "Stand up and wipe that mud from Jesus' face, even if it means that I stay for ever without a husband!"

I want to thank my wife for one thing. In all the striving to get to heights of giving to God, no day did I have to argue with her. She has come along very willingly, when each step has meant a reduction in her allowance, in food money, and in everything along this pilgrimage, right to the point where we are today. Even the savings I started to make in 1979 as some reserve to be responsible as a husband and father, are being turned over to the Gospel. We have not had one second of squabble. We have had no disagreements about money. But I also want to tell the brothers that I have paid all the bills. Don't go and tell your wife that there is no food because you have given all the money to God and that she should eat oxygen because God has eaten the money. God gave me the gift of handling money and she has believed me.

At the age of 11, I was going from a place called Ngie to Mbengwi for the National Day, what used to be the Empire Day. It took six days; one day to go, one day to rest, three days of sports and one day to come back. My father gave me six pence in those days for pocket money. Only those who know what six pence meant then can understand its value. I took the money, got to Mbengwi, and then I remembered that my godmother (you know I come from a Presbyterian background) was living at a place 5 kilometres away. I went to live with her. So I had breakfast, then I walked to the field, and in the evening I went back home and ate. And I didn't spend the 6 pence. I didn't spend even one penny. All the things they were selling, groundnuts and the rest, I didn't see why I should spend the money for them when I ate breakfast and supper. Finally, when we got home on the evening of the sixth day, I gave the six pence back to my father. He asked me, "What happened?" So I said, "I went to live with my godmother and since I ate in the morning and in the evening, I didn't see why I should spend the money." Then he asked me, "Do you love me so much that you would not want to waste my money?" He said, "O.K., from this day you are my friend." It is that friendship that has altered all my life! It was just six pence. From that day he gave me the name "Z.T." And the last words he uttered in this life were, "Where is Z.T.?"

So money is important. When you have to increase giving to God, and you have to convince a woman over long discussions on the table! A missionary went somewhere, I won't tell you where, and did some job. When they paid him, he phoned to me and said he wanted to give all the money to the Lord as the first-fruits. Three days afterwards he said they had had a disagreement with the wife. The wife wanted a tithe and an offering given and that's all. I told him, "You had better give in. Agree with her."

Song:

> *Whether na police Oh, na ma choice Oh Oh! Na ma choice*
> > *Oh Oh!*
> *Whether na soldier, na ma choice Oh Oh! Na ma choice*
> > *Oh Oh!*
> *Whether na missionary, Na ma choice Oh Oh! Na ma choice*
> > *Oh Oh!*
> *Whether na soldier, Na ma choice Oh Oh! Na ma choice*
> > *Oh Oh!*
> *Whether she follow you Oh, Na ma choice Oh Oh! Na ma*
> > *choice Oh Oh!*
> *Whether she fit allow you give all for God Oh, Na ma choice*
> > *Oh Oh! Na ma choice Oh Oh!*

Whether she show you thing wey you never buy am Oh, Na
ma choice Oh Oh! Na ma choice Oh Oh!
Whether she show you house wey you never build am Oh, Na
ma choice Oh Oh! Na ma choice Oh Oh!
Whether she show you that new clothes for shop Oh, Na ma
choice Oh Oh! Na ma choice Oh Oh!
Whether she show you that new pair of shoes Oh, Na ma
choice Oh Oh! Na ma choice Oh Oh! Na ma choice
Oh Oh!

The song means: Whether she is a policeman or a soldier or a missionary, whether she can allow you to give all to God, whether she shows you what you have not bought for her – the house, the clothes or the new pairs of shoes, she is your choice. You made the choice.

You don't need to be a perfect woman. But, What radical contribution have you brought into the man's life? Or is it only far-reaching hindrances? The liberty to run the monies unquestioned, with no explanations to give, gave me the freedom to move the family to where we are now in our giving. Do you have such liberty? My wife has never reminded me about what is lacking. She has never reminded me about what I have not bought.

One of the missionary couples sold their property, and their house, in Yaounde. They want to buy a plot and build their house on the mission field. In fact, they expect that in two years they will not need any franc from home. They plan to already be in their own house; therefore, they will not pay any rents, and they are planning to open a poultry. One day, we got a fax. The man told me, "The foundation is laid. I have taught '*The Way of Life*' for 22 weeks. So the foundation is laid. For 22 weeks he taught his young Church '*The Way of Life*,' two hours every Tuesday, and wrote home to say, "The foundation has been laid. We will now start to build on it." Is that aggressiveness? Yes, that's aggressiveness. Then he says he will teach '*The Way Of Obedience.*' All he will do will be just to teach one book after another, so that the people will have the book while he is teaching it. Then they will read it at home. We have some crooks who don't know how to teach the Word, but they want to become their own originals and confuse the Church.

We got a message from a Church leader in Australia. They were having the convention for their Work, so the top leaders were coming together, thirty of them. He asked us for thirty copies of '*The Way Of Christian Service.*' He said that that was what they would study during their annual convention. And we sent them to them. He was not looking for something original. "The foundation is laid!"

Somebody told me that in one Bible School, the teachers use our books, but they remove the covers because they don't want to admit the fact that it is our material. But one student who had the book was following the teacher as he taught. He was just taking the thing paragraph by paragraph. I didn't blame them.

But what are you teaching the people?

These Churches where every year, every time there is a new list, it is because there is no systematic teaching. When a pastor cannot say, "My people have been taught this. This has been taught. This is settled. We will move to this," he is confusing the people. He is pretending to be a teacher.

What have you already given the people?

What are you giving them now?

Where are you taking them next?

What do you put the young converts on?

We were talking about the tribe of Levi. You know, the priests came from the Levites — the self-ordained priests. When they came to the Jordan, the Levitcal priests had to carry the ark. They were to go ahead. There was a gap between them and the people. There was a gap. The Jordan was flooded at that time. It was flooded, but these Levitical priests, representing the overcomers, had to step into the flooded Jordan. They were to enter the Jordan at risk because they could be swept away. The Jordan was flooded. They were ahead. So at personal risk, they had to step into the Jordan while it had overflowed its banks . That is what it means to be a leader.

That is what it means to be a self-ordained priest - that you step into the place of death for the people.

Their lives were in jeopardy. Carrying the ark, they had to step in the Jordan. Leadership is a matter of really standing in the place of death. But when they stepped into the Jordan, when they entered into the place of death, Oh! the Jordan stopped flowing and a way was created! When they entered into the place of death, the Jordan stopped flowing and there was a pathway, a way created, as it were, at the price of death, just as a way was created for us by the death of the Lamb. Death creates ways. Until they stepped into the Jordan, the Jordan was flowing and overflooded. But when they entered in the place of death, risking their lives and risking everything, the Jordan stood still. "Unless a grain of wheat falls down and dies, says the Lord,... Unless a grain of wheat falls down and dies...."

John 12:24-25 "I tell you the truth, unless a grain of wheat falls to the ground and dies, it remains only a single seed. But if it dies, it produces many seeds. The man who loves his life will lose it, while the man who hates his life in this world will keep it for eternal life."

And we tell people who love their lives that they are going to heaven. The Apostle says "Death worketh in us so that life might work in you."

Life in the Churches is at the price of death in the leaders, death by extra sacrifice.

<u>Joshua 4:10</u> "Now the priests who carried the ark remained standing in the middle of the Jordan..."

In the middle; yes, in the centre. They were in the very centre of death. There was no hope that if the Jordan came back, they could escape. They stood in the place of death. Please get "The Ministers And The Ministry Of The New Covenant" and read it very many times over. It is the companion to the Christian worker. As they stood in the place of death, the Jordan stood still and all the people crossed in safety. There was no risk for them. These people had, first of all, taken the position of death by taking sides with Moses, and then ordaining themselves at personal cost. They had put a knife to personal relationships. They had killed sons, daughters and everything else; and now it was their own lives. They stood there, at the place of death so that the others might cross over in safety. The question is, "Do we have people in Nigeria who will stand in the place of death so that the millions of Nigerians that will be saved should enter into the salvation of our God?" Do we have self-ordained priests, people in Benin ordained and at great cost?

Ask yourself: "Am I making more costly sacrifices now or have I backslidden?" Backsliding is not going to the world because you will never go back to the world. If the sacrifices were at a certain level and now they are at a lower level, they remain sacrifices, but they are the sacrifice of a man who has abandoned the heights.

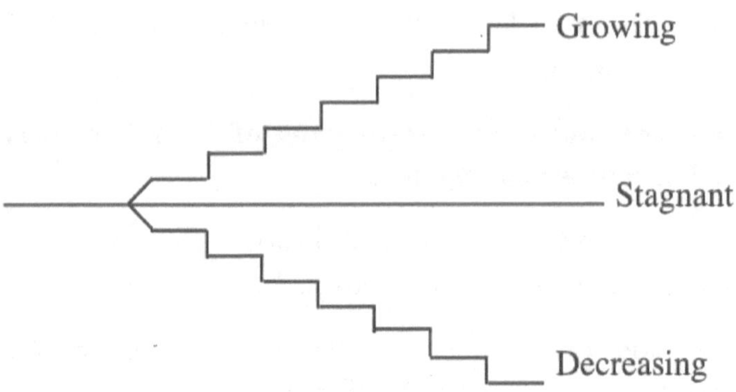

As your Ministry grows, two pathways are possible:

1. that you continue to make more and more increasingly great sacrifices,
2. that you stay at the same level,
3. or that you start to decline, enjoying yourself more and more and suffering less and less. And in ten years you will see the cumulative effect in your life.

Are you making more and more sacrifices?

Are you growing in sacrifice or are you growing in self-sparing?

What does the Holy Spirit say of you?

Where are the sacrifices of this year? Where are the nail-prints of this year? I wish I could stand where the missionaries are and ask each of them personally.

But listen, is it costing you more this year than it did last year? Is there bleeding for the Gospel this year that was not there last year?

Is it costing you more?

Do you live daily under the grip of the agony of the Cross?

Is it causing you more pain this year than in the past, than when you first beheld the Lord? Is it causing you greater pain than ever before? Where are the wounds?

The overcomers stood in the centre of the place of death; the others were passing without any problem.

Listen, there is a freedom which the non-overcomers will have in the Christian life. They will have freedom to own some things, go to some places, do some things and live a certain kind of life, which if the overcomer attempts, he will be finished. That is why if you listen to the people and accept what they offer, you may become like them and go where they go. Samson had his hair making him look clumsy. Wherever he appeared, he looked terribly clumsy. But he was also unusually strong. The day he became like others, he also became like others in strength.

Unusual strength and unusual separation from the common are invariably tied together.

To have what the others have, enjoy what they enjoy, dress like them, go where they go, have all the rest that they have, is also to be like them. So, why not? C.T. Studd did not improve on his tent. He would have become a different man.

Have you become another man or were you never an exceptional man?

What is there, distinctively yours, of the knowledge of the Word, and of the Word known and lived that sets you apart from all the other people in the Work? Where is your distinctive knowledge of God?

Where is your distinctive service that makes you say, "Let people come from 200 countries. I will give them God, flowing forth from my life. I will teach them to serve God as I have served"?

And you people going as missionaries: There are many believers in the countries where you are going to. What is distinctively yours that they do not have? What is written in your life? Because they have Bibles, they know doctrine.

What is written in your life that is lacking there?

What is the justification for your going there? Have you ever thought about it?

What are you taking to them, not as a doctrine, but as a life lived, not only in the past but even more intensively now? What was there in miniature form that is now in full development? Has the spring become a river? Is it something of the past? Are you the former man of God?

It is for you something to face now. There is no future in the question. It is a question that demands an immediate answer. You don't have to give it aloud. But on it may hang your qualification for the mission field before God. You owe the answer to no man. But you owe it to God. And honesty means that you owe it to yourself.

Do you know what, Brother? It is stark dishonesty, for a man to be selling books which he has not read. When a man is selling books which he has not read, it is pure corruption. It means his dishonesty has reached the supreme point. When a man does not read the books he is producing, it is extreme wickedness because he kills the books. I want to challenge you. I am busier than most of you, but I have read 48 books this year. When a man affords to sell books he has not read, I cannot understand it. And you ask God to bless the sales of books that talk of what you don't know. How do you expect God to act?

Once in Uganda, a brother in charge of the Scripture Union, whose name I want to withhold, was introducing books. He said, "This book, which I have not read, is very good." And he said it without worry. I said, "I am face to face with the first Christian sorcerer."

If you are not prepared to read the books, don't sell them! When people are trying to force the books to other people, books they have not read, where have they kept their consciences? They are just doing the same thing as the brother who said, "This book, which I have not read, is very good." It is witchcraft!

In Pensacola, the pastor bought thirteen copies of the Indian edition of, "The Way Of Victorious Praying," one for each leader in the Church. He said they were going to read one chapter per week. He said he would give them the book so that nobody might say that he didn't know where to get the book. It is the birth of a revolution. Next year, God willing, I will speak for three days in that Church.

The priests were in the place of death so that others might cross over into the Promised Land. The question is, "Shall we have overcomers?"

When a man goes to a nation with nothing that sets him apart from all the other people there, he goes to

add to their numbers, waste his life and produce others like what is already there.

The overcomers stood in the centre of the Jordan until all the people crossed over. It is a place of sustained death. It is not something you just jump there, and then you get out, because that is the game many people play. It is standing in a sustained way in the place of death through sustained fasting, sustained praying, sustained bleeding in giving, sustained bleeding holiness, which goes on and on and on, and not just occasional trips. It is sustained victory! They stayed there until the last Israelite crossed over.

Brother Joe Mbafor, do you know what that means? When you go, tell your wife what it signifies. When you go, tell the Elders what it means.

It is signing off for ever the possibility of ever being normal.

It is abandoning for ever the possibility of ever being normal again.

It is not sacrifice for the time being.

Oh Brethren, it is a covenant for life. It was in the purpose of God that Samson be a Nazirite for life. He went for some time but lost it. It is a sacrifice to be poor because of the Gospel until Jesus comes, not because you will not make more and more money, but because you will give more and more away; to fast ever increasingly; to put yourself under increasing restrictions, because it will take standing in the place of death until all the ransomed Church of God is saved, as it were, to sin no more.

For you, my dear Brother, it means standing in the place of death until you have the 500,000 believers without spot, without wrinkle, without blemish. It is to know increasing hardship. Yes, increasing hardship. It is to know that next year, you will be making sacrifices that you have not yet made; to stand in the place of death until the last Israelite gets over. Oh! But I see a new possibility. I see a new joy, that the whole Church will rise and enter into the Promised Land, provided God finds overcomers, and they are prepared to stay in the centre of the Jordan, in the place of death, in the very centre of the place of death, not at a corner of it but in the very centre of the place of death, because they can function only from there, until the last believer is in the Promised Land. Oh I see a new possibility, I see a new hope! The weakest believer shall be found in the Promised Land! I believe that God will find His overcomers! God will have His overcomers!! And they will stay in the centre of the Jordan, in the place of total renunciation and total sacrifice, and then they shall have the joy of seeing the whole Church in the Promised Land. Hallelujah! The Church in the Promised Land!! The whole Church in the Promised Land! Then it will make their sacrifice worthwhile. The whole Church in the Promised Land! Oh, I see a new day coming! I see a day coming at the return of the Lamb - the Church, all of overcomers, because the overcomers stayed in the centre of the Jordan, in the place of death, because they did not give up, because they did not go on holidays, because they did not compromise, because they did not seek ease. Does that excite you? I want to tell you that it excites me. I am tremendously encouraged. Oh, the whole Church will be in the Promised Land because the overcomers will stand in the very centre of death, hazarding their lives, hazarding their all, out of an inexplicable love for the coming King and out of inexplicable love for each sheep, for even the weakest sheep. Because of their profound love for the coming King, no price is too big, no price is too great to be paid for every sheep whose name was written in the

Lamb's Book of Life from the very foundations of the world. They share God's love for the world. Because of God, they love the world that God loves. Oh yes, the Church shall come to victory! Oh, the whole Church shall get into the Promised Land!

Are you going to be an overcomer or will you be one of those who shall be seen across?

All will have gone through the Jordan. All the divided hearts will be in the Promised Land — their hearts no longer divided. Oh, we behold a glorious Church without spot, without wrinkle and without blemish in the presence of God. And because of that we pay any price.

What is the reward? The reward is this: After everybody had crossed over, the overcomers did not remain at the back. Everybody waited and they went ahead, and there was a gap between them and the others. It is that gap between them and the others that is the reward. It is that extra closeness to the Lamb that those who stayed in the Jordan shall know throughout eternity that the others shall not know — that is the reward. Because there will be rewards in heaven in proportion to what we have suffered for Him, in proportion to what we have denied ourselves of for Him, in proportion to what the salvation of the lost has cost us, we shall not be the same.

There will be those who will wear crowns and those who will not.

There will be those who will have more than one crown and others will not.

There will be others who will have special rewards and others will not have.

It is like they say, "All of you have degrees." They say in a class, "All of you have passed." Some have "Average Pass," some have "Third Class," some "Second Class," some "First Class."

- First class
- Second class
- Third class
- Average pass.

Redemption has freed us from failing, but:

What is going to be your class?

And you will bear it for ever.

Others will come, take their crowns and place them at the feet of the Saviour; and you will stand there gaping with no crown to lay at His feet, because you had the pleasure of just crossing over while they stayed there. The rewards that some got by their consecrated service in the past, because they have backslidden from that service, those rewards will be taken and given to others. Some shall have a partial reward, others shall have a full reward.

<u>2 John 8</u> *"Watch out that you do not lose what you have worked for, but that you may be rewarded fully."*

That you may get a full reward. Some shall be rewarded partially, and throughout eternity bear the mark of a partial reward. The crowns of others will be taken from them...

<u>In Revelation 3:11</u> The Word of God says, *"I am coming soon. Hold on to what you have, so that no one will take your crown."* The crowns of some will be taken. They did labour, they did have crowns. But they backslid

- from that standard of life,
- from that standard of service,
- from that standard of sacrifice,
- from that standard of suffering.

And the Lord lifted their crown and gave it to another person. Does it frighten you? In heaven, the overcomers shall be leading, even though they had spent all their lives in the place of death so that the others might get through to victory.

DAY FIVE

Before Jericho could fall, crossing the Jordan was already a supernatural act of God. It was not a conflict as such. Aggressiveness was not needed there. It was the spirit of willingness to stand in the position of death that was required from the overcomers. The battle for Jericho was the first major conflict of Joshua. But before that,

Joshua 5:14 "Now when Joshua was near Jericho, he looked up and saw a man standing in front of him with a drawn sword in his hand. Joshua went up to him and asked, "Are you for us or for our enemies?"

"Take sides," Joshua was saying.

Verse 14-15 "Neither," he replied, "but as commander of the army of the Lord I have now come." Then Joshua fell face down to the ground in reverence, and asked him, "What message does my Lord have for his servant?" The commander of the Lord's army replied, "Take off your sandals, for the place where you are standing is holy." And Joshua did so.

The impure cannot serve the holy God.

Service begins with radical holiness!

Service begins with holiness that is acceptable to God. It is the function of the sanctified, of the holy. Brethren, we want you to confront this:

Before God can use any man, the man has to be separated from all sin.

Until then, it is religious amusement. May we first get you to see it from Scriptures. God called Moses to serve Him,

Exodus 3:4-5 "When the Lord saw that he had gone over to look, God called to him from within the bush, 'Moses! Moses!' And Moses said, 'Here I am.' 'Do not come any closer,' God said. 'Take off your sandals, for the place where you are standing is holy ground.'"

"Take off your sandals, for (the place) where you are standing is holy ground." And now to Joshua, at the beginning of service:

Joshua 5:15b "Take off your sandals, for the place where you are standing is holy." Forty years had elapsed. A new leader is in the lead, and the conditions for serving God have not altered.

Only the holy can serve God.

Only those who are separated from all sin can serve God.

The rest are wasting their time. I don't want to leave it there. Look at

Isaiah 6:1-5 "In the year that King Uzziah died, I saw the Lord seated on a throne, high and exalted, and the train of his robe filled the temple. Above him were seraphs, each with six wings: With two wings they covered their faces, with two they covered their feet, and with two they were flying. And they were calling to one another: 'Holy, holy, holy is the LORD Almighty; the whole earth is full of his glory.' At the sound of their voices the doorposts and thresholds shook and the temple was filled with smoke. 'Woe to me!' I cried. 'I am ruined! For I am a man of unclean lips, and I live among a people of unclean lips, and my eyes have seen the King, the LORD Almighty.'"

"Woe to me!" Why? He confronted the holiness of God. And he encountered the God of all holiness.

People must confront the holiness of God and come into communion with the God of all holiness. People must contemplate the holiness of God, and encounter the God of all holiness. If not, big gifts, long prayer crusades, long fasts are just wood, hay and stubble. If there is sin in your life, sin in your heart or sin in your thoughts, all that you have done and all that you are doing for God is wood, hay and stubble. It is less than useless. And there are many people who have wasted their lives. Whether it is lying, or gluttony, or adultery in desire, or adultery in thought, or covetousness, or greed, or pride, or laziness, without encountering the holiness of God and encountering the God of all holiness, all that you have done and are doing is useless. Isaiah said, "Woe to me! I am ruined!" When did you ever say, "Woe to me for I am ruined"? Do you know that you are ruined? Justified but ruined. Not going to hell but ruined. "Holy, holy, holy is the LORD Almighty." "Woe to me for I am ruined!"

Exodus 28:36 "Make a plate of pure gold and engrave on it as on a seal: HOLY TO THE LORD."

Exodus 29:37b "Then the altar will be most holy,..." All that pertains to God in Scripture is His holiness; that cannot be negotiated. Because of a people confused about "eros" and holiness and real love, they have painted a God of love, a sentimentalist.

The first thing about God is His holiness.

"Holy, holy, holy...." He beheld the holiness of God, then he said, "I am ruined! Woe to me! I am ruined!" The problem is that many believers know nothing of the holiness of God. No wonder, they never say, "Woe to me!" They have never confronted the fact that they are ruined. They have never confronted the fact that they are men of unclean lips, unclean hearts, adulterous and idolatrous thoughts, with the world on their hearts. "Woe to me! I am ruined!" Why? Because of unclean lips, lips that lie, lips that exaggerate, lips that confess one thing and live another, insincere lips, lips that flatter, lips that exaggerate. "I am a man of unclean lips and I live among a people of unclean lips."

Isaiah 6:6-7 "Then one of the seraphs flew to me with a coal in his hand, which he had taken with tongs from the altar. With it he touched my mouth and said, "See, this has touched your lips; your guilt is taken away and your sin atoned for."

It is then, and only then,

Verse 8 "Then I heard the voice of the Lord saying, 'Whom shall I send? And who will go for us?' And I said, 'Here am I. Send me!'"

The one whose sin has been totally dealt away with could be sent. Others cannot be sent.

Revelation 4:8 "Each of the four living creatures had six wings and was covered with eyes all around, even under his wings.

Day and night they never stop saying: 'Holy, holy, holy is the Lord God Almighty, who was, and is, and is to come.'"

From heaven, the proclamation of the living creatures is: "Holy, holy, holy!" I want to ask you:

What do you know about the holiness of God in your own life?

What do you know about an encounter with the God of holiness, an encounter with the holiness of God?

Listen, if there is one sin in your heart, maybe a sin in desire, or a sin in thought, or a sin in look, or a sin in touch, or a sin in word, or a sin in act, and you have not confessed and forsaken it permanently, you are ruined and you cannot serve Him. I want to ask you:

Is there a testimony from heaven that says, "This man, this woman has forsaken all sin for evermore"? Is there a testimony that says, "This man, this woman has abandoned all sin for ever and is walking in that abandonment"?

If there is no such testimony, your service is a waste of time.

God cannot negotiate His holiness.

He cannot accept sacrificial services in exchange for corruption of heart, instead of a pure heart. Purity first, and then service.

Until there is purity, there is only a waste of time.

How is it like in your heart?

How is it like in your desire?

Can you afford to deceive yourself all your life, to suffer all the suffering that you are suffering in vain, because there is one thing in your heart or one thing in your life that tarnishes all and you will not let it go? Only you know. Only you know whether you desire something or someone that Jesus would not have desired. It may be occasional desire but you are ruined.

What is the testimony of the Holy Spirit?

What is the testimony of your own heart?

Can you say, "God, You know that there is no secret desire in my heart that I would not want written across the skies"? Can you go to the mission field and afford to waste your life like that? There is financial corruption; things are not straight; your figures are twisted; there is no truth in financial matters!

When a man has separated himself from all sin for all time he may begin to serve God.

Until then, he is deceived and he is wasting his time. For Moses, he encountered the inescapable holiness of God. For Joshua, it was the same thing. For Isaiah, it was the same thing.

Who deceived you that with an impure heart you could go into the service of God?

You are not accepted. You have disqualified yourself. You can come to God, expose your sin, hate it, abandon it, and separate yourself from it for ever.

Are your hands clean for the Work?

Is your heart pure for the Work?

If not, you are the greatest idiot who ever lived, because all that you are suffering to do is a waste of time. God is not mocked.

What is the testimony of the Holy Spirit? Does it say, "Free from all sin"?

That there are no thoughts that leave much to be desired?

That there are no thoughts that contradict the Cross?

That there are no desires that are foreign to the heart of God?

After the holiness of God has been encountered, a man may go and serve God.

Until then, he is wasting his time. Joshua was appointed but he had to face the holiness of God.

Sin is confessed, one after the other, in total detail and then forsaken before it can be forgiven.

All the other things are wicked noises that harden the heart. To mention sin and to confess sin are two different things. Listen,

There can be no confession of sin before it is hated, because no one can forsake sin until he hates it.

And

In real confession, no one can confess sin and still keep it because hatred of sin precedes confession of sin.

You hate sin.

You confess it.

You forsake it.

No one can keep a sin after he has confessed it. But a man can keep sin after he has announced it. The missionaries awaiting their send-off, unless you can say to God that there is no falsehood anywhere in your life, don't appear for the send-off, because you will be appearing for total judgment.

And the Elders coming for ordination, unless they can say to the Holy Spirit, "There is no falsehood in my life," it will be consecration unto judgment.

Tell those people who will want to be ordained someday, if all falsehood has not been parted with, it will be ordination to the wrath of God.

And if there is any falsehood in your own life, you are a ruined man and God's fiercest enemy!

Any missionary practising sin in any form whatsoever will be removed from the mission field; and God may act by very drastic methods. To sit in a foreign country with a heart made impure even by one sin is to hinder God completely. There is a choice to make. Put God to the test and see.

Any head of department who keeps even one sin in his life will face the full wrath of God. God's Name has been dragged into mud for too long. If the holiness of God could not be bypassed by Moses, if the holiness of God could not be bypassed by Joshua, if God would not allow Moses to move on before he had terminated for ever with sin, if God would not allow Moses to begin to serve Him before he had confronted the purity of God and the God of all purity, listen, Brethren, you are deceived to think that justification is enough:

In Joshua 5:9. There was circumcision. It was like a reaffirmation of justification. "Then the Lord said to Joshua, 'Today I have rolled away the reproach of Egypt from you.'"

They had just faced justification afresh, but it was not enough. Joshua had to confront sanctification, the holiness of God. Only after that could he go on to God's battles.

Only the sanctified can go into God's battles.

If the unsanctified go into God's battles, they go unto total judgment. The reproach of Egypt was rolled away, but the holiness of God had to be encountered. Because the God of holiness had to come and lead Moses, and because God, the God of holiness had to lead Joshua, they had to be holy in order that they could move in the companionship of the God of holiness.

Now, that is the message God has for each leader.

Joshua 5:14c-15. "What message does my Lord have for His servant...? 'Take off your sandals, for the place where you are standing is holy.' And Joshua did so."

He separated himself unto the holiness of God and separated himself unto the God of all holiness. He could testify, "God, You know it is all holiness within." Isaiah could say, "God, You know this touched my lips and my iniquity has been purged. God, I can now go into service."

To go into another country, to lead a department with sin in the heart, is the most terrible thing that anyone can do for himself! And I want to beg you, don't do it. What will happen after that is too horrible to put into words, because God must have a spotless Bride. And "When the best bucks are changing ground...." Woe unto you if you are in the way. You will not live to tell the story. The bits of you will not be found. And at this new beginning in the work, if you offer to obstruct God, you will see.

To plan God's work,

to teach the Word,

to preach,

to pray,

to fast,

to give,

to read the Bible,

to meditate,

to counsel,

to write a book or a tract

with one sin in the heart is to practise witchcraft.

No one can confess sin before he has hated it.

No one can keep a sin after he has confessed it, because the confession and abandonment of sin are inseparable.

Forty-day fasts,

forty-day prayer crusades,

bleeding gifts,

extreme hard work,

plus one sin that is known but not confessed and forsaken, is a sheer waste of time. All it is, is wood, hay and stubble.

A life with a sin known but not confessed and radically forsaken, is wasted, regardless of what seems to have been accomplished.

Is yours a wasted life? Will you continue to waste it? Only you can answer that.

Do you know what, Brethren? When people have sin in their hearts and they do not forsake the sin, if they pray for you, they are actually practising sorcery against you because their prayers become acts of sorcery.

If you send your prayer topics to someone who has a sin in his life, which he knows about but he has not abandoned it, the more he prays for you, the more you are destroyed; because since all that he does is sorcery, you are the object of his sorcery. If somebody asks you for your prayer topics, ask him, "Have you separated yourself from all sin?" But you cannot ask him that unless you yourself have separated yourself from all sin. If you have, and may you, you ought to.

If he hasn't, don't give him your prayer topics. You will not still be the same after he has uttered some words of prayer for you.

Immediately after that, the Bible says, "And Joshua did so." He entered into the holiness of God.

Joshua 6:1 "Now Jericho was tightly shut up because of the Israelites. No one went out and no one came in."

If someone brings a gift to you, ask him, "Have you separated yourself from all sin?" If the answer is: "No," give him back his gift because you will be contaminated. You will begin to share his sin. You will begin to be tempted towards his sin.

Listen, Brethren, the strategy must come from God; God cannot call you to His task and you create your way of serving Him.

Joshua 6:2

> *"Then the Lord said to Joshua, "See, I have delivered Jericho into your hands, along with its king and its fighting men."*

God gave the instructions:

Verse 3

> *"March around the city once with all the armed men. Do this for six days."*

With all the armed men! Do this for six days.

It was sustained.

Joshua 6:4-5

> *"Have seven priests carry trumpets of rams' horns in front of the ark. On the seventh day, march around the city seven times, with the priests blowing the trumpets. When you hear them sound a long blast on the trumpets, have all the people give a loud shout; then the wall of the city will collapse and the people will go up, every man straight in."*

The detailed instructions were from God. When you sit and plan your thing and set out to execute it and ask God to come and bless it, are you not deceived? The goal must be from God; the method from God; and the price to be paid from God.

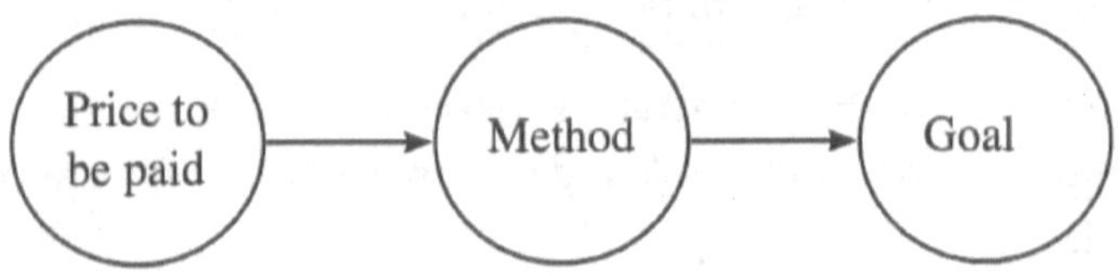

The goal must come from God, as well as the method, and also the price to be paid.

The goal must come from God.

The method must come from God.

And the price to be paid must come from God.

I say, Brother, when you decided on those 40-day fasts or 40-day prayer crusades, or was it 21, who asked you? Who asked them of you? Who set that as the price—God or you?

It is extreme arrogance to set your own goal, set your own method, set your own price to be paid and then you call it a work of God.

Was the overthrow of Jericho Joshua's initiative? No.

Was the way to win Joshua's making? No.

Was the price to be paid Joshua's initiative? No.

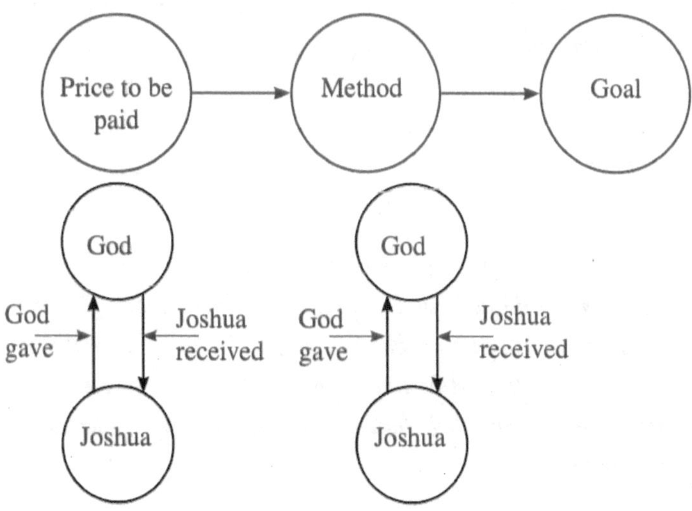

The goal was from above. God revealed it and it was received. God gave, Joshua received. The method: God gave, Joshua received. The price to be paid: God gave it, Joshua received it and paid it.

May the Holy Spirit convict you about what we are saying now! May He convict you! There is a difference between convincing and convicting.

Listen, when leaders have sat and set their own goals, and set their own methods, and set their own prices, and they want God to come and stamp them, they are fortunate that the Holy Spirit has not scattered the whole thing and scattered the people, because they are constructing a modern Tower of Babel.

<u>Genesis 11:1-9</u>

"Now the whole world had one language and a common speech. As men moved eastward, they found a plain in Shinar and settled there. They said to each other, 'Come, let's make bricks and bake them thoroughly.' They used brick instead of stone, and tar for mortar. Then they said, 'Come, let us build ourselves a city, with a tower that reaches to the heavens, so that we may make a name for ourselves and not be scattered over the face of the whole earth.'

But the Lord came down to see the city and the tower that the men were building. The Lord said, 'If as one people speaking the same language they have begun to do this, then nothing they plan to do will be impossible for them. Come, let us go down and confuse their language so they will not understand each other.'

So the Lord scattered them from there over all the earth, and they stopped building the city. That is why it was called Babel - because there the Lord confused the language of the whole world. From there the Lord scattered them over the face of the whole earth."

Come, let us do this! They had a goal, they had methods, and a price to pay. And God was outside. God came in as a visitor! And He scattered it!!! The visitor God! I see people who have those placards saying, "God is the Unseen Guest,..." Yes, He is a guest. He doesn't dwell there. He comes when people want. After that, they send Him away. "The Silent Listener...." When He comes on invitation, He must be silent until He is invited to speak. The third thing they say is He is present at every meal. So that they may eat and not die.

I remember when I just returned home, I was invited by the Prime Minister. He was the Minister of the Public Service then. He said, "Doctor, they say you are a pastor. Pray that we may eat and not grow fat." How do you pray that people should eat and not grow fat?

Is your Ministry a modern Tower of Babel? The goal is set by you, the method by you, the price to be paid by you. And you want God to stamp it and come occasionally to bless it, to bless what you have created and what you are working on. Listen, Brethren, there are very many modern Towers of Babel.

When did God give you that goal?

When did He give you that method?

When did He give you the price to pay?

Brethren, I am asking a serious question.

Who is the author of the goal; is it God or yourself?

Who is the author of the method; is it God or you?

Who is the author of the price to be paid; is it God or you?

When did God give you that goal?

When did He give you that method for its accomplishment?

And when did He dictate that price to be paid?

"Nous avons planifié." = "We have planned." When the goal is already self-created, all else is a wreck. That is what the serpent told Adam and Eve: "You will be like God." And you are acting like the serpent said, creating your own goals, your own methods, setting your own price and, therefore, producing your own results.

How many people have read, "The Way Of Christian Service"? If you have read it less than five times, I consider that you have not read it because without two, three, four times of reading a book, you will not come to grips with it. If I were to have written only one book, that is the book I would have written. It is the first message God gave me and everything is tied around it. The other 73 books are only an expansion of that one.

We presuppose that people are listening to what God is saying and that they are thinking the message through. Until people are hungry, you can't feed them. You can give them food. They will touch it and leave it.

Have you seen these cats that live in the houses of the wealthy? Do they catch rats? No. They eat delicacies. In fact, in the U.S. it was found that what the Americans spend on cats' and dogs' food is more than what they give to foreign missions in all the denominations. They have food for cats to slim. They have slimming food for dogs. Two years ago, I met a sister I had first met with her husband four years before. The husband is a Captain in the Navy. They were very fond of me. And God reached out to them through me and ministered very deeply to them. Two years ago, immediately I arrived, the woman came to the house. When my hostess in Boston talked about the problem she was having with her child since she began to work, this woman said, "I'm having the same problem with the dog." I asked her how much she spent on the dog. It came to $40.00 a month, i.e. 20,000 CFA francs for its food. I told her that the blood of men was on her because of this wastage. I told her to go and kill the dog and give the money to the Gospel. From that day, she never saw me again. And this time, even though they knew I was coming, they didn't appear.

God reveals the goal that He wants accomplished!

Man receives the goal of God and commits himself to it, saying, "Woe to me if this is not accomplished!" When you establish your own goal and you don't accomplish it, nothing has gone wrong. You just establish another one and keep going. But if God has given you His goal, not to accomplish it is the worst thing that has happened on Planet Earth.

Is it God's goal or is it man's goal?

If it is God's goal, then you know that if you don't accomplish it, you are a wreck! You are disqualified! Another will take your place. But if it is your goal, there is no consequence, whether the goal is accomplished or not.

Is it God's goal for you?

Is it God's goal for that project?

Is it God's goal to be accomplished in that unit of time?

What if it is not accomplished?

God reveals the goal that He wants accomplished!

The Director of the Magazine ought to ask God:

- When do You want the first newsletter out?
- How many pages should it be?
- What articles should it contain?
- Who should write the articles?
- What should the cover be like?
- Who should design it?

These are the basic questions which when a man acts without hearing God about, he is carrying out witchcraft! It is a Tower of Babel. I beg you, get "The Way Of Christian Service" and read it 10 times and never forget its message.

Who is the author?

Elders, if they say, "Come and bless a marriage," and you just run there and put your hands, and lift up your voices and talk. Who is the author of the marriage? After that, you say: "No divorce." After that you say, "What God has put together, let no man put asunder." When did God tell you that He has put it together? Should the Elders not ask, "Who has put these people together?" If not, you get there and say, "These people, who have put themselves together, have told me that I should recognise that they have put themselves together. I declare here that they have put themselves together, and that the public accepts what they have done for themselves ." If you say that, you have sanctified God's Name. Brethren, is that not honesty? Any way, there was room for blessing Ishmael because Abraham interceded.

I know God wants us to send 18 missionary couples out next year. If we don't send them, we have failed God. I was asking that question to God for three weeks. I lay on the floor for hours, waiting on God. If I were to create the figure, I would not have been that "mad." I now know, "Woe to me if 18 missionary couples do not leave for the mission field next year!"

Where will they come from?

When will they be trained?

Where shall we have the monies from?

The only thing I know is that God wants it. This year He asked for 12. By the end of the month there will be 9. If by the end of the year another 3 go, we shall have freed ourselves from failure and from His anger.

I asked God how many nations were to be represented here. He told me 10. When the Gabonese delegation could not come, I said, "I'm done for." But in His love, by bringing the delegation from Paris which I didn't foresee, the 10 nations are here.

And when you begin to face God's will approximately, it is a most dangerous matter. Now I want to say it to you, Brethren, that the primary function of leadership is: To seek, to know and to declare God's will so that it may be executed.

The primary function of leadership is to seek, to know and to declare God's will.

That is why the leader is primarily a man who lives in God's presence. He is, first of all, not an activist. He must have another leader who is the executor. He receives the vision, imparts it and another leader executes it. He is the seeing leader and there is an acting or executing leader. The lack of this combination will cause failure. God must reveal what He wants accomplished, and man must receive the goal from God! It is not your goal. It is the goal of God - the goal of

God for your life. And man commits himself to it, saying, "Woe to me, if this is not accomplished!"

God reveals the method to be used to accomplish His goal. Man receives the divine method and makes it his only method, thus ensuring that all man-made methods are excluded.

Man receives the divine method and makes it his only method, or his only methods, thus ensuring that all man-made methods are excluded.

About the price, God reveals the price to be paid and man receives and submits absolutely and finally to God's revelation about the price, not adding nor subtracting anything. So it is not what he can do or what he wants done. It is what God wants.

About the conquest of Jericho, what God said was followed and none of it was illogical to man. It was the divine method and the divine price, and it happened, as it was followed scrupulously. The walls of Jericho fell and the city was taken. The last day they were to go around the city seven times. Man would have asked, "Why seven times?" "Why blast this trumpet?" "Why this order? "Why go like this?" That is why these thinkers' and analysers' failure is guaranteed. And God said, "Take the whole army for that going around the place." It was God's method.

Isaiah 55:8 "For my thoughts are not your thoughts, neither are your ways my ways," declares the Lord.

Yes, the thoughts and the ways of man should be abandoned.

Verse 7 "Let the wicked forsake his way and the evil man his thoughts. Let him turn to the Lord, and he will have mercy on him, and to our God, for he will freely pardon. 'For my thoughts are not your thoughts, neither are your ways my ways,' declares the Lord."

<u>Verse 9</u> "As the heavens are higher than the earth, so are my ways higher than your ways and my thoughts than your thoughts."

"Let the wicked forsake his way" - his ways! Oh there are too many of our ways! "And the evil man his thoughts" - his own thoughts: "I think!" "I thought!" The best thoughts of man are earthly, all God's thoughts are heavenly. To surrender God's thoughts or God's methods for man's thoughts or man's methods is tragic.

Is that why you are not making any progress? You are using the thoughts of man, the methods of man, the ideas of man, and you have put aside God's thoughts and methods.

Are you operating with God's methods or with yours?

<u>Jeremiah 2:13</u> "My people have committed two sins: They have forsaken me, the spring of living water."

That is the first sin. The second sin:

"and have dug their own cisterns, broken cisterns that cannot hold water."

God is saying, "My people have committed two evils. They have forsaken My goal for them, and they have created their own goal that will take them nowhere. My people have forsaken My own methods for the Work, and they have created their own methods. Their methods are broken cisterns that can hold no water, that can take them nowhere. My people have committed two evils. They have forsaken the price I want them to pay and they have committed a second sin. They have set up their own price that will take them nowhere."

So the first sin is forsaking God's own. If a man forsook God's own and didn't put away everything, it would not be horrible. But they went further, they hewed cisterns for themselves, broken cisterns that can hold no water. A lazy man is not as wicked as the man who leaves God's way and makes his own goals, makes his own methods, and accomplishes his own thoughts. If God told me to go and build a house on a certain plot and I didn't go, the plot would remain for the obedient person to go. But if on my own I go and build my own thing there, God will have to break it down and carry the debris away, before they start to build. That would be double work.

- Whose goal?
- Whose method?
- Whose price to be paid?

Joshua 6:15 "On the seventh day, they got up at daybreak and marched around the city seven times in the same manner, except that on that day they circled the city seven times."

On that day they circled the city seven times.

Verse 16-20 "The seventh time around, when the priests sounded the trumpet blast, Joshua commanded the people, 'Shout! For the Lord has given you the city! The city and all that is in it are to be devoted to the Lord. Only Rahab the prostitute and all who are with her in her house shall be spared, because she hid the spies we sent. But keep away from the devoted things, so that you will not bring about your own destruction by taking any of them. Otherwise you will make the camp of Israel liable to destruction and bring trouble on it. All the silver and gold and the articles of bronze and iron are sacred to the Lord and must go into his treasury.' When the trumpets sounded, the people shouted, and at the sound of the trumpet, when the people gave a loud shout, the wall collapsed; so every man charged straight in, and they took the city."

Hallelujah! Aggressiveness! Every man charged straight in and took the city. Every man charged straight in! Are you a charger? Every man charged in. Going round, it was just soft, and simple, but it was soldiers. Then they shouted, the city collapsed, and they charged in aggressively - everybody, all of them. There were no spectators! And they took the city. They said the gold, the silver, the bronze, and all those things were to be devoted to the Lord for the treasury. All of them heard.

Chapter 7 As Jericho collapsed, the fame of Joshua spread. It is wonderful when God backs a leader. It is normal that God backs a leader. I want to ask you as a husband, "Does God back you so that if your wife goes against your instructions, she will soon come repenting because God has backed you? Or are you such that when she follows you she has be sorry for it because it was all wrong?"

Does God back your leadership?

I am not asking whether your leadership is perfect. I am asking whether God backs your leadership. When people disobey you, do they realise afterward that God was with you and they were mistaken and they repent? Do people spontaneously know that not to obey you, the chances are high that God will not take their side?

Testimony - (Brother Theodore) Five years ago, I shared with Brother Zach that I was going to buy a piece of farmland in a village called Onguesse. After some days, he just told me that he didn't feel free about it. We had already made some deposit; so we stopped it. Later on, I discovered that the man who sold us the land had a son who was mad. My disciples in the village had gone and planted about 1300 fruit trees, plantains, etc. on it. The mad son went and told my disciple that if he saw him on that land which we had bought, he would cut off his head; that if that my disciple passed in the land we had bought, he would cut off his head. So we left him the plantains, he harvested all of them and I just thank God for saving us from the hands of a mad person. Of course, Brother didn't have the facts. He just felt uneasy. But we would have landed with about 16 hectares with a head-cutting land-owner.

Brother Joseph Gado: I too have something to say concerning logic. It is two matters. While we were building the hall at Obili in Yaounde, since I was in the committee, it was inaugurated and Brother Zach had announced that the next Monday was the last time we would be meeting in Etoug Ebe for the All-night prayer meeting. Everybody was therefore happy that the meeting was going to Obili. But there was a little incident during that prayer night and he just cancelled the project. And I was among those who within asked why he just spoiled everything that way. But the truth is that that same week, the wall collapsed from the back, such that the reason was not the same, but in every case, things just happened as he had said: The meeting did not move there. I just thanked God that He stopped us from going there because we worked on evacuating the debris of this wall for at least two to three weeks.

The other thing is recent. On our way here, the car in which I was, gave us a lot of trouble, such that the indicator for oil was always on the red; and I panicked, and said we must stop and go add some more oil so that the engine does not knock. We went past Edea. Brother Emmanuel said, "I do not at all feel that we should go back." I said in my heart, "Oh dear! This one, we should leave the matter of God aside. Mechanics is mechanics." Later on, he worsened things by saying, "If that is the case, let us just stop and park the car completely." I said, "But how? Instead of going a few more kilometres to spoil it, we are better off if we do the 2 kilometres back to Edea." Emmanuel stood his ground. I told myself, "Well, after all he is the leader. It doesn't matter." I stopped the fight and decided to yield to the leader. The truth is that we got to Douala with no incident. For me, when we took off and that light stayed continuously on the red, I told myself it could happen any time. But when we approached Douala and nothing happened, I said, "So much the better."

Brother Zach: Praise the Lord!

The Lord said that the silver, the gold, the articles of bronze, and the iron were sacred to the Lord and must go into the treasury. Oh Brethren, one thing, we must bear in mind is that,

When God has spoken, there is a finality about it. To come back to ask Him, that is when the voice of God becomes hazy and faint and the sharp edges are gone. Balaam came and asked God, "Should I go with these people?" God said, "No." Afterwards, he came again to ask. He was just saying, "God, let me go." And God said, "Go."

You know that the things about which you are struggling to know God's will, God had spoken before. You know what God said from the beginning. You know it. When instead of obeying, you raise it up again, you are saying, "Lord, I don't want Your will. Allow me in Your permissive will." And He will let you.

I know what God said to me the first time. Even if I loiter from it, I know I will come back to it because my heart can settle nowhere else. And later on when He says, "Go ahead," I still know that is not His perfect will and I don't accept it.

Nobody can, after he has heard God's voice, not know that he has heard it.

Mrs K. wanted me to go to Douala with her children. Immediately she said it, I was disturbed in my spirit. I felt angry. I had not even sorted then how I was going to travel to Douala, because up to that moment I was alone. In fact, I ought to have just told her, "No." The next day, when it was settled that we would bring the bus because we were to bring Jerome's bike, even when she came with the children, I was not offended but I just didn't like it. I told her to take her last son and go back because going to visit the unbelieving uncles was the way to get this young boy to be introduced to sin. But there was her second daughter; I said "She can stay, I will go with her." With increasing time, I was more and more disturbed. Finally, I gave her 4,000 CFA francs and said, "Go and see your mother and go to Douala on your own." Finally, when we were going, we found that there would have been no space for those people even if they had stayed. But I had to repent because the day before, I should have said, "No, my spirit says No."

We know. We walk close to God. We know. There is no mystery about God's will. There is no strain about knowing it. We know what God first said. If our fears and our unwillingness to obey cloud issues, we still know. Most of the time when people come to ask me, they know! The Lord has not left us without a witness. There is the witness of the Spirit of God.

Joshua 7:1 "But the Israelites acted unfaithfully in regard to the devoted things; Achan son of Carmi, the son of Zimri, the son of Zerah, of the tribe of Judah, took some of them."

The son of ...! Maybe the father was a thief who was not caught. So the Lord's anger burned against Israel.

<u>Verses 2-4a</u> "Now Joshua sent men from Jericho to Ai, which is near Beth Aven to the east of Bethel, and told them, 'Go up and spy out the region.' So the men went up and spied out Ai. When they returned to Joshua, they said, 'Not all the people will have to go up against Ai. Send two or three thousand men to take it and do not weary all the people, for only a few men are there.' So about three thousand men went up."

Did they ask God? They didn't. About Jericho God said, "Take the whole army."

In spiritual warfare it is not one to one in battle so that you ask how many of the enemy are there and then you decide how many to send. It is determined by what God says, and they were violating it here. Joshua did not say, "God, I hear there are few people; what should I do?" They chose their numbers: about three thousand. The presumptions of man! The calculations of man!

<u>Chapter 7:4-6a</u> "So about three thousand men went up; but they were routed by the men of Ai, who killed about thirty-six of them. They chased the Israelites from the city gate as far as the stone quarries and struck them down on the slopes. At this the hearts of the people melted and became like water. Then Joshua tore his clothes and fell facedown to the ground before the ark of the Lord, remaining there till evening."

He was now seeking God, whereas he should have done that before.

<u>Verses 6b-9</u> "The elders of Israel did the same, and sprinkled dust on their heads. And Joshua said, 'Ah, Sovereign Lord, why did you ever bring this people across the Jordan to deliver us into the hands of the Amorites to destroy us? If only we had been content to stay on the other side of the Jordan! O Lord, what can I say, now that Israel has been

routed by its enemies? The Canaanites and the other people of the country will hear about this and they will surround us and wipe out our name from the earth. What then will you do for your own great name?'"

<u>Verses 10-11a</u> "The Lord said to Joshua, 'Stand up! What are you doing down on your face? Israel has sinned.'"

Achan sinned = Israel has sinned.

<u>Verses 11b-12</u> "They have violated my covenant, which I commanded them to keep. They have taken some of the devoted things; they have stolen, they have lied, they have put them with their own possessions. That is why the Israelites cannot stand against their enemies; they turn their backs and run because they have been made liable to destruction. I will not be with you any more unless you destroy whatever among you is devoted to destruction."

Listen, God said, "I will not be with you any more unless you destroy whatever among you is devoted to destruction." But we think that God can come along when there has been no repentance and a destruction of that which is meant for destruction. How deceived we are!

<u>Verse 13</u> "Go, consecrate the people. Tell them, 'Consecrate yourselves in preparation for tomorrow; for this is what the Lord, the God of Israel, says: That which is devoted is among you, O Israel. You cannot stand against your enemies until you remove it. '"

"You cannot stand against your enemies until you remove it." God cannot close His eyes. He cannot jump over things. But you can deceive yourself and lose many years. Is that what you are doing? You think that with a lot of time God will forget. God does not forget, He cannot forget.

Verse 14 "In the morning, present yourselves tribe by tribe. The tribe that the Lord takes shall come forward clan by clan; the clan that the Lord takes shall come forward family by family; and the family that the Lord takes shall come forward man by man."

Now God has taken over again; He is giving instructions. 'In the morning, present yourselves tribe by tribe.' And He went on:

Verses 15-21 "He who is caught with the devoted things shall be destroyed by fire, along with all that belongs to him. He has violated the covenant of the Lord and has done a disgraceful thing in Israel!" Early the next morning Joshua had Israel come forward by tribes, and Judah was taken. The clans of Judah came forward, and he took the Zerahites. He had the clan of the Zerahites come forward by families, and Zimri was taken. Joshua had his family come forward man by man, and Achan son of Carmi, the son of Zimri, the son of Zerah, of the tribe of Judah, was taken.

Then Joshua said to Achan, "My son, give glory to the Lord, the God of Israel, and give him the praise. Tell me what you have done; do not hide it from me."

Achan replied, "It is true! I have sinned against the Lord, the God of Israel. This is what I have done: When I saw in the plunder a beautiful robe from Babylonia, two hundred shekels of silver and a wedge of gold weighing fifty shekels, I coveted them and took them. They are hidden in the ground inside my tent, with the silver underneath."

"I saw, I coveted, took, I hid." Is that you? You saw! You coveted! It is in your heart - that shirt, that pair of trousers, that pair of shoes, that car, that house, those chairs. "I saw, I coveted, I took and I hid."

Verses 22-25. "So Joshua sent messengers, and they ran to the tent, and there it was, hidden in his tent, with the silver underneath. They took the things from the tent, brought them to Joshua and all the Israelites and spread them out before the Lord. Then Joshua, together with all Israel, took Achan son of Zerah, the silver, the robe, the gold wedge, his sons and daughters, his cattle, donkeys and sheep, his tent and all that he had, to the Valley of Achor. Joshua said, 'Why have you brought this trouble on us? The Lord will bring trouble on you today.'

Then all Israel stoned him, and after they had stoned the rest, they burned them."

What are you doing to your family?

What are you doing to your children?

There is no substitute for radical dealing with sin.

How long have you been hiding what you saw, coveted and took? The punishment included Achan's whole family.

Do you know the fear of God?

Achan thought that he could somehow sneak away. The whole camp was blocked. All the more than two million people were blocked. Because there were six hundred thousand men, so normally there were six hundred thousand women. So the adults were 1.2 million. If there were two children per family, the total was 2.4 million. Two million people were blocked because of one man. Listen, the logic is this: that a son will continue to commit the sins of the father. That is why the whole family was wiped off. Do you know? They don't mention his wife because a wife does not necessarily continue to commit the sins of the husband. Her genes are different. But the children carry the genes of the father and obviously those of the mother; but since he was the thief, to allow his children to continue, would have been to allow potential thieves to continue. So God settled the matter, God eliminated them.

We look at sin too lightly.

We have very superficial answers.

That is God acting.

<u>Chapter 8 Verse 1a</u> "Then the Lord said to Joshua, 'Do not be afraid; do not be discouraged.'" That was God's own verdict.

<u>Verses 1b-2a</u> "Take the whole army with you, and go up and attack Ai. For I have delivered into your hands the king of Ai, his people, his city and his land. You shall do to Ai and its king as you did to Jericho and its king, except that you may carry off their plunder and livestock for yourselves."

For Jericho it was total destruction, or total devotion to God. For Ai, the instructions were different. They were to keep the plunder and they were to set an ambush. Now, do you see the need to go to God for each battle and not just to ask, "How was it done in the past?"

God has fresh instructions for each battle.

So no one can just work on the basis of the yesterdays and make it. "You may carry off their plunder and livestock for yourselves." This time they were not to march around the city blowing horns. It was to be a total attack by ambush, even though it was a small city.

God's evaluation is not man's.

God's methods are not man's.

May all fear and walk before God!

Verse 3 "So Joshua and the whole army moved out to attack Ai. He chose thirty thousand of his best fighting men and sent them out at night."

It was a full-scale war. This man said three thousand but just at night he already sent thirty thousand.

Verses 4-5a The orders were: "Listen carefully." The problem with many people is that they don't listen. "Listen carefully. You are to set an ambush behind the city. Don't go very far from it. All of you be on the alert. I and all those with me will advance on the city."

Thirty thousand went just for the ambush. And all of the rest of the army was with Joshua.

Verses 5-7a "I and all those with me will advance on the city, and when the men come out against us, as they did before, we will flee from them. They will pursue us until we have lured them away from the city, for they will say, 'They are running away from us as they did before.' So when we flee from them, you are to rise up from ambush and take the city."

"...and take the city." Before, it was different methods. But now, it is "...take the city." Now there are other methods.

Verses 7b-8 "The Lord your God will give it into your hand. When you have taken the city, set it on fire. Do what the Lord has commanded. See to it; you have my orders."

Leadership is to provide orders.

The thing is that some wicked men want suggestions. Leadership is to release orders. How do you act when orders are given? Do you say, "Let's sit down and discuss"? "These are my orders."

They were God's orders but they were also the leader's orders.

Verse 9a "Then Joshua sent them off, and they went to the place of ambush and lay in wait between Bethel and Ai, to the west of Ai."

Do you remember Abraham between Bethel and Ai? He first pitched his tent between Bethel and Ai and built an altar. They were back there after 430 years. The iniquity of the Amorites had reached its fullest. God was now justified to eliminate them.

Verses 10-13a "Early the next morning Joshua mustered his men, and he and the leaders of Israel marched before them to Ai. The entire force that was with him marched up and approached the city and arrived in front of it. They set up camp north of Ai, with the valley between them and the city. Joshua had taken about five thousand men and set them in ambush between Bethel and Ai, to the west of the city. They had the soldiers take up their positions - all those in the camp to the north of the city and the ambush to the west of it."

So putting them all together, it was 35,000.

Verses 14-18 "When the king of Ai saw this, he and all the men of the city hurried out early in the morning to meet Israel in battle at a certain place overlooking the Arabah. But he did not know that an ambush had been set against him behind the city. Joshua and all Israel let themselves be driven back before them, and they fled toward the desert. All the men of Ai were called to pursue them, and they pursued Joshua and were lured away from the city. Not a man remained in Ai or Bethel who did not go after Israel. They left the city open and went in pursuit of Israel.

Then the Lord said to Joshua, 'Hold out toward Ai the javelin that is in your hand, for into your hand I will deliver the city.' So Joshua held out his javelin toward Ai."

Oh, the javelin of Joshua was held towards Ai! What is that? Prayer. Who is in prayer? The leader. Those corrupt people who say, "I have hired people to pray for me." It is like hiring somebody to worship an idol. Somebody who also preaches told me, "I have hired somebody to pray for me," so that I can have results. The Moslems do it all the time. The big person doesn't have to pray. He hires a Mallam to pray for him and pays him a lot of money. There is one in my office who does that. So, the five times of prayer a day are covered by the man who prays. He will do the special prayers but hires that one for protection, success, or when he sins. Is indulgence not part of those sins?

<u>Verses 18b-19a</u> "So Joshua held out his javelin toward Ai. As soon as he did this, the men in the ambush rose quickly from their position and rushed forward." In the first battle, as soon as they shouted and prayed - the walls collapsed. As soon as the javelin was up, the men in ambush rose quickly and rushed forward.

<u>Verses 19b-20</u> "They entered the city and captured it and quickly set it on fire. The men of Ai looked back and saw the smoke of the city rising against the sky, but they had no chance to escape in any direction, for the Israelites who had been fleeing toward the desert had turned back against their pursuers."

<u>Verses 24-26</u> "When Israel had finished killing all the men of Ai in the fields and in the desert where they had chased them, and when every one of them had been put to the sword, all the Israelites returned to Ai and killed those who were in it. Twelve thousand men and women fell that day - all the people of Ai."

So the estimate that just said two, three thousand was totally off!

<u>Verses 25-26</u> "Twelve thousand men and women fell that day - all the people of Ai. For Joshua did not draw back the hand that held out his javelin until he had destroyed all who lived in Ai."

He remained in the position of prayer until all of the enemy was smashed. Be strong and very courageous. If it had been a weakling given a javelin....! He did not put it down to go and urinate. Some people are always urinating. He did not put it down to go to toilet. He didn't put it down to scratch himself. As long as the javelin pointed towards Ai, victory was established. So the battle was won by the prayer of the leader.

After that, Joshua built an altar to the Lord.

Aggressiveness is filing the whole army into the conflict.

Aggressiveness is filing the whole army.

It is total consecration.

It is the investment of a man's all.

That is part of the lesson from the battle of Ai.

We were asking ourselves, "Can believers stand two such Courses in a year? You know, when I spoke in France, they said it would take two years for them to digest it. I went there again after two years. Then they said it would take four years. Then they said they would have some speakers in the interim who don't tax people - so that after the convention they have nothing to work on. The question was not just the sharpness. I remember the Elder's wife was just weeping and saying, "C'est trop!" = "It is too much." And we were not giving them this type of thing. We were just laying the foundation. How could we get to such deep things? But it was a foundation, and when you are laying a foundation, you have to chip the stones. It is not these foundations laid with cement blocks. You know, in the village they had to shape stones and build foundations. And those houses are solid. So the bricklayer was, first of all, the stone-shaper. And we want to tell the missionaries, "First of all, be stone-shapers." It may take some time for it to stabilise the Assembly. Don't worry; it will stabilise. But don't comfort yourself with some false peace.

After we had been going on in Yaounde for about eight months, I went to Ibadan for research, for two months. When I came back, at the All-night, everybody was just sleeping. Then after two and a half years, when I went to Germany, by then Brother M.A. was put in charge of the Work. By the time I came back, there were very many conflicts because the leadership had not emerged, and also because the leader was not a shepherd. Even a young shepherd knows how to keep the flock together. In fact, for the two and a half weeks that we left the Church with Joe in 1978 and went for the Bamenda Crusade, when we came back, things were holding together, even though he was just six months old in the Lord.

You cannot skip over spiritual gifts.

A young cock is a cock. An old hen is not a small cock. And this is where we really just have to be honest.

Are we deceived about what we are?

If an evangelist believes with his whole heart that he is a pastor and works very hard; will it make him a pastor?

Before I went to bed this morning, I was rethinking what we were saying about people selling books and not reading them. Then I said to myself, "To what extent can people be forced to read books? To what extent can you force a man to read the Bible?" You can't force anybody.

- **The reading of books, a spontaneous reading of books, is the characteristic of all Bible teachers.**

- **And the many times reading of the Bible is a characteristic of all Bible teachers.**

You know Watchman Nee who read the New Testament one time every month and would read it late into the night. Even when he was visiting brethren late at night, he would be carrying the Bible because he had not finished what he had to read for that day. And Watchman Nee was so desirous to read books by others. Miss Barber was the one building him up. He went to Miss Barber and asked for three books. The three books were beyond his level; so she refused to get them for him. He went through somebody else and got the books and had to repent afterwards.

When a man is not interested in books he is no Bible teacher.

He can stand in that office but he is no Bible teacher. He does not hunger for the Word. It is something that is second nature.

I shared with you the fact that before I left the primary school, I had read the Bible twice. I took my father's Bible and I was underlining in my Bible all that he had underlined in his. It was a Bible that he had long stopped using. I didn't know why he was underlining but I said, "There must be some reason why he underlined this, so I will underline it in my own Bible." At 1.00 or 2.00 a.m., I would still be reading. The year I consecrated my life to the Lord at university, I read fifty books. And I bought very many books. When I had to go back home, the problem was books – how to carry them. And when you get to Etoug Ebe, you see there are books there; even though three boxes of books were burnt when my father's house was burnt. It is an effortless affair. There is a hunger for what the other people have written, because you know that you are only part of (let me call it) a tradition that has been going on for years.

I told you about John Wesley. He was one of the top Bible teachers of all time, fabulously interested in books. Either he was reading, translating, printing or publishing — four hundred books in all.

When a man finds these marks lacking in his life, and he says he is a Bible teacher, he is just deceived, because these are not things that are self-created.

- **Bible teachers love to sit under other Bible teachers:**

There is a Ghanaian — Godfred Osei Mensah. He is one of the top Bible teachers of the continent. When I was a student at university, each time he was coming, my joy was full. I would sit with him and ask him all the questions I could ask because I had very many questions. If I heard today that he was preaching somewhere in this town, I would go there immediately and sit down and listen. In fact, what I have shared before about Christian Reward, he was the first person I heard speak on the Christian's Reward. And you all know my indebtedness to Watchman Nee. I have read everything written by Watchman Nee and I own the books. I read "What Shall This Man Do?" eight times. The first time I read it for over four months on my knees, crying out to God for revelation. He is without equal.

- **Another mark of the Bible teacher is that he knows what the other versions are saying.**

For some things I say, "Read it to me from the Revised Standard Version." For other things I say, "Read it from the King James Version." What I am using now is the New International Version. But for seven years I read only the King James Version. Then I read the Revised Standard Version for ten years. This is my sixth year of reading this New International Version. So the comparative thing is in my head.

If there is no commitment to know where the thing may be better presented, you are no Bible teacher. There are some verses in the Bible which are best expressed only in the Living Bible: In Galatians, where Paul says, "God forbid that I should glory except in the cross of our Lord Jesus Christ. By that cross, all the attractive things of this world have long since been dead to me, and I to them," they communicate it the best. It is an effortless affair. It is just the overflow of the teacher's life.

- **<u>And the teacher spontaneously wants to know, "What is it in Hebrew and Greek?"</u>**

So, if he cannot read Hebrew and he cannot read Greek, he has a Greek New Testament and a Hebrew Old Testament with the literal translation; not polished, just translated word for word, what it says. When there is some confusion in the versions, he spontaneously checks, "What did He say in Greek? What did He say in Hebrew?" If these are not things that he struggles to put on, that is the teacher!

To love the name "Teacher" and to be a teacher are very different things. The problem is that many exhorters deceive themselves that they are teachers, just as there are many exhorters who deceive themselves that they are prophets.

Then to be deceived saying that you are a pastor without a flock, without clear evidence of people you have built for years, of whom you can say, "I took this one as a baby; now I present him as a mature man," is also tragic. The pastoral ministry has to do with a long term interest, commitment and transformation of men from babyhood to adulthood.

It is like those evangelists in America who can only evangelise on television. The evangelist normally goes looking for sinners where they are. When you want people to gather them, and have good music and everything and then you stand on the rostrum and proclaim, you are more in show business. That is why Wilkerson does not spare them. He has the sword of God in his limbs, on his lips and on his pen. In his last publication that came out before I left, he was bemoaning the hirelings of America who call themselves pastors. And he described the experience he had in one Church. He said he found himself there and said, "Oh, what a privilege just to sit in someone's congregation instead of having to preach," since he is a pastor himself. What happened was so sickening that he said, "I couldn't stand it to the end. I walked out," and he went out weeping for the flock in America that does not have shepherds. He said it was all gimmick, the singing was gimmick, the preaching was gimmick, all was gimmick.

About eighteen years ago, I remember going to one of the Pentecostal denominations in Yaounde with a Frenchman. It was money-raising gimmick of the worst kind, and the preaching was terribly out of tune with the Bible. The Frenchman said that the preaching had no spirit. He was not talking about the Holy Spirit. It had no place where it held together. There was nothing of flow. It was a heap of stones. It was not a building.

When I am saying this, I say it with a great burden because I would like to have a workshop with the teachers of the Word so that I can help them with the little I have learnt over the years. Many years ago, it was said that the Church in Africa had first class evangelists and first class pastors, but that teachers were extremely rare on the continent. I believe the people because they did a lot of research and they didn't want to be negative, or else they would not have been talking about the first class evangelists and the first class pastors. The question before me is, "Can this shortage be remedied?" Knowing that in every miracle there is what God does and there is what man does, that is why I am asking myself, "Can we do something to make a human contribution to the raising of teachers on the continent?"

The thing is that if we could discover those who have the gift, we could help them to develop it, because the gift can lie dormant without the person knowing that he has it.

Apart from the private characteristics like loving books and writing down a summary of every book I read, and writing down the quotations from the speeches of people, because I was thrown into leadership six months after I believed, I became the General Secretary of the Scripture Union. I had to whether teach or preach, I don't know which. So there may be some teachers with the dormant gift. But one thing I know, if there is the gift, there will be

- a hunger to read and read and read and read the Bible
- a hunger to read other books, and
- a burning desire to sit under a teacher.

But how to cultivate the gift and how to clarify it, may need the help of another.

I also want to tell the brethren that my baptism in the Holy Spirit was the single greatest event in my life. This thing I was telling you about running after sinners in the streets, spending all those nights on the streets, was the spontaneous flow from the baptism in the Holy Spirit. It was as if I had to tell someone about Jesus Christ or break. There was no Church. On Sunday, we went to an Anglican Church just because that was the tradition, even though whatever the man was saying in the front there, you didn't bother to listen because even if you listened you had nothing to benefit from it. But we were very loyal because we always took the communion. Why you took it, you didn't know. We just knew that they took it, so we took it. So there was no one saying, "Go and evangelise." There was no Assembly to want to build in number. It was just that from inside, these rivers burned in my heart. They were flowing. I went to the streets to get them released. It is a serious thing in the Ministry - people who have baptism in the Holy Spirit without a crisis! The question is, "What have they had?" That was where the prayer life was born in me. It was after that that I spent the first night in prayer alone. It was not that there was a Work and so I had to pray the prayer topics through or that I had to pray the Work through. It was not because somebody's Ministry had to be supported. My whole being was just burning to talk to God. It was not goal-directed outside God. Everything with the Ministry stems right from that time. The vision of hell came out shortly after I was baptized in the Holy Spirit. The vision of heaven came after the baptism in the Holy Spirit. The public ministry in the real sense started that day when I was baptized in the Holy Spirit. It is something that we ought to ask:

Why is it that many people say they are baptized in the Holy Spirit but it is like a duck that has passed through water?

Why is it that it does not leave profound effects?

When I think about Brother Firmino's work, in a sense, their fabulous growth is the overflow of the price he paid, and the fact that the Holy Spirit came upon them. Over a hundred of them were baptized in the Holy Spirit two years ago, and the fact that they have grown to six hundred is just what should happen normally. The Apostle Paul said to Timothy, "What you have heard from me before many witnesses, commit to faithful men." So Timothy received what Paul gave, and then there was a divine revelation.

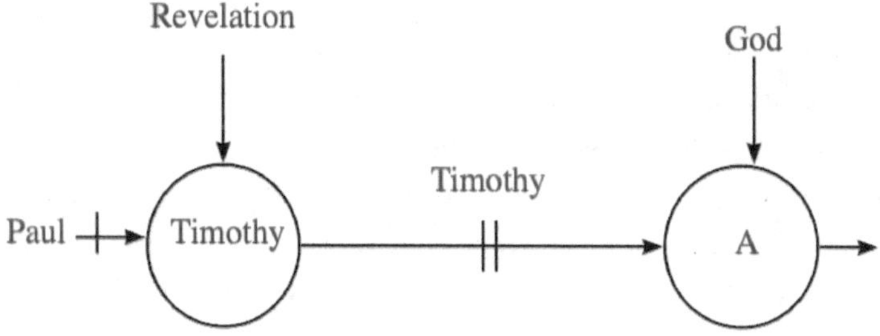

So he had what he received from Paul and what he got from God to now constitute Timothy's deposit, which he would then hand over to somebody A, who now has what he has got from Timothy, plus what he got from God, and so forth. Now, this is the tradition of teachers. But when somebody wants to be the beginning, he hinders himself or reduces where he could have got to. "What you have heard from me..., commit to faithful men who will be able to teach others. They don't just regurgitate what they receive. They mix what they have received from man with what they have received from God to have their own Teaching Ministry.

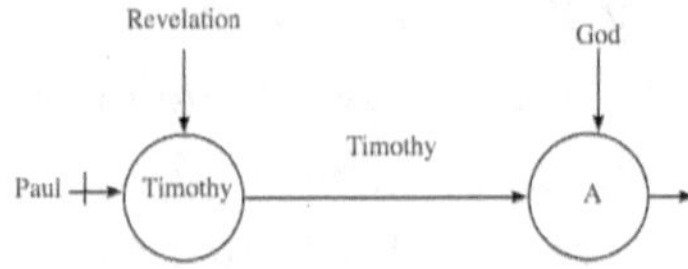

If you cut that, you have destroyed the teacher. And it is something that is inward.

When a teacher touches the spirit of an older teacher, he cleaves to him.

It was in 1969 that Dr. Powell gave me: "Changed Into His Likeness." I was going to Uganda. By then I had read at least 150 books on the Christian life, but as I read it, it was like distilled nectar. I read and reread it! And I began to seek every book by Watchman Nee. Wherever I found it at whatever price, I bought it. It was something flowing out. And that is it! The biography of Watchman Nee - "Against The Tide" - I have read it five times. I wanted to get to the spirit of the man. Then I read the other book, "Meet Watchman Nee." Also, I want to say that it was not something made up. I didn't even know that I would one day be a Bible teacher; so I was not doing what you do to become a Bible teacher. It was just the spontaneous flow of the heart. I didn't even know that Watchman Nee was a great Bible teacher.

It is possible to quench the Spirit by pride.

It is possible to block the River by independence.

It is also possible to block God by suspicion.

Let's come with Joshua to the Gibeonites' deception.

<u>Joshua Chapter 9</u> "Now when all the kings west of the Jordan heard about these things - those in the hill country, in the western foothills, and along the entire coast of the Great Sea

as far as Lebanon (the kings of the Hittites, Amorites, Canaanites, Perizzites, Hivites and Jebusites) - they came together to make war against Joshua and Israel."

However, when the people of Gibeon heard what Joshua had done to Jericho and Ai, they resorted to a ruse: They went as a delegation whose donkeys were loaded with worn-out sacks and old wineskins, cracked and mended. The men put worn and patched sandals on their feet and wore old clothes. All the bread of their food supply was dry and mouldy. Then they went to Joshua in the camp at Gilgal and said to him and the men of Israel, 'We have come from a distant country; make a treaty with us.'

The men of Israel said to the Hivites, 'But perhaps you live near us. How then can we make a treaty with you?'

'We are your servants,' they said to Joshua.

But Joshua asked, 'Who are you and where do you come from?' They answered: 'Your servants have come from a very distant country because of the fame of the Lord your God. For we have heard reports of him: all that he did in Egypt, and all that he did to the two kings of the Amorites east of the Jordan - Sihon king of Heshbon, and Og king of Bashan, who reigned in Ashtaroth. And our elders and all those living in our country said to us, "Take provisions for your journey; go and meet them and say to them, 'We are your servants; make a treaty with us.'" This bread of ours was warm, when we packed it at home on the day we left to come to you. But now see how dry and mouldy it is. And these wineskins that we filled were new, but see how cracked they are. And our clothes and sandals are worn out by the very long journey.'

The men of Israel sampled their provisions but did not inquire of the Lord. Then Joshua made a treaty of peace with them to let them live, and the leaders of the assembly ratified it by oath.

Three days after they made the treaty with the Gibeonites, the Israelites heard that they were neighbours, living near them. So the Israelites set out and on the third day came to their cities: Gibeon, Kephirah, Beeroth and Kiriath Jearim. But the Israelites did not attack them, because the leaders of the assembly had sworn an oath to them by the Lord, the God of Israel.

The whole assembly grumbled against the leaders, but all the leaders answered, 'We have given them our oath by the Lord, the God of Israel, and we cannot touch them now. This is what we will do to them: We will let them live, so that wrath will not fall on us for breaking the oath we swore to them.' They continued, 'Let them live, but let them be woodcutters and water carriers for the entire community.' So the leaders' promise to them was kept.

Then Joshua summoned the Gibeonites and said, 'Why did you deceive us by saying, 'We live a long way from you,' while actually you live near us? You are now under a curse: You will never cease to serve as woodcutters and water carriers for the house of my God.' They answered Joshua, 'Your servants were clearly told how the Lord your God had commanded his servant Moses to give you the whole land and to wipe out all its inhabitants from before you. So we feared for our lives because of you, and that is why we did this. We are now in your hands. Do to us whatever seems good and right to you.'

So Joshua saved them from the Israelites, and they did not kill them. That day he made the Gibeonites woodcutters and water carriers for the community and for the altar of the Lord at the place the Lord would choose. And that is what they are to this day."

The Gibeonites came and deceived Joshua.

<u>Verse 8</u> "We are your servants," they said to Joshua. But Joshua asked, "Who are you and where do you come from?"

Then all that deceit.

<u>Verse 14</u> "The men of Israel sampled their provisions but did not inquire of the Lord." They used their logic. They used what they could see. They used what they could analyse. But they did not ask the Lord. They used sense knowledge, what the eyes could tell them. Oh those words:

<u>Verse 14</u> "The men of Israel sampled their provisions but did not inquire of the Lord." ...they did not inquire of the Lord!

<u>Verse 12</u> "This bread of ours was warm when we packed it at home on the day we left to come to you. But now see how dry and mouldy it is." See, see how dry it is!

<u>Verse 13a</u> "And these wineskins that we filled were new, but see how cracked they are." See! Analyse! Think!

Is that you? Are you a man moved by what he thinks, by what he sees, by what he feels?

There is the natural man.

There is the carnal man.

There is the spiritual man.

The natural man is led by his soul and his body. And the soul is his will - his mind - his emotions. His body is what he sees, what he tastes, what he feels, what he hears, and what he smells.

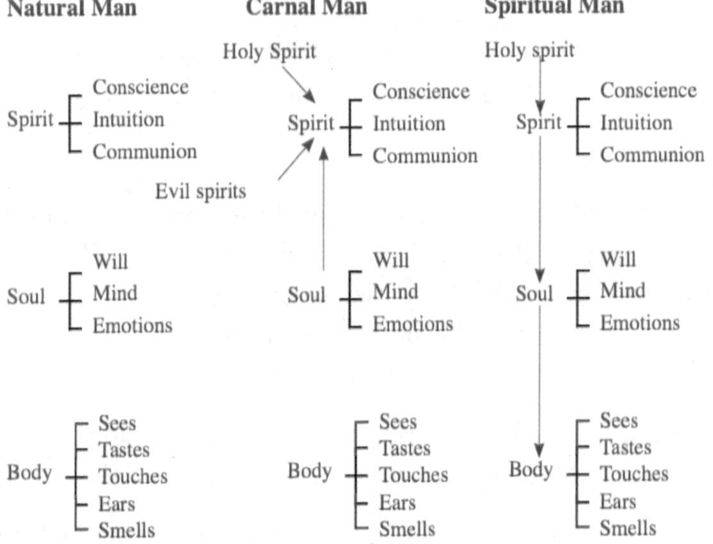

The natural man has a very strong will. These are the decision-making mechanisms of the natural man. They govern him. The carnal man is governed by the same thing. But, occasionally, he may allow his spirit to intervene. And the spirit is the conscience, intuition, and communion. Now, I want to say that the natural man also has a conscience. He also has intuition and he has communion. These are parts of his spirit. Please listen very carefully. The thing is that the spirit of the natural man is severed from the Holy Spirit; therefore it acts at will, independently. And it is often controlled by the Wicked One. That is why a satanist enters into communion with the Devil. There is communion between the spirit of an unbeliever and evil spirits. Just as the believer would commune with God, the unbeliever communes with evil sprits. So he can have supernatural knowledge given to him by evil spirits. That is why you can have the spirit of divination. But, normally, the natural man is controlled by the soul and body. In the carnal man, the Bible says that the spirit of the natural man is dead. It is dead in the Bible sense, which means "lacking communion with God," because death in this Bible sense does not mean the cessation of existence. The Bible says, "The soul that sinneth, it shall die." It doesn't mean that that soul will cease to exist. It means that it will not have communion with God. When they say a man is dead, what do they mean? He no longer responds to environment; and when a man is dead spiritually, he no longer responds to God. So when a man sins, communion with God is broken; he is dead. The natural man is dead, not because his organs are not functioning, but because they are out of union with God.

In the new birth, the spirit of man is quickened. The Apostle says, "You who were dead in trespasses and sin, he made alive." He quickened. What did He quicken? Not the body, because the body was always there. Not the soul, because the soul was always alive. Not the emotions, because unbelievers can have positive and negative emotions. It is the sprit. It comes alive in the fact that it comes into live union with the Holy Spirit. It gets into touch with God. It can now be controlled by God and led by God. I will stop here because there is no time to develop the theme. We need to spend seven days on this. In fact, one of the books that we will be writing will be: "The conscience of the believer," because many brethren are suffering from a destroyed conscience. By refusing to obey the dictates of conscience, from a bad conscience they finally have a seared conscience, so that they can do the wrong thing untouched. The conscience is seared.

Intuition is the organ of knowledge by revelation - knowledge that does not come by reason. It is communicated in the spirit. Normally, it ought to be from the Holy Spirit to the human spirit. I want to tell you that the spirit of the believer can be influenced by the Holy Spirit. It can also be influenced by evil spirits. In the carnal believer the spirit is underdeveloped. The soul may be hypo- or hyper-developed. Now, in the development of the soul, there may be unequal developments. Some people just have overdeveloped emotions, so their capacity to feel is so overriding. Some people have overdeveloped minds, some people, an overdeveloped will. That is why you can have soulical fasts. The man has a strong will; so he says, "No food," and he goes on until he finishes the fast. It is just a strong will. A man can approach the Scriptures just with an intelligent mind. With a mental grasp he sees how all holds together. So he can be under the influence of the spirit, be under the influence of the devil, and could also be under the influence of the flesh. Of course, the flesh is part of the satanic trinity.

In the carnal believer, his capacity of being influenced by the Holy Spirit is underdeveloped, while his capacity of being influenced by the soul is very developed. And this is a coup d'état because the spirit should dominate the soul, but now the soul begins to dominate the spirit. So what the will demands or what the mind demands, or what the emotions demand, is what is executed. So immediately there is a question to settle, the man turns to his mind, and analyses or he turns to his emotions and acts as they dictate and seals it with his will. The carnal believer is someone who is led principally by the soul. The Holy Spirit can intervene from time to time, but his decisions are based upon his will, his mind, his emotions. If the conscience raises some question, he brings the mind to impose, or he brings his will to crush, or he brings his emotions to rule in the situation.

A carnal believer is someone who though born again, and having the Holy Spirit within, is guided principally and led by the soul - his will, his mind and his emotions. And he prides in it. Such people are so desperate that everything must be orderly and logical. They cannot really be true prophets. Why? God says to Isaiah, "Go tell this king Hezekiah that he is going to die, he will not live." He goes and tells him. When he is going away, he is still in he courtyard when He says, "Go and tell him that I have added his years." Such a man will say, "No,... A few minutes ago, this man was to die, now You are saying this man has 15 years more." He can't be a messenger of God that way because his logical mind cannot allow him to flow. God tells him, "Don't fast." Soon afterwards God tells him, "Fast." God tells him, "Fast for 40 days." Afterwards God tells him, "Stop it." He says, "No, this must be the Devil. I will finish my fast." And he finishes it. It is his fast. It is not God's fast. That is why after some fasts people are so far away from God. Remember that in the long fast of Jesus, He was led by the Spirit into it. He was not led by the will. He was led by the Holy Spirit. He was led to the wilderness by the Holy Spirit.

There are people with weak wills; there are people with strong wills. There are people with intelligent minds; there are others with unintelligent minds. There are people with strong emotions; there are some people who are emotionally dry like dry bones. We do not need people with strong wills or people with weak wills. We need people with wills that are controlled by the Holy Spirit; so that when they have to be strong they are as strong as steel, and when it is necessary to change the mind immediately, they are just so soft that they change without bothering about the consequences. We need Spirit-filled wills so to say; Spirit-controlled wills - totally controlled by the Holy Spirit. What we need is wills totally controlled by the Holy Spirit. What we need is minds totally controlled by the Holy Spirit. What we need is emotions totally controlled by the Holy Spirit.

As you know, C.T. Studd married a beauty. When you are married to a beauty, to leave her and go away and never see her again, something has to have happened to you. He was going away contrary to natural desires. Why? He had Spirit-controlled emotions. He was not there burning, "O my darling!"

There are Spirit-controlled emotions. That is why a woman can lose her husband and the emotional love she had for him is totally taken away or put under control, and she functions fully normally emotionally. That is why a Spirit-filled man or a Spirit-filled woman can decide, "I am going to be single." People say, "I am burning! What is happening about my burning?" What has happened to the burning? Because the emotions are Spirit-filled emotions, they can express themselves differently. They can express themselves in a friendship that is not "eros" but is deep and fulfilling.

So in a spiritual man there is the conscience, there is the intuition, and there is communion. There is still the will, the mind, and there is the emotion; there is the body. The Holy Spirit is in control in the Spirit-filled man. He controls the spirit, the spirit controls the soul and the soul controls the body. So it is the will of the Holy Spirit that is executed. So what should happen in the course of spiritual growth is that the believer cooperates with the Holy Spirit for the building of his conscience, that he has a mature, strong, perfect conscience; so that he has a fully developed intuition, a capacity to receive facts by revelation from the Holy Spirit. He has the capacity to enter into intense union, intense communion with the Lord because of the Holy Spirit having developed his capacity for communion. Then with a fully developed spirit, the will and the mind and emotions are under control. Then with a fully developed spirit, the will and the mind and emotions are under control. So the soul wills what the conscience has approved. Yes, the soul wills what the conscience has selected to be the will of God. The mind proclaims the knowledge that has been received from the Holy Spirit as the true knowledge. And the emotions with which relationships are established are governed by the intense communion with God.

So, actually, the purpose of the Christian life, in a sense, is to bring the spirit to maturity. But I find that many believers have not worked on their conscience, they have not worked on their intuition, they have not worked on their communion. They are just absolute babies, governed by their minds. Occasionally, something may come through.

So when the Gibeonites came, if the Israelites had asked God, they would have got from the Holy Spirit the facts intuitively, but they turned to the soul, the soul turned to the body, and the body said, "See!" and they took the decision. They did not turn to the Lord. That is my problem with many believers: They don't turn to the Lord.

They turn to the facts.

They turn to the evidence.

They turn to what seems good to them, to what gives them advantages.

The problem with many people is that with these things underdeveloped, people function without any developed intuition or with just natural intuition.... And the intuition of women is natural intuition. It is not a Spirit-controlled intuition. And the logic of men is the logic of the mind. Both are of the flesh.

Without harsh and radical consecration and without a release of the spirit from the slavery of the soul, the

soul will control, and so they will be guided by the natural intuition and saying, "This is how I think." Or by the natural mind, saying, "This is what I reason." Because you have the human spirit there, it can be under the control or rule of the soul. It is as if the spirit and the soul were married.

The release of the spirit is the separation of the spirit from the soul. After that separation, then the spirit controls the soul.

Until then, the spirit is under the control of the soul. There is indeed a separation. <u>Hebrews 4:12a</u> "For the word of God is living and active. Sharper than any double-edged sword, it penetrates even to dividing soul and spirit, (joints and marrow)."

Dividing soul and spirit! The soul and the spirit must be separated; so that the spirit is released from the bondage to the soul to be controlled by the Holy Spirit.

Watchman Nee wrote the book on this: "The Release Of The Spirit." First of all, that is the most complicated book he wrote. When I was hungering to know the release of my spirit, it was the only book I saw on the subject. I don't know why he didn't make it simpler. By the time I got into the experience I had read the book seven times.

The dividing of soul and spirit is necessary; so that even if you have a lot of natural intelligence your decisions are not based on the natural. You know how to put the natural aside. Again, I am yielding to the temptation of being in this area. Some people have thought that people were spiritual because they did not sin, because they were sanctified. Every believer is supposed to be sanctified. In fact, people should stop sinning the day they believe. There are many carnal believers who do not sin. They are just led by the soul. It is a question of: Who is in control? Who governs? Who has the final word - the soul or the spirit? I am saying that from the lesson now, bringing out the difference between a carnal believer and a spiritual man, it is clear that the spiritual man, submitting himself totally to the control of the Holy Spirit, is able to work hard at the reading of the Word and therefore to grow. When I started hungering for books and read 50 of them in the first year of my faith, I was a carnal believer. When I read the Bible twice before I left the primary school, I didn't even know the Lordship of Jesus. I was barely justified. The release of the spirit will not make a man into a lover of books.

The baptism in the Holy Spirit is not the release of the spirit because, as you see, the Corinthians with all those spiritual gifts were carnal believers. They were all baptized in the Holy Sprit. They were manifesting spiritual gifts, but they were carnal. Therefore, whatever desire was raised by their soul, it took hold of them. If it was sex, they responded. If it was anger...they gave full vent to it. That is why the other man went and slept with his father's wife. That is why there were so many divisions. It was the overflow of the soul.

Once upon a time on Planet Earth, a lover of the Lord was engaged and the girl fell into fornication with somebody else. I was in the seat of decision-making. My decision mattered. And we called off the relationship. I was gripped last month for reasons which I don't want to give here, to confront the fact that we did not ask the Holy Spirit. I stop there.

To bring it home, seven years ago, most brethren said Sister A. could not be Brother T.A.'s wife. Brother T.A. is a colossal intellectual. Sister A. is a simple-minded woman. She is not an intellectual. But that's the wife God meant for him. As we see his Ministry developing, if he had married some woman who had a Ph.D. but could not fast, when you declared a fast she would bring the books on nutrition to tell you why... Obviously then, nobody saw what Brother T.A. would become and what Sister A. has become was not obvious. And Brother T.A. is the man who if he had a wife who opposed him, by this day the whole place would have been torn apart. It is absolutely correct! "An oversabi woman" = "a woman who knows too much" for Brother T.A. would have been impossible, unthinkable. He might have ended up like John Wesley who separated from the wife. In fact, that was the problem; the woman was strong and John Wesley needed a woman who would just follow him. And one day her folly made her go out of the home. When she wanted to come back, John Wesley said, "No, just stay where you are." And she stayed away until she died. They never came together again.

When you have a strong man and a strong woman it is disaster. You can manage to put the pieces together, but it doesn't work. When you have a man who hears from God and a woman who would like to raise questions and try to push through her will, it cannot work, because these people who hear from God are intolerant of discussions. If they have heard, they have heard. And often they are honest to say, "We have not heard." But when they have heard and you want it to come to the debate table, it is another story. So

What seems correct now and what will be correct in the horizons of time could be two different things.

There is compatibility and there is compatibility.

Finally, unless a wife helps a man to get to the heights that God has for him, all that she does for him will not help in anything, it will not interest him.

So, as time goes on, it is the power of the woman to help the man to get to the heights that God has called him to, that matters. She ought to have that from the beginning, and that ought to be the deciding factor.

I want to say one other thing about this. The Gibeonites deceived Joshua but a treaty was signed, a covenant was made. When later on they discovered that it was deceit, the covenant was still respected. Later on, when King Saul killed the Gibeonites, God judged Israel with a famine which was only lifted when the grandsons of Saul were hanged. It was a covenant made in error; nevertheless, it was binding.

Even if you discover that you married the wrong person, you are nevertheless bound. You can't walk out of a covenant without confronting the judgment of God.

14

THE SUN STANDS STILL

Joshua 10:1-15: Now Adoni-Zedek king of Jerusalem heard that Joshua had taken Ai and totally destroyed it, doing to Ai and its king as he had done to Jericho and its king, and that the people of Gibeon had made a treaty of peace with Israel and were living near them. He and his people were very much alarmed at this, because Gibeon was an important city, like one of the royal cities; it was larger than Ai, and all its men were good fighters. So Adoni-Zedek king of Jerusalem appealed to Hoham king of Hebron, Piram king of Jarmuth, Japhia king of Lachish and Debir king of Eglon. "Come up and help me attack Gibeon," he said, "because it has made peace with Joshua and the Israelites."

Then the five kings of the Amorites - the kings of Jerusalem, Hebron, Jarmuth, Lachish and Eglon - joined forces. They moved up with all their troops and took up positions against Gibeon, and attacked it.

The Gibeonites then sent word to Joshua in the camp at Gilgal: "Do not abandon your servants. Come up to us quickly and save us! Help us, because all the Amorite kings from the hill country have joined forces against us."

So Joshua marched up from Gilgal with his entire army, including all the best fighting men. The Lord said to Joshua, "Do not be afraid of them; I have given them into your hand. Not one of them will be able to withstand you."

After an all-night march from Gilgal, Joshua took them by surprise. The Lord threw them into confusion before Israel, who defeated them in a great victory at Gibeon. Israel pursued them along the road going up to Beth Horon and cut them down all the way to Azekah and Makkedah. As they fled before Israel on the road down from Beth Horon to Azekah, the Lord hurled large hailstones down on them from the sky, and more of them died from the hailstones than were killed by the swords of the Israelites.

On the day the Lord gave the Amorites over to Israel, Joshua said to the Lord in the presence of Israel: "O sun, stand still over Gibeon, O moon, over the Valley of Aijalon." So the sun stood still, and the moon stopped, till the nation avenged itself on its enemies, as it is written in the Book of Jashar.

The sun stopped in the middle of the sky and delayed going down about a full day. There has never been a day like it before or since, a day when the Lord listened to a man. Surely the Lord was fighting for Israel!

Then Joshua returned with all Israel to the camp at Gilgal."

Praise the Lord!

Our commitments to the Lord will be tested!!

God does not accept empty words.

This covenant was entered into with the Gibeonites.

<u>Verse 2b</u>

"...Gibeon was an important city, like one of the royal cities; it was larger than Ai, and all its men were good fighters."

It tells you something about the power of Israel.

<u>Verses 3-4</u> "...Adoni-Zedek king of Jerusalem appealed to Hoham king of Hebron, Piram king of Jarmuth,...'Come up and help me attack Gibeon,' he said, 'because it has made peace with Joshua and the Israelites.' Although the Gibeonites used ruse, they were wise. Why go fight with a man who will destroy you? Make peace with your adversary. It is not the making of peace that was the problem. It was the way they did it.

Brother M.A. is a very able man capable of making peace with his adversaries. He can swim in very difficult waters. It is a compliment because some people just go knocking their heads until the heads are in bits. But Brother M.A., I was just asking myself the other day, *"How will you negotiate with your wife?"* You understand the question? Because he is going to be the national leader. Brother T.A., he is your disciple. Have you thought about it? No, he will survive. He will not drown. There are many men who drown.

John Wesley was coming on the road, and it was a narrow road where only one person could pass at a time. Then there was a man coming, saying, "I never give way to fools." John Wesley went to the other side and said, "I always give way to fools." He had a very deep sense of humour. But he could also be very insolent. If you stepped on his toe, you would have it! He would give you two punches. Because he could have just stepped aside without announcing that he always gave way to fools. "We have this treasure in earthen vessels that it may be obvious that transcendent power belongs to God and not to us." So I think Brother M.A. will not say, "I always give way to fools." It is very true that he will be safe in very troubled waters.

There are many possibilities. But he is wise. He doesn't go on head-on collision. I think when he is walking he says, "What's the safest way out of this?" And that is wisdom. Why go and cause unnecessary war?

In the United States I was talking about some people who say a chair must always be placed a certain way, and some people who think that chairs have no sides. One brother just came and told me, "Look, I am the one for whom chairs have no sides, but for my wife every chair has a side." And the brother does just exactly what Brother M.A. does. They have had no quarrel on any day. He is a totally relaxed man; the type of man who can never have high blood pressure and the wife is the person who can have high blood pressure. So while she is fighting about the sides of the chairs, he just relaxes and does what he considers important. But what I found, because I lived with them for some time, in that case she is older than the Brother physically, she is older than him spiritually, she is a more mature believer, and she's putting him under spiritual discipline; because he is also the man who can say, "I will meditate at 10 o'clock." And he acknowledges the positive impact of her interventions. I think Brother just has to know where when he speaks, there is no talking and no discussion; because for every leader, that point must be arrived at. Sooner or later, it will come; because the revelation for the national Work will be given to him, not to her. And if people think differently, it is what he says that has to be adopted.

Submission, to me is obedience without grumbling. Obedience with grumbling is no submission, because if you are a spiritual surgeon, you have to deal with hearts. If someone follows singing, "It is Not An Easy Road-O" that is saying, "If it were possible for you to be beaten, you would have been beaten; but you are too big to be beaten." My wife will not refuse following but she could follow singing a song like that. She says she is encouraging herself. But I have the liberty to take the decisions that I want taken because she does follow, most of the time without grumbling. But I want to say **submission is something heavenly.**

Anybody who has a woman who is naturally submissive, one day you will find that that submission has ended and you will be very shocked. In fact, you will be totally overtaken. If a woman says, "I am a rebel, I cannot submit," only then can she submit.

When people easily say they submit, they don't understand. They don't know the deceitfulness of their hearts. If you ask me, "Do you love your wife?" I will say, "No, but I'm learning."

No man loves his wife naturally.

Natural excitements, those are vanities of vanities.

The power to love a woman is the power to love like God loves.

It has to be received from the Lord. No man has it naturally. If it was something that could be done without divine intervention, God would not have insisted upon it. He insists upon it because it can never be done by man without divine intervention. So when God insists that the woman should submit, it is because she cannot submit naturally.

Every woman is born a rebel.

If by the grace of God she comes to the end of herself and then turns to the Lord and receives from God as a gift the power to submit, then there will be no submission with songs. It will be an inward bang that comes immediately in response to the Holy Spirit. That submission will stand any condition. It is divine submission. Many people think that they can submit naturally and they justify the fact that they can submit, even though there are blatant acts of insubmission. It is the deceit from Eden. If there was understanding from the Holy Spirit, there would be a cry: "Lord, I cannot submit. I am not submissive. I may be calm outside but I am boiling inside. God, give me God's submission, God's power to submit. My own submission will fail. My own submission will not pass the test. Yours will do. Natural submission will go up to a limit. But it will finally fail. I don't want it. I don't want to depend on it. I want divine submission because it will not fail."

No woman can serve a man because you can't serve apart from submission.

Or you can serve as long as he is nice with you. When he is hard and rude, to continue to submit, to continue to love, to continue to serve, it has to be God's submission. May all these fleshly submissions be torn down and overthrown, because they will not do. Either it leads to rebellion or to self-pity. "The flesh profiteth nothing."

Another thing that the sisters should ask is God's power to please a man. Because many of them are struggling to please a man in the flesh, sometimes it only offends.

Have you come to grips with the fact that you can't please that man - the humility to come to that, that what you are, what you do, cannot please him?

What could have been said to men is being said in a book, "A Successful Marriage: The Man's Making." Brother, go and receive God's power to love a woman.

When the Gibeonites were attacked,

Joshua 10:6a "The Gibeonites then sent word to Joshua in the camp at Gilgal: 'Do not abandon your servants.'" They had accepted to be servants.

Verse 6b-11 "Come up to us quickly and save us! Help us, because all the Amorite kings from the hill country have joined forces against us."

So Joshua marched up from Gilgal with his entire army, including all the best fighting men. The Lord said to Joshua, 'Do not be afraid of them; I have given them into your hand. Not one of them will be able to withstand you.'

After an all-night march from Gilgal, Joshua took them by surprise. The Lord threw them into confusion before Israel, who defeated them in a great victory at Gibeon. Israel pursued them along the road going up to Beth Horon and cut them down all the way to Azekah and Makkedah. As they fled before Israel on the road down from Beth Horon to Azekah, the Lord hurled large hailstones down on them from the sky, and more of them died from the hailstones than were killed by the swords of the Israelites."

Yeah! When God is on your side it is wonderful! And when He is against you, if you escape the sword, it will be famine; if you escape famine, it will be hailstone; if you escape hailstone, it will be the flood. Those who were running very fast thought they would be safe, until the weapons began to come from the air.

<u>Verse 12-13a</u> "On the day the Lord gave the Amorites over to Israel, Joshua said to the Lord in the presence of Israel: 'O sun, stand still over Gibeon, O moon, over the Valley of Aijalon.' So the sun stood still, and the moon stopped, till the nation avenged itself on its enemies."

The elements, on the side of God. "If God is for us who can be against us?" You can tell when God is in a thing. And you can say when God is out of it. Have you faced a situation where God walked out completely? Here, God was fully in. But it was the power of God through men. "Sun, stand still. Moon, stand still" - the elements were at the command of leadership. I believe that he sorted this out with God before he started speaking. It might be better to read it, "Joshua, at the command of God, said, 'Sun, stand still. '" Don't just stand up one morning and say, "Sun, stand still." The other thing is this: The nation was in danger. There are things that leadership can ask and receive from God in times of great difficulties that cannot be asked and received in times of peace.

If some day I have no money, I shall tell God to drop me dollars from the air. And the dollars will start descending.

1. Look, the prophet was fed by birds.
2. We are in God's hands.
3. His hand is not shortened.
4. His methods are not limited.
5. Fear not.
6. Be very courageous.
7. Don't take stock of the enemy.
8. God is not compelled to use the method He used in the past.
9. But He will act.
10. And the enemy will collapse.
11. Put aside your methods.

12. Put aside your worries!
13. Put aside your fears.
14. Go into God's battles.
15. Go into God's missionary field.
16. Go ahead into the work God has called you to.
17. Don't take stock of the needs.

God's work done God's way will never lack supplies!!

There are no prayers that are too big.

Could anything be bigger than this?

<u>Verse 12b, 13a and c, 14</u> "'O sun, stand still over Gibeon, O moon, over the Valley of Aijalon.' So the sun stood still, and the moon stopped,...

The sun stopped in the middle of the sky and delayed going down about a full day. There has never been a day like it before or since, a day when the Lord listened to a man. Surely the Lord was fighting for Israel."

There never has been a day like that before or since, when God listened to a man in such an unusual way! God is ready to do the unusual, to do something for the first time to back His servants as they serve Him. God is prepared to do the unusual, to do what He has never done. But listen, it doesn't happen for people who are on safe grounds. It is as people obey God into real difficult situations that the divine intervention comes. There never was a day like it. God had to win. Joshua had to win. Therefore God acted.

Will you by obedience to Him let God have an opportunity? Not that you create a difficulty and ask God to step in.

God will step into that which He ordered.

God will step into that which is the fulfilment of His covenant. If you go and start your own war, thought by you, planned by you, and you expect God to step in, you are mistaken.

God sent Elijah to confront and punish the prophets of Baal on Mount Carmel. It was not something that the prophet initiated. Throughout this book you see that the leader did what God said. God said!

Leadership does not initiate. Leadership obeys.

Many girls start saying, "God, give me a husband." They should first ask, "God, is marriage Your design for me?" Because God may have called you to be a eunuch for the Gospel. There are three classes of eunuchs:

Those who were born eunuchs, biologically incapable of being anything else but a eunuch.

There are those who were made eunuchs by men.

And there are those who have made themselves eunuchs for the Gospel. The Lord may intend that you make yourself a eunuch for the Gospel. If that is God's plan, and you say, "God, give me a husband!" And you do a 40-day fast for a husband; because people have converted fasts into something like the drug for all diseases...

Is it the will of God?

Do you want God's will?

It is better to be single than to marry outside God's will. Your prayer should be: "God, have You ordained me to marriage?" If God says, "Yes," then you say, "God, bring me the man of Your choosing, not the man of my choosing. God, give me the man of Your choice because I do not know what I want." Or,

"God, give me the man of Your choice because my heart might deceive me. What I want now, I may not want tomorrow."

Leadership is not to initiate. It is to execute. Therefore we must find out what God has in His own mind, and then bring it into existence IN EVERYTHING! Along that pathway, if it is necessary for the sun to stand still, if it is necessary for the moon stand still, God will tell us to command the sun and command the moon and they will stand still. **But do you want God's will or do you want your own will?**

God's will will glorify God.

Your own will will glorify you.

You know what you want; you will have it.

When once you know God's will you put in everything — you take no rest, and give Him no rest until you have done everything required of you. Because He has revealed His will to you, you are responsible for executing it. When He has shown you His goal for your life, woe unto you if you don't accomplish it! When He has shown you His methods, woe unto you if you don't follow them! If He has shown you the price to be paid, if you don't pay it, you are done for. So,

Spiritual aggressiveness is the imposing of the will of God on myself, on my environment, on His world.

And to impose it, I must know it. But whatever barrier is on the way, I must be adamant. If they say lions are in the way, the lions will be tamed and ridden. If there is no money to buy bullets, I must go on. Hailstone will do the job.

The Lord has sent you. Go, and aggressively fill Planet Earth in the shortest possible time.

We have been commanded. AMEN.

You know this was in the time of Joshua, and then Saul came in long afterwards. Because he violated this covenant, God judged the nation with a famine. And things were only restored when the sons of the sons of Saul were hanged. It tells you the gravity of covenants.

That is why there can be no place for divorce.

That is why there can be no place for remarriage, because the other covenant is there. You can get the court to annul it, but God has not annulled it.

1 Timothy 5:11-12

> *"As for younger widows, do not put them on such a list. For when their sensual desires overcome their dedication to Christ, they want to marry. Thus they bring judgment on themselves, (because they have broken their first pledge)."*

I want some of our people to rise and study Greek and Hebrew and give us a translation of the Bible. You know, in this Bible (New International Version) the people don't like fasting. There are three passages on fasting that these people have removed. Yes, it is the Bible of today. And the word "loyalty" is not there. "Beloved" is "dear." I use it but I only use it because I know what the other versions say. It is better than the other versions but there are many weaknesses. If you read only this Bible you may not fast. In the Corinthian passage where it says that husband and wife should not deny themselves except they have decided for a season to give themselves to prayer and fasting, they have removed the fasting there. Where the Lord says, "This kind goes out only by prayer and fasting," they have removed the word "fasting." Paul says "in fasting often,..." They have removed that word "fasting." You see, the thing is that when a man has never fasted, when you say "in fasting..." the man doesn't know what you are talking about.

In the Bible in Mungaka[1], since they were deceived by the Swiss to put water on people's heads, when they were translating the Bible, they said, "Go and make disciples of all nations, putting water on their heads, in the name of the Father, and of the Son and of the Holy Spirit." "...putting water on their heads..." Now when a man reads that, he will defend it to his last drop of blood. On the other hand, in order that they might bear witness to God, for John the Baptist they say, "John, he who immersed the people..." I believe that God allowed them to translate it that way so that someone will know that even though they are putting water on the head, John was the one who plunged people into water. In all the manoeuvres of man, God has maintained a witness to Himself and a witness to His Word. "John, he who immersed the people...", then: "...putting water on their heads..."

If you are deceived into a covenant, you are bound by it.

You can't say, "Well, they deceived me, so let me get out." No, you are bound by it. This matter of the Gibeonites is a very serious matter. You aggressively stick to the covenant that you have made at any cost to yourself.

Who here has a covenant with someone? At least if you are married, you have a covenant. You signed. O.K. Outside that, who has a covenant ratified by signature?

I want to encourage you who have made covenants to document them, to ratify them in writing, because we are in a generation that does not know covenants.

The more superficial a person is, the fewer covenants he has. The more superficial a person is, the fewer definitive declarations he has. Every door is open.

Brethren, this morning I had to confront the fact that I cannot throw off the "do's and don'ts" of my life because they were ratified in writing before God. I would just be a covenant-breaker. They will make my life very restrictive, but that is it! That's it! So from this morning, I have just renewed what I wrote and what I said to God, with all the inconveniences that go with it; so that I may not be a covenant-breaker, regardless of the misunderstanding that will go with it. And when I was preparing this message the conviction became even stronger.

You can't say things before God, write them in His presence, and walk away from them without consequences.

And these women who said they would not get married and then they went and got married, the Bible says that afterwards they desire to get married; and that they bring judgment upon themselves for having broken their first commitment.

This morning when I was praying, I was praying for a sister who was close to me and who is in a marriage that is not working. Then I just received light. Two covenants were broken for the marriage to take place: First of all, a covenant to God that she would stay single, and another covenant which I will not announce. To violate two covenants and hope to have a wonderful marriage is self-deception at its worst.

Thinking about what I said to God and to which I immediately came back when I confronted the matter, what concerns the brethren most is the matter of not receiving gifts for my personal needs beyond food and hospitality. I came to the conclusion by reaction because of the covetousness of a number of spiritual leaders. It is easier to quote an example from somewhere else. In the book "The Happiest People On Earth" on the Full Gospel Business Men's Association; that man who preached started asking for gifts and the people were bringing gifts, and giving gifts; he kept asking for more gifts. They filled one basket and he kept on asking for more. Women even removed their ornaments and gave him; but he just asked for more and more; and he took them and ran out of town. And he was a man whom God had used mightily.

A brother told me a missionary from some country (I don't want to name) went to a rich country and they gave him a lot of gifts and money. He was living in a hotel and he bought a revolver to protect himself. Yes. Look at it this way: Your salary is about 100 thousand. If you go somewhere and they give you 2 million, that is one year's salary, isn't it? This man had to buy a revolver which was under his pillow, for fear that thieves might come.

The last thing was that, now where I am in the Ministry is a dangerous position concerning the matter of gifts. Once we received a very expensive gift from a sister. Later, on she acknowledged that it was in order to outrival a certain sister that she got the gift for us. Because she is close to me, she owned up. Now when you keep the fruits of rivalry! And in some cases the gifts are bribes...! Somebody gives to you so that you may not look into some matters. And if you want to be honest, gifts have power.

Listen, if a man tells a girl, "Let me give you a lift," and she enters his car. When she is coming out, if the man says, "When can I see you again?" She won't say, "What for ? Get out!" She may say, "I'm very busy." She has lost the power to give the man the true answer for what it is, hasn't she? And why so? She has received the gift.

A son of one of the Elders in Yaounde said that my wife and I could not give what we were giving to God but for the gifts of the Brethren. We are giving for the glory of God, but we are also giving to speak to the Enemy, and to talk to coming generations, to provide a model. If people have ways of running away from it, they should not be allowed to run away from it.

And you know, Brethren, of the people with big Ministries in our generation, almost all of them have got wrong with money. In one big Church with 5,000 people in the United States, when you enter they give you an envelope. You put a cheque and sign, is it for the Church, is it for the pastor, is it for missions? Now can you imagine how many cheques are for the pastor?

Tom Skinner, a leading black evangelist and the author of "Black and Free"…wrote another book entitled, "Revolution Now." I read only the first two chapters, because I was reading it in the plane when I was returning from Nigeria, and when I got to Yaounde the security men in the airport took me to a special room and said, "Revolution Now!" And they took away the book. They said they would read it. But Tom Skinner talked about what happens in the black Churches, that they first take the general offering. Then the pastor gets the people prepared to give the pastor's offering. When the people are saying, "Hallelujah!" and everybody is caught up in the frenzy, then they take the pastor's offering.

In the book entitled "Black and Free," one pastor said, "Guess what, I preached a very great sermon today. How do I know? The people paid me well for it." Leadership is very slippery ground. Please permit me to return to this with rigour starting from today; so that no fault may be found with our Ministry.

The other problem is that I am here today - gifts! I am there tomorrow - gifts! I am here in this House Church - gifts! gifts! So that the whole man can be gifts, gifts. I am not setting a standard because that is not what the Word says. I taught you very clearly what the Word says. Follow it. Ask for gifts and receive gifts. Some of you, even after you have asked, will receive very little anyway. Allow me to confront the problems that have to do with my lot in the Ministry, because of where God has placed me.

The other thing has to do with embracing the brethren. I did say to God, "No." It is painful to go back, but let me be true to myself and to God, so that God may not be limited in His backing of me just because I said it.

The other thing has to do with eating meat and fish and the like. When I studied and found that a man could live without meat and fish and live a healthier life, I calculated what a piece of meat would cost and what it could mean for the Gospel if I didn't eat meat. And I decided that I would not eat meat for the sake of perishing souls. Again, it is not your problem. I am a travelling man. Normally, when you have a visitor, you give him what you don't even eat yourself and it is very expensive.

I remember when we went to Bertoua. And a man in short supply of money prepared two chicken, and he prepared other things. When you tell such a man you are coming again, he will calculate the chicken. Please, that is simply true!!

Sister V.A. takes care of me when I go to Garoua. The time I went there not eating any meat or fish, she said that my stay cost 7,000 C.F.A. francs less. When you confront that, and you are always travelling, and always costing 7,000 or 14,000 francs more, you could do something about it. And again I want to say that God gave meat to man. So, eat it with thanksgiving. The decision is peculiarly mine, and I beg you not to enter into it because you will need to first become Zach Fomum before you put your neck into things you don't understand.

Please, don't go and cook extra soup for me that has no meat. I will eat what you cook and I will leave the meat aside so that you don't have to cook some food for the brethren and some different food for me. Please just allow me that aspect of my walk with God without imitating it.

There is another reason, Brethren. There is the book, "The Ministry of Supplication." I told you I read 24 books on prayer. It was in order to write Chapters 1 and 2 of the book because I'm just quoting what others — Spurgeon and all the rest — have said about prayer. But it was also an enriching experience. I was touched by the depth of Spurgeon. In fact, I learnt something in his book, "Twelve Sermons On Prayer." The book was produced in Nigeria. I strongly recommend the book to you. It is pearl. You know, in the life of Hannah, she took the vow that she would give Samuel back to God and she kept her vow, and the nation had a prophet. If I don't go back to my own commitments, I cannot write that chapter because I have covenanted with God that I will not write anything that is not true in my life, or which I am not actively putting on. So a covenant-breaker cannot write that book. It is so that I may be able to write all the things that God will want us to write. Normally, that brings a restricted life. So please bear with me and understand.

Now, there is another thing that affects the brethren. If you want to tell me anything negative about somebody, go and bring the person along. It is one of the things I covenanted with God but which unfortunately I have broken many times. It was that I would not listen to someone make negative comments about an absent party. If you want to discuss or say something negative about somebody, go and bring the person or keep quiet. And if you catch me doing it, pull my ear and say, "You are violating your covenant."

The last thing we want to look at about Joshua and spiritual aggressiveness: I met a brother in the United States. He is 52. He told me he had lived for 21 years without a woman, without a wife. He was married. He told me, "My wife told me she wanted to buy some things. I said, "No, we don't have money now but we shall have money tomorrow." She said, "No, I just want to go and compare prices so that when we have money tomorrow I will know where to go to." He said, "I want to come with you." She said, "No!" As she went, God told him, "Put on your jogging clothes." Then He said, "Jog to that shop that she said she was going to." He went there and didn't see her. Again He said, "Jog to the other shop that is a possibility." He went there and did not see her. Then the Lord said, "Jog to that motel." He jogged there and found her car parked there. He forced his way into the room and she was committing adultery with somebody. He went home and when she came, they talked the whole night and he forgave her. In her shame, she went and divorced him. He forgave her and they started to live normally but she went and divorced him, and in his integrity he has not married another woman. But he told me another story. He told me that a prophetess came and told him that God had sent her to be his wife. So she came right to where he was. He refused. She said, "Let's go for a meal, I'll pay for it." You know in America, they eat outside. Then she told him, "My last husband left me a lot of money, so you have no problem. I will sponsor our joint ministry. You will lack nothing." Then the man asked, "What happened to your first husband?" "He died". "What happened to your second husband?" "He died". Then the man said," Let us order a coffin first because what happened to the first two people...." He kept true to his covenant. She since got married to somebody else. But he has maintained his covenant. He has been true to his covenant.

I pray to God that it will be characteristic of our Ministry that we are true to our covenants; that the covenants of friendship are unbroken, and that the covenants of friendship are extended to our children, because that is what the Bible says.

Brethren, listen, <u>Joshua 9:20</u> "This is what we will do to them: We will let them live, so that wrath will not fall on us for breaking the oath we swore to them."

An oath to crooks nevertheless had to be respected. In the church, when a young man promises to a girl that he will marry her, for him to change his mind, it must be very gravely studied, weighed very very heavily, because it is walking on the wrath of God. So to promise one here, and promise one there, and then take the sixth to the altar to be blessed is a frightful thing.

Integrity is the translation of one's word into action.

It is corresponding one's act to one's word. And don't let the devil tell you that this is legalism. It is just truth. In America, I heard of preachers who marry one woman, divorce her; marry the next one, divorce her; marry another one, divorce her; and go on preaching the gospel because God has cancelled the past. He is a God of covenants. What of Jephthah who swore that the first thing that would come out of his house he would give unto the Lord? And it was his only child. He kept his vow at the greatest cost possible. And the daughter said, "Since you have made this vow...." And when she came back, he sacrificed her to the Lord to remain childless all his life in order that he might be a man of integrity.

---

1. Mungaka is a language predominantly used by the Presbyterians from anglophone Cameroon

BACK MATTERS

VERY IMPORTANT!!!

If you have not yet received Jesus as your Lord and Saviour, I encourage you to receive Him. Here are some steps to help you,

ADMIT that you are a sinner by nature and by practice and that on your own you are without hope. Tell God you have personally sinned against Him in your thoughts, words and deeds. Confess your sins to Him, one after another in a sincere prayer. Do not leave out any sins that you can remember. Truly turn from your sinful ways and abandon them. If you stole, steal no more. If you have been committing adultery or fornication, stop it. God will not forgive you if you have no desire to stop sinning in all areas of your life, but if you are sincere, He will give you the power to stop sinning.

BELIEVE that Jesus Christ, who is God's Son, is the only Way, the only Truth and the only Life. Jesus said,

"I am the way, the truth and the life; no one comes to the Father, but by me" (John 14:6).

The Bible says,

"For there is one God, and there is one mediator between God and men, the man Christ Jesus, who gave himself as a ransom for all" (1 Timothy 2:5-6).

"And there is salvation in no one else (apart from Jesus), for there is no other name under heaven given among men by which we must be saved" (Acts 4:12).

But to all who received him, who believed in his name, he gave power to become children of God..." (John 1:12).

BUT,

CONSIDER the cost of following Him. Jesus said that all who follow Him must deny themselves, and this includes selfish financial, social and other interests. He also wants His followers to take up their crosses and follow Him. Are you prepared to abandon your own interests daily for those of Christ? Are you prepared to be led in a new direction by Him? Are you prepared to suffer for Him and die for Him if need be? Jesus will have nothing to do with half-hearted people. His demands are total. He will only receive and forgive those who are prepared to follow Him AT ANY COST. Think about it and count the cost. If you are prepared to follow Him, come what may, then there is something to do.

INVITE Jesus to come into your heart and life. He says,

"Behold I stand at the door and knock. If anyone hears my voice and opens the door (to his heart and life), I will come in to him and eat with him, and he with me" (Revelation 3:20).

Why don't you pray a prayer like the following one or one of your own construction as the Holy Spirit leads?

> *"Lord Jesus, I am a wretched, lost sinner who has sinned in thought, word and deed. Forgive all my sins and cleanse me. Receive me, Saviour and transform me into a child of God. Come into my heart now and give me eternal life right now. I will follow you at all costs, trusting the Holy Spirit to give me all the power I need."*

When you pray this prayer sincerely, Jesus answers at once and justifies you before God and makes you His child.

> *Please write to us (**ztfbooks@cmfionline.org**) and I will pray for you and help you as you go on with Jesus Christ.*

THANK YOU

For Reading This Book

If you have any question and/or need help, do not hesitate to contact us through ztfbooks@cmfionline.org. If the book has blessed you, then we would also be grateful if you leave a positive review at your favorite retailer.

ZTF BOOKS, through Christian Publishing House (CPH) offers a wide selection of best selling Christian books (in print, eBook & audiobook formats) on a broad spectrum of topics, including marriage & family, sexuality, practical spiritual warfare, Christian service, Christian leadership, and much more. Visit us at ztfbooks.com to learn more about our latest releases and special offers. And thank you for being a ZTF BOOK reader.

We invite you to connect with more from the author through social media (cmfionline) and/or ministry website (ztfministry.org), where we offer both on-ground and remote training courses (all year round) from basic to university level at the _University of Prayer and Fasting (WUPF)_ and the _School of Knowing and Serving God (SKSG)_. You are highly welcome to enrol at your soonest convenience. A FREE online Bible Course is also available.

Finally, we would like to recommend to you another suitable title - _Laws Of Spiritual Leadership_:

The choice of leadership among God's people is God's sole prerogative.

In this book, *Laws of Spiritual Leadership,* Professor Z.T. Fomum convincingly shows from Scriptures <u>why God chooses certain people</u>, as well as <u>the kind of people He chooses</u> for leadership.

The content carries a strong voice of Scripture on <u>simple down-to-earth godly leadership principles</u>, with examples from both the Old and New Testaments. Both the aspiring as well as those already involved in Christian leadership will find their lot.

The leader must set and maintain a leadership gap between himself and those he is leading. The author suggests twelve such domains in which the potential leader should seek and establish distinction. For, no one can honestly lead from behind. <u>You cannot lead those who are ahead of you in the knowledge and pursuit of God.</u> Never! Leadership is a call to give God to the people.

This will be a priceless gift for your leader!

Professor Zacharias Tanee Fomum was born in the flesh on 20th June 1945 and became born again on 13th June 1956. On 1st October 1966, He consecrated his life to the Lord Jesus and to His service, and was filled with the Holy Spirit on 24th October 1970. He was taken to be with the Lord on 14th March, 2009.

Pr Fomum was admitted to a first class in the Bachelor of Science degree, graduating as a prize winning student from Fourah Bay College in the University of Sierra Leone in October 1969. At the age of 28, he was awarded a Ph.D. in Organic Chemistry by the University of Makerere, Kampala in Uganda. In October 2005, he was awarded a Doctor of Science (D.Sc) by the University of Durham, Great Britain. This higher doctorate was in recognition of his distinct contributions to scientific knowledge through research. As a Professor of Organic Chemistry in the University of Yaoundé 1, Cameroon, Professor Fomum supervised or co-supervised more than 100 Master's Degree and Doctoral Degree theses and co-authored over 160 scientific articles in leading international journals. He considered Jesus Christ the Lord of Science ("For by Him all things were created..." – Colossians 1:16), and scientific research an act of obedience to God's command to "subdue the earth" (Genesis 1:28). He therefore made the Lord Jesus the Director of his research laboratory while he took the place of deputy director, and attributed his outstanding success as a scientist to Jesus' revelational leadership.

In more than 40 years of Christian ministry, Pr Fomum travelled extensively, preaching the Gospel, planting churches and training spiritual leaders. He made more than:

- 700 missionary journeys within Cameroon, which ranged from one day to three weeks in duration.
- 500 missionary journeys to more than 70 different nations in all the six continents. These ranged from two days to six weeks in duration.

By the time of his going to be with the Lord in 2009, he had preached in over 1000 localities in Cameroon, sent over 200 national missionaries into many localities in Cameroon and planted over 1300 churches in the various administrative provinces of Cameroon. At his base in Yaoundé, he planted and built a mega-church with his co-workers which grew to a steady membership of about 12,000. Pr Fomum was the founding team-leader of Christian Missionary Fellowship International (CMFI); an evangelism, soul-winning, disciple making, Church-planting and missionary-sending movement with more than 200 international missionaries and thousands of churches in 65 nations spread across Africa, Europe, the Americas, Asia and Oceania. In the course of their ministry, Pr Fomum and his team witnessed more than 10,000 recorded healing miracles performed by God in answer to prayer in the name of Jesus Christ. These miracles include instant healings of headaches, cancers, HIV/AIDS, blindness, deafness, dumbness, paralysis, madness, and new teeth and organs received.

Pr Fomum read the entire Bible more than 60 times, read more than 1350 books on the Christian faith and authored over 150 books to advance the Gospel of Jesus Christ. 5 million copies of these books are in circulation in 12 languages as well as 16 million gospel tracts in 17 languages.

Pr Fomum was a man who sought God. He spent between 15 minutes and six hours daily alone with God in what he called Daily Dynamic Encounters with God (DDEWG). During these DDEWG he read God's Word, meditated on it, listened to God's voice, heard God speak to him, recorded what God was saying to him and prayed it through. He thus had over 18,000 DDEWG. He also had over 60 periods of withdrawing to seek God alone for periods that ranged from 3 to 21 days (which he termed Retreats for Spiritual Progress). The time he spent seeking God slowly transformed him into a man who hungered, thirsted and panted after God. His unceasing heart cry was: "Oh, that I would have more of God!"

Pr Fomum was a man of prayer and a leading teacher on prayer in many churches and conferences around the world. He considered prayer to be the most important work that can be done for God and for man. He was a man of faith who believed that God answers prayer. He kept a record of his prayer requests and had over 50, 000 recorded answers to prayer in his prayer books. He carried out over 100 Prayer Walks of between five and forty-seven kilometres in towns and cities around the world. He and his team carried out over 57 Prayer Crusades (periods of forty days and nights during which at least eight hours are invested into prayer each day). They also carried out over 80 Prayer Sieges (times of near non-stop praying that ranges from 24 hours to 120 hours). He authored the Prayer Power Series, a 13-volume set of books on various aspects of prayer; Supplication, Fasting, Intercession and Spiritual Warfare. He started prayer chains, prayer rooms, prayer houses, national and continental prayer movements in Cameroon and other nations. He worked with leaders of local churches in India to disciple and train more than 2 million believers.

Pr Fomum also considered fasting as one of the weapons of Christian Spiritual Warfare. He carried out over 250 fasts ranging from three days to forty days, drinking only water or water supplemented with soluble vitamins. Called by the Lord to a distinct ministry of intercession, he pioneered fasting and prayer movements and led in battles against principalities and powers obstructing the progress of the Gospel and God's global purposes. He was enabled to carry out 3 supra – long fasts of between 52 and 70 days in his final years.

Pr Fomum chose a lifestyle of simplicity and "self- imposed poverty" in order to invest more funds into the critical work of evangelism, soul winning, church-planting and the building up of believers. Knowing the importance of money and its role in the battle to reach those without Christ with the glorious Gospel, he and his wife grew to investing 92.5% of their earned income from all sources (salaries, allowances, royalties and cash gifts) into the Gospel. They invested with the hope that, as they grew in the knowledge and the love of the Lord, and the perishing souls of people, they would one day invest 99% of their income into the Gospel.

He was married to Prisca Zei Fomum and they had seven children who are all involved in the work of the Gospel, some serving as missionaries. Prisca is a national and international minister, specializing in the winning and discipling of children to Jesus Christ. She also communicates and imparts the vision of ministry to children with a view to raising and building up ministers to them.

The Professor owed all that he was and all that God had done through him, to the unmerited favour and blessing of God and to his worldwide army of friends and co-workers. He considered himself nothing without them and the blessing of God; and would have amounted to nothing but for them. All praise and glory to Jesus Christ!

facebook.com/cmfionline

twitter.com/cmfionline

instagram.com/cmfionline

pinterest.com/cmfionline

youtube.com/cmfionline

ALSO BY Z.T. FOMUM

https://ztfbooks.com

THE CHRISTIAN WAY

1. The Way Of Life
2. The Way Of Obedience
3. The Way Of Discipleship
4. The Way Of Sanctification
5. The Way Of Christian Character
6. The Way Of Spiritual Power
7. The Way Of Christian Service
8. The Way Of Spiritual Warfare
9. The Way Of Suffering For Christ
10. The Way Of Victorious Praying
11. The Way Of Overcomers
12. The Way Of Spiritual Encouragement
13. The Way Of Loving The Lord

THE PRAYER POWER SERIES

1. The Way Of Victorious Praying
2. The Ministry Of Fasting
3. The Art Of Intercession
4. The Practice Of Intercession
5. Praying With Power
6. Moving God Through Prayer
7. Practical Spiritual Warfare Through Prayer
8. The Ministry Of Praise And Thanksgiving
9. Waiting On The Lord In Prayer

PRACTICAL HELPS FOR OVERCOMERS

SPIRITUAL LEADERSHIP

GOD, SEX AND YOU

OFF-SERIES

PRACTICAL HELPS IN SANCTIFICATION

MAKING SPIRITUAL PROGRESS

1. Vision, Burden, Action
2. The Ministers And The Ministry of The New Covenant
3. The Cross In The Life And Ministry Of The Believer
4. Knowing The God Of Unparalleled Goodness
5. Brokenness: The Secret Of Spiritual Overflow
6. The Secret Of Spiritual Rest
7. Making Spiritual Progress, Volume 1
8. Making Spiritual Progress, Volume 2
9. Making Spiritual Progress, Volume 3
10. Making Spiritual Progress, Volume 4
11. Moving on With The Lord Jesus Christ

EVANGELISM

1. God's Love And Forgiveness
2. The Way Of Life
3. Come Back Home My Son; I Still Love You
4. Jesus Loves You And Wants To Heal You
5. Come And See; Jesus Has Not Changed!
6. 36 Reasons For Winning The Lost To Christ
7. Soul Winning, Volume 1
8. Soul Winning, Volume 2
9. Celebrity A Mask
10. The Winning of The Lost as Life's Supreme Task
11. Salvation And Soul-Winning
12. Encounter The Saviour
13. Meet The Liberator
14. Soul Winning And The Making Of Disciples
15. Jesus Saves And Heals Today
16. Victorious Soul Winning

17. The Salvation Of The Lord Jesus: Soul Winning
(Vol. 3)

WOMEN OF THE GLORY

1. **The Secluded Worshipper**: The Life, Ministry,
And Glorification Of The Prophetess Anna
2. **Unending Intimacy**: The Transformation, Choices
And Overflow of Mary of Bethany
3. **Winning Love:** The rescue, development and
fulfilment of Mary Magdalene
4. **Not Meant for Defeat**: The Rise, Battles, and
Triumph of Queen Esther

ZTF COMPLETE WORKS

1. The School of Soul Winners and Soul Winning
2. Making Spiritual Progress (Volumes 1-4)
3. The Complete Works of Z.T.F on Holiness
(Volume 1)
4. The Complete Works of Z.T.F on Basic Christian
Doctrine
5. The Complete Works of Z.T.F on Marriage
(Volume 1)
6. The Complete Works of Z.T.F on The Gospel
Message (Volume 1)
7. The Complete Works of Z.T.F on Prayer (Volume 1)
8. The Complete Works of Z.T.F on Prayer (Volume 2)
9. The Complete Works of Z.T.F on Prayer (Volume 3)
10. The Complete Works of Z.T.F on Prayer (Volume 4)
11. The Complete Works of Z.T.F on Prayer (Volume 5)
12. The Complete Works of Z.T.F on Prayer (Volume 6)
13. The Complete Works of Z.T.F on Prayer (Volume 7)

SPECIAL SERIES

ZTF AUTO-BIOGRAPHIES

THE OVERTHROW OF PRINCIPALITIES

OTHER BOOKS

DISTRIBUTORS OF ZTF BOOKS

These books can be obtained in French and English Language from any of the following distribution outlets:

EDITIONS DU LIVRE CHRETIEN (ELC)

- **Location:** Paris, France
- **Email:** editionlivrechretien@gmail.com
- **Phone:** +33 6 98 00 90 47

INTERNET

- **Location:** on all major online **eBook, Audiobook** and **print-on-demand** (paperback) retailers.
- **Email**: ztfbooks@cmfionline.org
- **Phone**: +47 454 12 804
- **Website**: ztfbooks.com

CPH YAOUNDE

- **Location:** Yaounde, Cameroon
- **Email:** editionsztf@gmail.com
- **Phone:** +237 74756559

ZTF LITERATURE AND MEDIA HOUSE

- **Location:** Lagos, Nigeria
- **Email:** zlmh@ztfministry.org
- **Phone:** +2348152163063

CPH BURUNDI

- **Location:** Bujumbura, Burundi
- **Email:** cph-burundi@ztfministry.org
- **Phone:** +257 79 97 72 75

CPH UGANDA

- **Location:** Kampala, Uganda
- **Email:** cph-uganda@ztfministry.org
- **Phone:** +256 785 619613

CPH SOUTH AFRICA

- **Location:** Johannesburg, RSA
- **Email:** tantohtantoh@yahoo.com
- **Phone:** +27 83 744 5682